Heaven and Hell in Western Art

Robert Hughes

Dearest Barbara —
I don't know if you are
Beatrice but you have a good ax
for the dark woods and some day
I'll dedicate a book to you instead
of just scribbing on the flyleaf
such phrases
as
"with love from"
Bob.

Stein and Day/*Publishers*
7 East 48 Street New York

© 1968 by Robert Hughes
Library of Congress Catalog Card No. 68-27617
All rights reserved
Designed by Bruce Robertson
Printed in Germany
by K. G. Lohse Graphischer Grossbetrieb,
Frankfurt am Main
Stein and Day/*Publishers*/7 East 48 Street,
New York, N.Y. 10017

contents

part 3 Hell

In 1833, the emperor of Vietnam issued an edict to suppress Christian missionaries. It began:

I, Minh-Mang, the king, speak thus. For many years men from the Occident have been preaching the religion of Dato [Christianity] and deceiving the public, teaching them that there is a mansion of supreme bliss and a dungeon of dreadful misery. They have no respect for the God Phat [Buddha] and no reverence for ancestors . . . Could anything more contrary to reason and custom be imagined?

Perhaps not by Minh-Mang, nor by a modern humanist: but the unalterable fact is that the prospect of Heaven and Hell was, for more than fifteen hundred years, the chief religious obsession for most of the population of Europe. It remains so today, but for a dwindling number of Christians. Our modern ideas of Heaven and Hell are diluted. Heaven is vaguely thought of as a stretch of blue sky, with pearly gates like those in a hairdresser's movie ad, harps, clouds, and angels in long white caftans flapping their technicolour wings in time with the strains of Mario Lanza wafted faintly through some celestial Muzak system. It is all as clean as the inside of a new ice-box and to anyone with a trace of blood in his veins it is a prospect of appalling boredom, like being confined forever in Disneyland with nobody to talk to but Norman Vincent Peale and the dithering secretary of the local Methodist Ladies Bridge Auxiliary. Hell, on the other hand, is equally a cliché: a prospect of grid-irons and spits, beclouded with heavy sulphur fumes, through which intermittently dance figures in red tights and long red opera cloaks, with horns, Mandrake the Magician moustaches, and whippy spiked tails. The Christian Hell has become unreal for us in comparison with the concrete and much more dreadful-sounding hells which men have managed to construct for others in the last fifty years, in Siberia, on the frozen compounds of Belsen and Auschwitz, and in Vietnam. Reality has outstripped myth. The art of the twentieth century, despite a fitful interest in demonic and ecstatic images among the Surrealists, includes no significant paintings on eschatological themes.

This is emphatically not true of earlier art. Because Heaven and Hell were the two master images of a system of moral organisation built on the idea of punishment and reward, western art from the dawn of Christianity to the middle of the nineteenth century abounds in representations of God-imposed torment and bliss. The changes, shifts and elaborations of these images tend to be excessively complicated. No book of this length can do full justice to them. The complete story of Heaven and Hell

preface

7

in European art would also have to be a history of moral theology, of social morality and, to no small extent, of religious literature as a whole, spread across the total panorama of European history. I would like to hope that such a work will presently be written, but this book is not it. My intention is limited to noting certain recurrent images and themes in paintings and carvings of Heaven and Hell, showing (in the broadest of outlines) how and why they changed their *basic* features, and thus constructing an elementary outline of the iconography of Heaven and Hell in the art of the Christian west. To begin with, it will be useful to look at what the doctrine of the existence of a Heaven and a Hell meant – and, by the way, what it did *not* mean.

The Dead before his Judge from the Rohan Book of Hours, Bibliothèque Nationale, Paris. The Judge, overwhelmingly large in proportion to the dead man, is both the Father and the Son – as indicated by the cruciform halo. As lord of the world he holds an orb in his left hand, and as judge the sword of justice in his right. The dead man quotes (in Latin) Psalm XXX v. 6: 'Into thine hand, O Lord, I commit my spirit: thou hast redeemed me, O Lord God of truth.' God replies (in French): 'Do penitence for thy sins; in the judgment thou shalt be with me.'

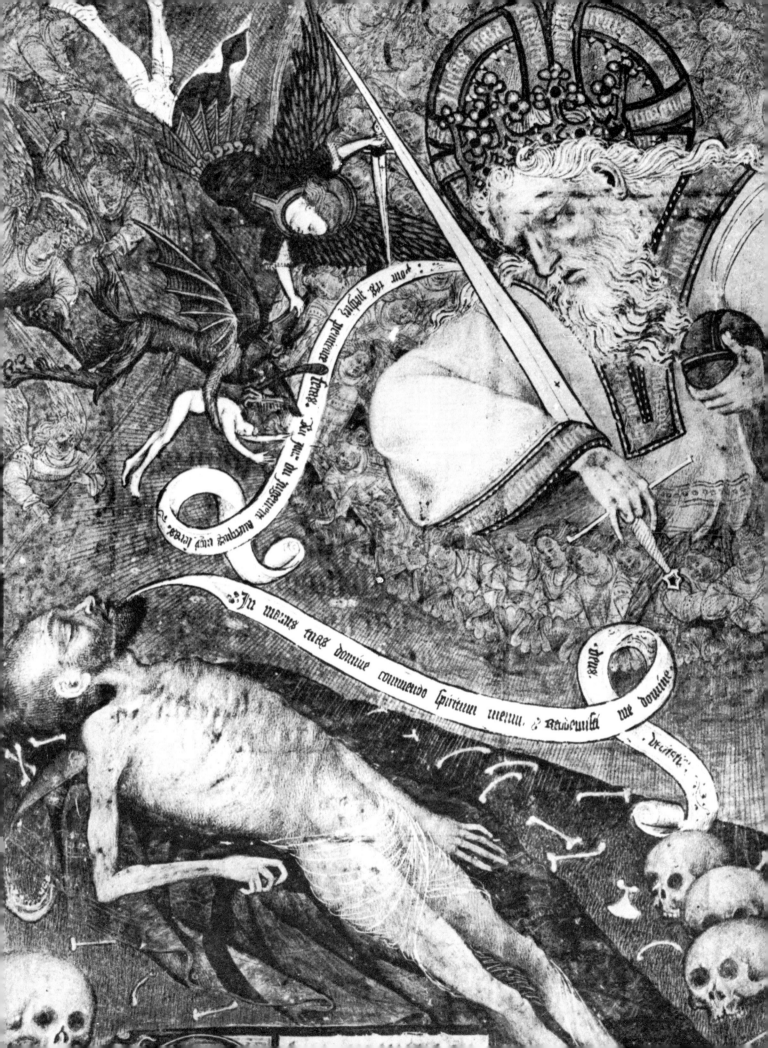

part 1

Judgment

Day of wrath and doom impending,
David's word with Sibyl's blending:
Heaven and earth in ashes ending.

Oh, what fear man's bosom rendeth
When from heaven the judge descendeth,
On whose sentence all dependeth!

Wondrous sound the trumpet flingeth,
Through earth's sepulchres it ringeth,
All before the throne it bringeth.

Death is struck, and nature quaking,
All creation is awaking,
To its judge an answer making.

Dies Irae *13th cent.*

chapter 1

The Mansion and the Dungeon

There can be very few religions which do not hold, somewhere near the core of their mythology, that men have souls or spirits which go on living after their bodies have died. But there is a staggering variety of theories about what happens to these souls. Are they immortal, or do they too die after a while? Do they evolve from lower states of being to higher, or does the death of the body freeze them in an inflexible moral *stasis* under the eye of God? Can the acts of the living help them – as the prayers of living Christians are supposed to shorten the length of time Christian souls spend in Purgatory, or as the virtuous behaviour of a good Buddhist is believed to be transferable to the *petas*, the souls of the dead, and turn them into *devas*, blessed ones; or can nobody's intercession release them from the existence into which they are bound at the moment of death? Can God extend clemency to a damned soul or is he the prisoner of his own laws? Are the souls, in fact, judged or not? Once judged, are the innocent rewarded and the guilty actively tortured; or are they all left wandering, as if lobotomised, on a level of consciousness whose deficiencies they are not equipped to understand?

The traditional Christian answer is brutal: judgment by God, followed by the dispatch of the soul to Heaven or to Hell – or, under certain conditions, to Purgatory, where it is tortured for a finite period in order to purify it so that it is fit to enter Heaven. Wherever it goes, the soul will live forever; and at last, on the day of the Final Judgment, all the souls of saved and damned alike will be reunited with their bodies.

This vision of the Four Last Things – Death, Judgment, Hell and Heaven – was often given a unified form by Christian artists; the whole eschatological drama was combined in one picture. Such is the twelfth-century mosaic at Torcello (opposite). The scenes are stacked in five tiers. At the top, flanked by the immense angels Gabriel and Michael, St John the Baptist points to the figure of Christ, who is seen trampling down the doors of Hell and striding across the recumbent form of their guardian devil, as he leads a soul out of Limbo. In the second tier, below it, the Last Judgment is in session; God sits in an oval mandorla, with the Virgin Mary on his right and St Joseph on his left hand. On either side of him the choirs of the blessed – saints, evangelists, fathers of the Church – are drawn up; and below his mandorla a pair of Cherubim hover, in company with two wheels, symbols of another kind of angelic being, Thrones. In the centre of the third tier (p. 14, top), angels and seraphs are seen guarding God's seat, behind which rise emblems of his sacrifice – spear, sponge, crucifix, crown of thorns. On the left (p. 14, bottom), a pair of angels trumpet the resurrection to the earth, and

The Last Judgment, Torcello. 12th-century mosaic. The theme is set by the large figures in the top row: Christ as saviour of souls. In the second tier, Christ is seen in glory, as judge of mankind, with saints and confessors. In the third, angels blow the last trump, and sea and land give up their dead; in the fourth, the damned are separated from the saved; in the fifth, the elect are seen in Paradise and the condemned in Hell. Note the stream of fire flowing from Christ's mandorla to Hell, signifying that the *Inferno* is kept alight by God's direct will.

13

the dead, wrapped in their cerements, emerge from their tombs, while a leopard, a griffin, a lion, two crows, a bear and, incongruously, a man-eating elephant regurgitate bits of people. On the right, the same thing is happening in the sea, as dogfish and sea-leopard surrender fragments of drowned sailors (opposite). Below, in the fourth tier, a company of martyrs, saints and confessors watch on the left as the archangel and a pair of demons dispute, on either side of the scales, over the fate of souls weighed in the balance; while on the right, the damned are being harried into Hell by two more of God's angelic messengers. It is a democracy of suffering: kings, knights and peasants, priests and laymen, Europeans and Orientals are in the flames, which lick around the dragon throne of Satan and its two sinner-chewing heads (p. 17). To emphasise that Hell is kept in existence by God's constant will, the river of fire which feeds its conflagration flows directly across the wall from the bottom of Christ's mandorla. In the fifth and bottom tier, the contrast between reward and punishment is stressed again; on the left, Christ blessing a crowd of little children, with Mary by his side, and John the Baptist, St Peter and an angel pointing out the gate to Paradise, inside which the 'cherub with a flaming sword' stands like a sentry in a box; while on the right, more sinners broil and lament in the flames and thick darkness, and beneath them lies a charnel-house of skulls through whose empty sockets worms crawl.

On the day of Judgment, according to the more radical

Christian millenarians, the hills will dance, Antichrist will be destroyed, and a reign of absolute justice will descend on the transfigured inhabitants of a renewed and Paradisal earth while Hell burns on below.

The doctrine of the Last Judgment is supported by a number of biblical texts, of which the most important is *Matthew* xxv, 31–46.

When the Son of Man comes in his glory, and all the angels with him, then he will sit on his glorious throne. Before him will be gathered all the nations, and he will separate them one from another as a shepherd separates the sheep from the goats, and he will place the sheep at his right hand, but the goats at his left.

Then the King will say to those at his right hand, 'Come, O blessed of my Father, inherit the kingdom prepared for you from the foundation of the world; for I was hungry and you gave me food, I was thirsty and you gave me drink, I was a stranger and you welcomed me, I was naked and you clothed me, I was sick and you visited me, I was in prison and you came to me.' Then the righteous will answer him, 'Lord, when did we see you hungry and feed you, or thirsty and give you drink? And when did we see you a stranger and welcome you, or naked and clothe you? And when did we see you sick or in prison, and visit you?' And the King will answer: 'Truly I say to you, as you did it to the least of these my brethren, you did it to me.'

Then he will say to those at his left hand: 'Depart from me, ye

The Last Judgment, Torcello. **top left** the adoration of Christ's throne, with its emblems of the Passion – sponge, spear, cross and crown of thorns. **bottom left** the resurrection on earth: angels summon the animals, including a griffin and a man-eating elephant, to vomit up their victims for judgment. **below** the resurrection of men lost at sea. The marine god derives from Neptune but his pose, on a sea-leopard, may allude to Antichrist riding on the back of the sea-monster Leviathan.

cursed, into everlasting fire, which was prepared for the devil and his angels; for I was hungry and you gave me no food, I was thirsty and you gave me no drink, I was a stranger and you did not welcome me, naked and you did not clothe me, sick and in prison and you did not visit me.' Then they, too, will answer, 'Lord, when did we see you hungry or thirsty or as a stranger, or naked or sick or in prison, and did not minister to you?' Then he will answer them: 'Truly, I tell you, as you did not do it to the least one of these, you did not do it to me.' And they will go away into eternal punishment; but the righteous into eternal life.

God, in creating souls, makes them incomplete but endows them with a potential for completing themselves; and this self-completion can only be achieved when they are able to participate in his own being. Such participation is the state of existence known as Heaven, and all the works of art which have taken Heaven as their subject-matter are, at best, imperfect metaphors of this state of being which is, strictly speaking, inexpressible – for to express something means that you must comprehend it first and Christianity maintains that nobody except a small élite of mystics can directly experience God before death. And when experienced, God's existence supersedes art, blotting all metaphors out. Even for Dante, words fail when the face of God is seen:

Power failed high fantasy here; but, swift to move,
Even as a wheel turns smoothly, free from jars,
My will and my desire were turned by love,
The Love that moves the sun and the other stars.

[*Paradiso* XXXIII, 142–5]

In la sua voluntate è nostra pace – 'In his will is our peace'. This renunciation of the ego, this willing absorption of consciousness and personality into the matrix of God's existence, is the joy of Heaven. Desire ceases because all potential is fulfilled. The fact that all the symbolic paraphernalia of harps, meadows, evangelical beasts, fires, choirs and golden gates was only a metaphor of this state was recognised early in the development of Christianity. The earliest full description of the orders of Heaven was given by a writer who worked under the name of Dionysius the Areopagite. The real Dionysius was converted by St Paul at Athens and was reputed, in the second century, to have been one of the early Christian bishops (he was later identified, in the ninth century, with St Denis of France), but it now seems clear that the Areopagite was a forger, writing his ornate and rhetorical prose later than the fifth century, and heavily in debt to the pagan neo-Platonist metaphysician Proclus (410–85). The Pseudo-Dionysius – as he is called – was well aware of the distance between symbol and reality when art dealt with Heaven. 'We might even think,' he remarked,

that the celestial regions are filled up with herds of lions and horses

The Last Judgment, Torcello. 'The democracy of Hell': men of all races and degrees are thrust into the flames, and over them Satan presides, holding Antichrist on his knee.

16

and re-echo with roaring songs of praise, and contain flocks of birds and other creatures, and the lower forms of matter, and whatever other absurd, spurious, passion-rousing and unlike forms the scriptures use for describing their resemblances . . .

– such as the ox, the lamb, the lion and the eagle. But, the Pseudo-Dionysius points out, truth is not dishonoured by the 'base' shapes it takes to make itself visible to the eyes of the profane; symbolism is necessary both to reveal the structure of Heaven and at the same time to conceal some of its esoteric significance from the vulgar who cannot use the knowledge:

. . . it must be said that the reason for attributing shapes to that which is above shape, and forms to that which is beyond form, is not only the feebleness of our intellectual power which is unable to rise at once to spiritual contemplation, and which needs to be encouraged . . . but it is also most fitting that the secret doctrines, through ineffable and holy enigmas, should veil and render difficult of access for the multitude the sublime and profound truth of the Supernatural Mind: for, as the Scripture declares, not everyone is holy, nor have all men knowledge.
[*On Celestial Hierarchies*, chapter 2]

In fact, using mundane symbols for Heaven can be a useful stratagem. They may direct the faithful to thinking in terms of the abstractions appropriate to heavenly order, instead of being overcome by the glamour of metaphor: simple food is best.

Nor, I suppose, will any man deny that discordant figures uplift the mind more than do the harmonious, for in dwelling upon the nobler images it is probable that we might fall into the error of supposing that the Celestial Intelligences are some kind of golden beings, or shining men flashing like lightning . . .

[*On Celestial Hierarchies*]

Such 'discordant figures' include biblical images of Christ and his Church: pot of ointment, cornerstone, bear deprived of its young, and even worm – '*Ego sum vermis et non homo*'.

The Pseudo-Dionysian position was retained by most Christian thinkers and constantly presented to their more intelligent audiences. John Donne, in his *Sermon of Commemoration of the Lady Danvers*, 1627, put it thus:

Here then the Holy Ghost intends the same new Heavens, and new Earth, which he does in the Apocalyps, and describes there, by another name, the New Jerusalem. But here, the Holy Ghost does not proceed, as there, to enamour us of the place by a promise of improvement of those things, which wee have and love here; but by a promise of that, which here we have not at all. There, and elsewhere, the Holy Ghost applies himself to the natural affections of men. To those that are affected with riches, he saies, that the new City shall be all of gold, and in the foundations, all manner of precious stones; . . . to those which delight in Musicke, he promises continuall singing, and every minute, a new song; To those, whose thoughts are exerciz'd upon Honour . . . hee promises

Priesthood, and if that be not honour enough, a Royall Priesthood ; and to those, who looke after military honour, triumph after their victory in the Militant Church ; and to those, that are carried with sumptuous and magnifique Feasts, a marriage supper of the Lambe, where, not onely all the rarities of the whole world, but the whole world it self shall be serv'd in ; the whole world shall bee brought to that fire, and serv'd at that table. But here, the Holy Ghost proceeds not that way, by improvement of things which wee have and love here ; riches, or beauty, or musicke, or honour, or feasts ; but by an everlasting possession of that which we hunger and thirst and pant after here, and cannot compasse : that is, Justice, or Righteousnesse . . .

If this beatific state is the natural culmination of the progress of the human soul through temporal into eternal life, it would be pleasant to suppose that such a transcendence happened, automatically, to everyone. But it does not. God gives his toys a tendency to break. The core of Christian doctrine on salvation is that you must *choose* Heaven. In other words, there must be free will. We will return to this rather problematical idea later, but for the moment it is enough to note that everyone is supposed to be able to make clear moral choices between good and evil, and that the choice he makes will decide whether he spends the rest of eternity in Heaven or in Hell. Thus a finite act is rewarded or punished to an infinite degree.

But while Heaven and Hell normally present themselves to the faithful as reward and punishment, a stricter theological approach might argue that such notions are beside the point when God and his actions are under discussion. God does not choose to send a good man to Heaven or a bad one to Hell in the same way as one chooses to send a sales executive to Bermuda or a criminal to jail. Even the idea of the Last Judgment is, in the last analysis, only a metaphor. The soul is already judged – that is to say, not judged at all : its previous actions automatically entail its fate to come. Sin *is* death. The issue is whether or not a soul, by its own choice, participates in God's being. God is unmoved. If I decide to eat an apple, I may enjoy it and it may nourish me. On the other hand, if I do not eat it I have deprived myself of the pleasure of tasting the fruit. But there is no sense in which the apple can be said to have judged me : apple-pulp or hunger, the choice has been mine all along, and in making it I have been dealing with natural reflexes which no amount of interpretation can change. In the same way, the soul does not 'please' God by acting virtuously, as a dancing dog might please its trainer ; if God is immutable and totally good, he can no more be placated, in that sense, than a metre-rule can be charmed into changing its length. Instead, the virtuous soul participates in God by moving to him as an absolute. Sin does not 'displease' God ; it is a direct rejection of his being, in which the soul becomes a negative image of its previous capacity for union with God. Sin is the anti-matter to God's reality. The sinner's soul is not punished; in a particular sense it becomes his sin.

But this is not a popular refinement on the idea of divine justice. Before this century few theologians and hardly any laymen were apt to think of Heaven and Hell in terms other than those of direct reward and brute vengeance, meted out by a satisfied or a raging God. In the Middle Ages, with the passion for category-splitting which was so typical of theological argument at the time, the Church's doctors were apt to go into preposterously elaborate classifications of the kinds of reward that the just might expect in Heaven. Thomas Cantimpratanus listed six, of which the last

> *will be to behold the damned on their left hand, to whom the Judge will say, 'Depart, ye cursed, into everlasting fire' . . . Some simple folk are wont to wonder that the saints, at the Last Judgment, will be in no wise disturbed at the sight of the damnation of their friends and parents ; but all faithful souls will account this their astonishment as mere folly, seeing that they know how the saints, confirmed in their perpetual exultation, can be touched by no trouble or grief . . .*

Cantimpratanus then described with relish how the Blessed Marie d'Oignies was sent a vision of her own mother in Hell, whereon she stopped crying over her death. What was the point of expending pity on the damned? Indeed, as Aquinas, the Angelic Doctor, had pointed out, it was a sin to commiserate with those in Hell, since this implied that you were siding against God. The thought of a row of saints peering over the lip of a cloud and tittering with glee at their roasting cousins below is not perhaps the most edifying of ideas today; it is a celestial equivalent of the aged Duke of Wellington's retort to a young officer who asked him why, whenever it rained, he spent the day glaring through the club window into St James' below. 'I am watching,' snapped the duke, 'all those damn'd people getting wet.'

Throughout the first fifteen hundred years of its activity, the Catholic Church developed an immensely elaborate superstructure of belief, legend and symbolism on top of its basic doctrines related to Heaven. The most striking example of this eschatological explosion is to be found among the angels.

Heaven, according to traditional Christian doctrine, has a complex hierarchy of angels. Various biblical texts refer to their number. Daniel (VII, 10) saw a million of them serving the Ancient of Days, and a hundred million standing before him. The *Apocalypse* of St John numbered them in 'myriads of myriads, and thousands of thousands'. Job (xxv, 3) could not count them at all. The Lord came down from Sinai, leaving behind 'ten thousands of the holy ones' (*Deut.* xxxiii, 2). In *Matthew* (xxvi, 53), Christ claimed to have at his disposal 'more than twelve legions of angels' – which, counting a legion as six thousand men, gives a grand total of seventy-two thousand.

Giotto: *The Last Judgment*, Scrovegni Chapel, Padua. Early 14th century. The traditional hierarchy of angels in nine tiers. The seraphim are nearest to God and surround the mandorla in which he sits. The other eight choirs are ranked vertically, one behind the other, on either side of the window.

As a Catholic priest, the Reverend R. O'Kennedy, of the diocese of Limerick, wrote in 1887, angels are powerful:

They can produce the most wonderful effects, as exciting storms and tempests, striking the earth with interior motions, causing foul dreams and diseases, or sometimes curing sickness and wounds, and bringing about health in man and beast when it pleases God to enable them to do so.

Angels destroyed Sodom and Gomorrah, slew the firstborn of the Egyptians and annihilated the army of Sennacherib; others, more benevolent, fed Elijah, shut the mouths of the lions in whose den Daniel was mewed up, wrestled with Jacob, cured Tobit's blindness and announced the birth of Samson to Manoah. Angels are the messengers of God, taking his instructions to earth and executing his will on its inhabitants, guarding men (one guardian angel was traditionally supposed to be assigned to each human soul), carrying the dead before the Judgment Seat, and fiddling with natural laws to produce miracles. According to St Thomas Aquinas, they are pure spirits, invisible, but apt to appropriate bodies of 'air or vapour' when they want to be seen. Their nature was created by God to enjoy Heaven and receive grace, but

as there were different choirs and different orders of spirits, and as variety adds to the beauty of a work, so it was fitting that there should be among the angels different degrees of grace[1].

In mediaeval theological practice this involved a rigid hierarchy of pure spirits in Heaven, of which the angels were the lowest. Going up, they run: angels, archangels, principalities; powers, virtues, dominations; thrones, cherubim, seraphim. Thus there are nine choirs (or species) of angels, in three groups of three (p. 21). This division of hierarchies was current since at least the fourth century, and it was confirmed as a reasonable hypothesis which the faithful might entertain without courting error (which is a different thing to defining it as dogma or stating it as doctrine) by the fifth Lateran Council (1512–17) under Leo x. It has persisted, with minor modifications and variations, until our own century. Only seven years ago, a Vatican spokesman in *Osservatore Romano*, the Vatican's newspaper, joined in the controversy over the question of intelligent life on other planets than earth. Indeed, he pronounced, such life could exist; and went on to list twelve different kinds of being, from seraphim to devils, that Russian and American spacemen might expect to meet on Mars.

St Augustine might have been less certain of recognising a bug-eyed green Throne:

That there are Thrones, Dominations, Principalities and Powers I firmly believe; and that they differ one from the other I hold as indubitably true; but what the differences are, and how great, I know not.

But St Bernard, St Bonaventure, St John of Damascus, the

Anonymous: miniature from Breviary of St Hildegarde, 9th century. The nine choirs of angels. The white disk at the centre is God's radiance and each concentric ring stands for a different angelic type. Note the thrones, in the third ring from the centre, symbolised by half-wheels.

Pseudo-Dionysius and St Thomas Aquinas were all convinced that this hierarchy was real and that its differences could be described. Its symbolical and allegorical ramifications were just as important as its structure. To begin with, the number of choirs in the hierarchy was nine, or 3 × 3 – the Trinity multiplied by itself, or repeated on three levels. Aquinas thought that each tier of angels represented one of the three types of divine act, while the three kinds of angel in each tier signified God's threefold manner of putting these acts into order. He classified them thus:

	Name of angelic type	Symbolic reference to
(1) GOD'S ACTS RELATING TO HIMSELF (E.g., self-knowledge)	Seraph	Father
	Cherub	Son
	Throne	Holy Ghost
(2) GOD'S ACTS RELATING TO UNIVERSAL CREATION	Domination	Creation
	Virtue	Preservation
	Power	Ordering
(3) GOD'S ACTS RELATING TO INDIVIDUAL BEINGS OR OBJECTS (E.g., Man)	Principality	Creation
	Archangel	Redemption
	Angel	Beatification

But if angels are pure spirits, how can one tell the difference between one type of angelic being and another? We can differentiate easily between one man and another since, although both belong to the category 'man', I can see that one has a bent nose and the other a straight, that one has black skin and the other yellow, and so on. Pure spirit, though, has no physiognomy. But it may have different intellectual functions. And so the grading of the heavenly hierarchy became a matter of separating out the different kinds of supernatural mind in it. Each of the nine angelic species was given distinct characteristics and tasks, as they all revolved in choirs round God. Seraphim, for instance, are the angels of Love, characterised by fire. Pseudo-Dionysius called them the 'Glowing Ones' and went on, at length and with maddening prolixity, about their

ceaseless and eternal motion about the Divine Principles, their heat and keenness, the exuberance of their intense, perpetual, tireless activity, and their elevative and energetic assimilation of those below . . . enlightening power, dispelling and destroying the shadows of darkness.

All fantasies of Nature idealised came, in Christian art, to be summed up in the vision of the Paradise Garden. **opposite** *The Madonna in a Rosegarden*, by Stefano da Zevio, Museo Civico, Verona. **overleaf** The elect greeting one another, with love, in Heaven, from *The Last Judgment* by Giovanni di Paolo (active 1420, d. 1482), Pinacoteca Nazionale, Siena.

Cherubim are the angels of Knowledge – one of them (*Genesis* III, 24) was placed with a flaming sword at the east entrance to the Garden of Eden, to prevent man's return to his original state of innocence. The function of thrones is less clear. They may symbolise the Holy Ghost, and they are commonly represented and described as winged wheels; but the Pseudo-Dionysius is masterfully obscure about that they do – except go round and round,

. . . ever moving onward, never turning back or going aside, [thrones] denote the power of their progressive energy on a straight and direct path in which all their intellectual revolutions are supermundanely guided on that straight and unswerving course. The figure of the spiritual wheels may also have another mystical meaning, for the prophet says that the name Gel, Gel *is given to them, which in the Hebrew tongue means revolutions and revelations . . .*

The dominations are there to worship the principle of authority embodied in God. Virtues – in the sense of the Italian *virtù* – signify virility, resolution, prowess. And so on. Summing up the general functions of the angelic hierarchy, St Bernard said that the seraphim, cherubim and thrones are the 'intimate counsellors' of God, whilst those of the second triad (dominations, virtues, powers) are the 'government' whose will is executed by the 'ministers' in the third triad, the principalities, archangels and angels. Bureaucracy goes about its mysterious ends in the upper rooms of the palace while Hell occupies the dungeons.

If one descends from the giddy rotations and pecking-orders of this celestial Ministry of Love, it is surprising – and rather heartening – to find that practically none of its immense structure was ever defined as dogma by the Catholic Church and that comparatively little of it was even codified as doctrine. (A dogma is an article of faith which, under pain of mortal sin, the faithful must accept.) The existence of Heaven was formally defined by Benedict XII, in a document issued on 29 January 1336. The souls of the virtuous

even before the resumption of their bodies and the Universal Judgment, after the ascension of Our Saviour Jesus Christ into heaven, were, are and will be in Heaven, in the heavenly kingdom and the celestial Paradise with Christ, together with the company of holy angels . . .

Heaven was announced to be a state, not a place – an important distinction. Later theologians took this 'state' to exist both ontologically and psychologically. Ontologically, Heaven is the state of union with God. Psychologically, it is the satisfaction and well-being (if such words are not too weak) which the soul experiences through this union.

As for angels and other sub-divine heavenly creatures, not a trace of the Pseudo-Dionysius' hierarchy is to be found in

opposite The ranks of saved souls in Paradise. Cassinese School, 12th century, S. Angelo in Formis. Note, in the background, the pairs of saints plucking fruit from the Tree of Life, represented as a date-palm.

Church doctrine. Angels are defined as spiritual beings who were created by God and are not part of God himself (a clause aimed at pantheists), but their properties are left – perhaps deliberately – vague. 'If anyone would not blush to affirm that nothing exists beyond material objects, let him be anathema,' announced the Twentieth Ecumenical Council, under Pius IX, in 1870. The Fourth Lateran Council laid it down in 1215 that God, 'with his omnipotent abilities', directly created at the start of time every creature, 'spiritual and corporal, out of nothingness; angelic creatures, for instance . . .'. Of the habits and activities of angels, the Church has little to say, except that they do not breed. This was stated in 1336 by Benedict XII in response to an Armenian heresiarch named Mechetriz who thought they did. Nor did the papacy ever take official note of the febrile speculations of mediaeval schoolmen about the size, sex and colour of angels, their weight and number, their maximum speed, and how many of them could dance on the point of that famous pin. However, Eugenius IV (1431–47) said that angels were good but capable of changing – 'good because they were made by the Highest Good, but mutable because they were made out of nothing'[2]; a useful qualification, since Lucifer and his followers had vigorously shown their changeability by rebelling against God.

The inhabitants of Heaven, then, are God in his triune form of Father, Son and Holy Ghost, the Virgin Mary (whose Assumption into Heaven was defined as dogma by Pius XII in 1953), an unspecified number of angels, and the saints. (The phrase 'saints in Heaven' is really a tautology, because there cannot be saints outside Heaven: a saint is a person whose soul, in the expressed opinion of the Church, has got there. Despite the plethora of saints, some of provable and others of fictitious historical identity, which infests the rubric of Catholicism, canonisation is still a rare event; and the list of canonised is not meant to exhaust the number of those probably in Heaven.)

In colloquial use, the words 'Heaven' and 'Paradise' are interchangeable. Not, however, in theological practice. The Heaven of Christian theology is not the Paradise of *Genesis*, the garden of innocence in which the first man was placed by a benevolent God. It is the confusion between them that has led to the popular vision of pearly gates and pie in the sky. In the encyclical against Armenian heresies quoted earlier, Benedict XII was at pains to attack the idea that 'the souls of children who were born of Christian parents after the Passion of Christ go, if they die before baptism, to the earthly paradise, in which Adam lived before Original Sin . . .' We will find, in Christian art as in theology, two systems of representation for Heaven: one which concerns itself with a strictly theological and, so to speak, metaphysical Heaven, the *state* in which saints, angels and apostles do nothing but live in rapt contemplation of God's being; the other deriving from Eden and the myth of the Golden Age, and represented as a *place*, sometimes with a definite geographical location and always with attributes like grass, rivers, perfumes, tame animals, walls of gold and pavements of emerald. Though these two ideas sometimes interlock in art, they should not be confused. For Paradise was the physical metaphor of the reality which was Heaven.

Purgatory and Limbo are a little outside the scope of this book, but for clarity's sake they should be mentioned. Those who die in venial sin go to Purgatory and are punished there for a time before they are released, with purified souls, into Heaven. It is therefore a temporary measure: sandpaper before the enamel. The existence of Purgatory was enunciated in 1254[3] on the strength of two New Testament texts. One was from Christ:

Therefore I tell you, every sin and blasphemy will be forgiven men, but the blasphemy against the Spirit will not be forgiven. And whoever says a word against the Son of man shall be forgiven; but whoever speaks against the Holy Spirit will not be forgiven, either in this age or in the age to come. [Matthew XII, 31–2]

By implication, there are sins which do not deserve eternal torture, and these are venial. Yet they will be punished:

The fire will test what sort of work each man has done . . . If any man's work is burned up, he will suffer loss, though he himself will be saved, but only as through fire. [1 Corinthians III, 13 and 15]

So the punishment will end in salvation: hence Purgatory.

Limbo, on the other hand, is reserved for the souls of those who merit neither Heaven (with or without a preliminary basting in Purgatory) nor Hell. To it went virtuous men who, being born before Christ, never received the grace of baptism. The usual mediaeval practice was to make Limbo a part of Hell. Dante located it in the first circle of the Inferno; Virgil describes the population of Limbo to him –

Or vo' che sappi, innanzi che più andi,
Ch'ei non peccaro; e s'elli hanno mercedi
non basta, perchè non ebber battesmo,
ch' è porta della fede che tu credi.
E se furon dinanzi al cristianesmo,
non adorar debitamente a Dio:
e di questi cotai son io medesmo.
Per tai difetti, non per altro rio,
semo perduti, e sol di tanto offesi,
che senza speme vivemo in disio.

ENGLISH TRANSLATION

– (*Inf.* IV, 33–42: 'I would have you know, then, before you go farther, that they did not sin; but though they have merits it is not enough, for they had not baptism, which is the gateway of the faith you hold; and if they were before Christianity they did not worship God properly, and of these I am one. For such defects, and not for any guilt, we are lost, and only so far afflicted that without hope we live in desire.')

Dante sees Limbo full of the heroes and poets of classical antiquity. It is a noble place, a bubble of light enclosed by the murk of lower Hell; Hector, Aeneas, Lucretia and Electra are there; Socrates and Plato, Democritus, Euclid, and Hippocrates; Horace, Ovid, Lucan and, of course, Virgil himself. The more common idea of Limbo among Catholics is, perhaps, closer to the Graeco-Roman Hades – a dismal, grey and excruciatingly boring place, filled with the mewling and puking of millions of unbaptised babies. It was into Limbo that Christ descended, after his death on the cross, to release the souls of the retro-spectively-saved elect. This became known as the 'Harrowing of Hell', a theme which recurs frequently in Christian art. Limbo was really a theological compromise forced on Christi-anity by the belief that one could only be saved by the blood of Christ. If one could not get to Heaven otherwise, what fate could be reserved for the great figures of the Old Testament, from Adam to Moses? Grossly unfair to damn them; better, it seemed, to invent Limbo, an ante-room or prison, in which they could await the reprieving sacrifice. The Harrowing of Hell is a minor incident in the New Testament – it is mentioned in the Apostles' Creed, and the first Epistle of St Peter briefly notes that Christ 'went and preached to the spirits in prison' *[1 Peter* III, *19]*. But its background must have given it an un-usual relevance, not only for Dante, but for many of the mediae-val and Renaissance painters who had been touched by the revivals of antiquity that took place between the tenth and sixteenth centuries, and whose reverence for the pre-Christian past could well have made it hard for them to take any pleasure in the thought of its makers cut off, irrevocably, from the divine vision. The Harrowing of Hell occupies a far more important place in Christian art than the doctrine of Limbo does in theology. Especially since, as we will see, it gave artists yet another of many chances to connect classicism with Christianity, by fusing Christ with Hermes Psychopompos, the Guide of Souls.

It may be difficult, in this last third of the twentieth century, to visualise the joys of Heaven, even through the net of paradisal metaphors which artists and writers threw, in the past, round Christian after-life. But even granted that our experience of pain is more immediate, in art as in life, than our understanding of transcendental bliss, it is still not by any means easy to recap-ture the sensations which paintings of Hell were originally meant to evoke. Even to try, one must do two things at the out-set. First, jettison the popular modern image of Satan, that moth-eaten, operatic joke who is fit for nothing better than ad-vertising sparkplugs and canned chili sauce. Second, remember that the existence of Hell, a fiery pit which yawned to engulf every sinner, was no metaphor, but an irreducible truth of reli-gious doctrine in which nearly every European for more than fifteen hundred years professed to believe. God did not live in Hampstead and was not expected to act like a liberal.

There are various reactions which a modern tourist is likely to have to a treatment of the Inferno like, say, Taddeo di Barto-

Taddeo di Bartolo: *Hell*, fresco in Collegiate Church of San Gimignano, c. 1320. In this dreadful image, Hell is seen in cross-section, divided into compartments, with ingenious and different tortures for each kind of sin. In the arch, three-headed Satan presides over his kingdom. The sinner hanging from his front mouth is the arch-traitor, Judas; those on either side, Brutus and Cassius.

32

lo's fresco of the Last Judgment and Hell in the Abbey Church of San Gimignano (p. 33); they are apt to end up as a compound of awe, pleasure and admiration, tied together by a sense of the sheer integrity of the myth; but only a minority is likely to see the fresco as what it was originally intended to be, a morality play with a strong documentary flavour aimed at one's conscience and designed to give a dreadful fright. The tendency is to enjoy eschatological nightmares of this sort in the same way as one approaches the Laocoon – as works of art built round a myth. Taddeo's vision of Hell has no more *documentary* reality to most visitors nowadays than the legend of Anchises' brother and the sea-snake. But we are unwise if we attribute our own reactions to the audience for whom, in 1320, Taddeo was painting. In all likelihood, the mediaeval peasant in the Abbey Church of San Gimignano was brought, by his primitive faith, into an immediate empathy with the sinners and their tortures: fornicators dismembered and scourged, fat sodomites spitted, like piglets, from anus to mouth on a pole and cranked over an open fire; foul air, iron claws, stake and blistering skin, Hell as an eternal reality. Before we come to the contents of this dungeon of the universe as they were recorded in art, it will be profitable to see what Christianity had to say about Hell.

One basic Scriptural text on Hell *[Matthew* xxv, 31–46, on the Last Judgment*]* has already been quoted. Others come from the *Book of Revelations :*

> *. . . And another angel, a third, followed them, saying with a loud voice : If anyone worships the beast and its image, and receives a mark on his forehead or on his hand, he shall also drink the wine of God's wrath, poured neat into the cup of his anger, and he shall be tormented with fire and brimstone in the presence of the holy angels and in the presence of the Lamb. And the smoke of their torment goes up for ever and ever ; and they have no rest, day or night, these worshippers of the beast and its image and whoever receives the mark of its name.*
>
> *[Rev.* xiv, 9–11*]*

> *. . . Then I saw an angel coming from heaven, holding in his hand the key of the bottomless pit and a great chain. And he seized the dragon, that ancient serpent, who is the Devil and Satan, and bound him for a thousand years, and threw him into the pit, and shut it and sealed it over him, that he should deceive the nations no more until the thousand years were ended. After that he must be loosed for a little while . . . And when the thousand years are ended, Satan will be loosed from his prison, and will come out to deceive the nations which are at the four corners of the earth, that is, Gog and Magog, and gather them for battle ; their number is like the sand of the sea. And they marched up over the broad earth and surrounded the camp of the saints and the beloved city ; but fire came down from heaven and consumed them, and the devil who had deceived them was thrown into the lake of fire where the beast and the*

34

false prophet were, and they will be tormented day and night for ever and ever.   *[Rev. xx, 1–3, 7–10]*

There are other references to Hell in the New Testament, but these contain all the fundamental aspects of the immense structure of fear which Christianity was to erect. The first is the idea of eternal punishment for crime; the goats, once condemned to their everlasting fire, can never be released from it. Nor does the torture consume them; they cannot escape from it into a second death; it, and they, are locked in a vice of excruciating pain for all eternity. Their pain is infinite in degree, because they are souls, without bodies and therefore without the physiological mechanisms of defence by retreat into coma or shock which the body supplies against pain: in Hell, the soul is utterly naked. Moreover, it is infinite in extension, because after death there is nothing left but the corridor of eternity. Naturally, all the Church's metaphors fell somewhere short of the full implications of its teaching on the tortures of Hell; nobody can imaginatively grasp the ideas of eternity and infinity or relate them adequately to his own existence. There is a point at which statistics, however thunderously presented by a preacher, become meaningless. One cannot arrive at a grasp of what the Final Solution meant by imagining one Jew choking in a cloud of Zyklon-B and then multiplying him by six million; the arithmetic cannot be performed since it eludes experience and will fit no context. In the same way, when a Catholic boy listens to a sermon like the famous fresco of damnation painted by Joyce in *Portrait of the Artist*, he will not be able to envisage what it will feel like to be punished for masturbation by being kicked, as a Jesuit once expressed it to me in a similar sermon in Australia fifteen years ago, in a certain part of the body, by a demon with a great clawed foot, twenty times a minute, sixty minutes an hour, twenty-four hours a day, for all eternity. But though the Christian doctrine of infinite and eternal pain in Hell is psychologically meaningless, its deterrent effect was immense. There is a parallel with the idea of 'overkill' in nuclear warfare. Some citizens of the United States derive a feeling of security from the fact that, whereas Russia has enough atom bombs and rockets to annihilate the population of the world fifty times over, the United States can do it seventy-five times. Retributive power can seem greater where size is meaningless, just as infinity and eternity of punishment can frighten where neither can be grasped.

The second aspect of traditional Christian teaching on Hell is that God does not punish the souls there in order to purge them or to make them reluctant to sin again. He punishes them vindictively. Sin is an offence against his nature; and God is infinite in all his characteristics. And so, as a seventeenth–century French theologian, Malebranche, put it:

The offence increases in proportion to the majesty offended. It is just to condemn an insolent subject, who has insulted his Prince, to be a galley-slave for life. Compare and judge whether God, without belying his nature, can be satisfied with a transitory vengeance.

For Malebranche, offence to princes was worse than offence to commoners precisely because it was a metaphorical act: the prince is the metaphor of the state, he sums up its authoritarian powers in his own person, and so, because insulting him means insulting the principle of moral order on which the state is presumed to rest, the galleys are prepared. The insult will not hurt the prince since it comes from an inferior – or, at worst, it will only hurt him in his private capacity as a person.

So with the sinner and God. God cannot be damaged by sin, since he is omnipotent and invulnerable. He cannot be changed by it in any way, since this would conflict with the traditional doctrine of his immutability.

No finite act, such as the murder of one man by another, can disturb God except in one of two senses. It may be a symbol of general revolt, on the one hand; or on the other (though the two are not mutually exclusive) he may see the murder as directed towards him. 'As you did it to the least of these my brethren, you did it to me.' In either case, it is *lèse-majesté*; and since the *majesté* is infinite, the offence is too, and so should the punishment be. There was some dispute among Church fathers and theologians about whether a pain could, under any circumstances, be infinite in degree. Some proposed that God's torturers would play upon the sinner like a virtuoso on a Wurlitzer keyboard, producing excruciating pains of the eardrum, then of the teeth, then of the shinbone, and so on through the whole miserable frame, in sums and combinations which would suit the particular crime for which he was in Hell. Others gravely (and perhaps rightly) objected that no matter how many bad pains you added up, they would never reach infinity; and so the sinner must be content with second worst, which, as both factions agreed, was the infinite length of time which he spent in Hell. It would be wearisome to go into the tangled academic disputes in which Church theoreticians indulged themselves whilst on the question of infinite pain, but it is certain that torture was not to be approached with an equally bureaucratic spirit until the rise of the Third Reich.

If the soul, once in Hell, cannot get out and must stay there 'night and day, for ever and ever', the punishment of Hell is automatically vindictive. It cannot be designed to reform him since there is no point in doing so; he will never be able to exercise the capacity for moral choice which alone makes the idea of virtue significant. There are no choices in Hell. Still less can it be meant to deter him from sinning again, since, according to Thomas Aquinas, the souls in Hell cannot sin; they have surrendered their free will (or had it taken away from them).

36

Detail of demons and tortured souls from *The Last Judgment*, a woodcut illustration to the Revelation of St John the Divine in the British Museum.

Traditionally, the Church teaches that the soul is incapable of moral change after it leaves the body. It will remain forever in the state in which it was when it went before the Judge – unless of course it is merely in a state of venial sin, which can be burnt away by a brief sojourn in Purgatory. The soul in Hell becomes totally evil; all its capacities are reversed; as souls in Heaven are absorbed into the presence of God's being and thus become totally good, souls in Hell are permeated with and absorbed by the presence of Satan. Thus they cannot choose. They cannot even choose to be evil, any more than I can 'choose' to have a ribcage. All that remains of their knowledge of good is the memory of the vision of God, however brief, at their judgment. There is Scriptural authority for the belief that souls in Hell can see those in Heaven – Dives, for instance, was able to call out to Lazarus from the depths of his sulphurous pit and be heard. But this is merely another psychological torture – that of the starving beggar with his nose pressed to the restaurant window. There is no communication between the damned and the saved.

The existence of Hell is intimately linked to the Catholic belief in free will. In order to sin at all the soul must choose between two courses of action, one of which it knows to be good, the other bad. It must choose to do wrong whilst aware that it is doing wrong, otherwise it cannot sin: for sin is a *conscious* offence given to God. (This, as we shall see later, did not inhibit St Augustine from consigning all unbaptised babies to Hell.) Hence the importance of free will, which states that one is always at liberty consciously to choose one's action, unhampered by factors of which one is not consciously aware. The doctrine of free will has emerged very tattered and reduced by modern psychological enquiries (in what sense can any decision be said to be consciously taken, considering the innumerable pressures which act out of the environment below the threshold of consciousness?), and it would be reasonable to say that no student of psychology could accept the idea of free will as it was originally promulgated by Christian eschatologists. Moreover, even though the findings of behavioural psychologists were not available to theologians in the twelfth century, or for that matter in the seventeenth, there were evident *philosophical* problems in the official notion of free will. These have been succinctly demonstrated by D. P. Walker[4]. Absolute free will is, as Leibnitz called it, a chimaera because it is an immediately self-contradictory concept, Walker argues:

> . . . *If the free will by which a man performs any action is free, not merely from specific constraints, external or internal, but from all determining causes, then his action must be a random one; but wholly random, haphazard actions are not called acts of will, free or otherwise, and, since they are performed by people who are unaware of what they are doing or are mad, they are rather the opposite of voluntary acts.*

Alternatively, man must be the absolute first cause of his actions, in which case we are involved in a polytheism [from the aspect of proof by causality of the existence of God] so vast as to be unintelligible.

Moreover, Walker adds:

... this chimaera does not exculpate God from being ultimately responsible for the sins he punishes, unless one takes from him his omniscience as well as his omnipotence ... For if, before the creation, he foresaw that most men would abuse their free will and commit sins, he could have refrained from creating them, in which case there would have been no sins to punish.

One of the fundamental questions in any discussion of Hell is for what sins a soul may be consigned there. Clearly, some sins are worse than others and therefore deserve to be punished more severely. You cannot decapitate a driver for speeding without voiding capital punishment of its exemplary powers and ridding it of whatever pretence to justice it may still be thought to have. If all sins are met with infinite punishment then in the eyes of God no sin is worse than any other – a situation which neither the Church nor any of the societies which based its laws on ecclesiastical morals could have been prepared to accept. The Scriptures are vague on the differentiation of sins. The passage I have quoted in *Matthew* refers entirely to sins against charity – failing to clothe the naked, visit the sick and so forth. The Ten Commandments themselves are general laws which, as the traditional Church was at ceaseless pains to emphasise, require interpretation and application. And so out of the problems arising from infinite punishment the difference between mortal and venial sins was promulgated. In practice, the difference between mortal and venial sins was not easily defined, except by the circular process of saying that mortal sins threw you into Hell whereas venial sins committed you to Purgatory. But the concept of venial sin and Purgatory, through which the soul finally reaches Heaven, did at least save God from the charge of being utterly indiscriminate. It also refined Hell's virtues as a deterrent. If all sins are equally to be punished by eternal torture, there will be some members of the flock who, having committed a minor sin, may feel that now they have given themselves to the devil they may as well make a thorough job of it; an expanded chance of salvation could, it was felt, expand the will to virtue. And some flexibility was certainly needed, considering what the seven capital sins were: Lust, Anger, Gluttony, Pride, Envy, Sloth and Avarice. It is easy to envisage a mortal sin of anger – murder is one; or of lust, which for traditional Christian teaching meant almost any sexual contact outside marriage beyond a peck on the cheek and did not exclude masturbation; or of avarice. But how to commit a mortal sin of gluttony? Does the chronic alcoholic commit one? And how, in principle, can one tell a mortal sin of pride from a venial one?

The division between mortal and venial sins was only a gesture: it shifted the limits of God's intolerance without making them realistic. It was like repealing the eighteenth-century English penal law which hanged children for stealing bread while keeping the death sentence equally in force for poaching, forgery and regicide. The spectrum of mortal sin remained absurdly wide and the Church made no serious effort to establish whether the infinite punishment allotted to rapists could justly be extended, as it was, to lovers. The doctrine of Hell retained the gross impartiality of fallout.

This affords one reason for the decline of belief in Hell among modern Christians. A God who consigns people to Hell for everlasting and vindictive punishment does not seem worth worshipping; he appears no more fit to be loved than a sadistic governor of Bridewell. God's vengeful omnipotence and his goodness seem directly in conflict. Archibald MacLeish made his character of Job, in *J. B.*, speak for a generation of Christians today: 'If God is God, he is not good; if God is good, he is not God.' It is possible to imagine a God with a maimed moral sense and to hold that only such a God could have created, as in a capricious game, both his creatures with their tendency to sin and their Hell as a punishment. But faced with the possibility that God might be capricious or actually evil, many Christians have preferred to let drop the idea of Hell as vindictive punishment.

The Revelations of Divine Love, by Juliana of Norwich, portray the impact of this traumatic contradiction between Divine Love and Hell. Juliana's revelations took place in May 1373 – she was a cloistered nun, one of a community supported by the church of St Julian and St Edward at Conisford – and the revelations turned on the nature of man's relationship to God. This, God revealed to Juliana, was wholly integrated in divine benevolence, which was without limit:

From the time these things were first revealed I had often wanted to know what was our Lord's meaning. It was more than fifteen years after that I was answered in my spirit's understanding. 'You would know our Lord's meaning in this thing? Know it well. Love was his meaning. Who showed it you? Love. What did he show you? Love. Why did he show it? For love. Hold on to this and you will know and understand love more and more . . .' And I saw for certain, both here and elsewhere, that before ever he made us, God loved us; and that his love has never slackened, nor ever shall.

But she is puzzled by the existence of sin in this scheme of embracing love and asks God about it. He replies, in a famous phrase, that sin is inevitable but 'all shall be well, and all manner of thing shall be well': words in which one may detect a trace of the ἀποκατάστασις παντῶν or Restoration of All Things, the universal salvation of everyone, including the devil, which, being the core of Origen's theory of eschatology, was also the

Demons carrying off damned souls, from a French mediaeval tapestry.

cause of his condemnation for heresy by the Council of Alexandria in AD 400. But this did not satisfy Juliana:

Another part of our belief is that many creatures will be damned; for example, the angels who fell from heaven through pride, and are now fiends; and those men on earth who die apart from the Faith of Holy Church, namely, the heathen; and those too, who are christened but leave unchristian lives, and so die out of love – all these shall be condemned to Hell everlastingly, as Holy Church teaches me to believe. This being so I thought it quite impossible that everything should turn out well, as the Lord was now showing me.

God, however, fobs her off with this reply:

What is impossible to you is not impossible to me. I shall honour my word in every respect, and make everything turn out for the best.

Juliana found this puzzling, but as a devout Catholic she had to resign herself. 'How this will be, no one less than Christ will know – not until the deed is done. At least, that is what I understood our Lord to mean at the time.' But her mystical experience continued to stand at odds with Church doctrine on Hell:

I wanted [as far as I dared] to get a real sight of Hell and Purgatory. It was not my intention, of course, to put any article of the Faith to the test, for I steadfastly believed that Hell and Purgatory existed for the same end that Holy Church taught. What I was hoping for however was to see [and thereby to learn] those things which are taught by the faith . . . but for all my desire I saw absolutely nothing, except . . . where I saw the devil reproved by God and condemned eternally.

Even the devil himself lacked the terrible power over souls which Catholics usually credited to him. Juliana perceives 'the emptiness of the Fiend's powerlessness', and sees him as a repulsive but comically inept Caliban:

Even if our enemy gains something from us when we fall . . . he loses very much more because of our love and humility when we get up again. This glorious rising up gives him such sorrow and pain [he hates our soul so much] that he burns and burns with envy. The very sorrow he would impose on us turns back upon itself. Which was the reason why our Lord spurned him – and the reason, too, why I laughed so much.

Only the orthodoxy of Juliana's Catholic discipline stopped her from drawing the logical but disastrously heretical conclusion from her visions: that the God of Love cannot be the God of Hell. In the end one is left with the impression that God created a Hell but could not, in his nature, use it to punish his creatures; that its only inhabitants are the original rebels, Lucifer and the other demons who revolted against God before the creation of the world.

The most advanced modern theologians, Catholic and Protestant alike, tend to share the view that the Hell of retributive punishment does not exist. This, in different forms, has been

The Last Judgment, from a 15th-century illuminated manuscript in the Bibliothèque Nationale, Paris.

proposed by Tillich and Barth, but it was at least implicit in the theory of Hell from its conception. It was foreshadowed by John Donne, in his seventy-sixth sermon, preached to the Earl of Carlisle and his company:

What Tophet is not Paradise, what brimstone is not amber, what gnashing is not a comfort, what gnawing of the worm is not a tickling, what torment is not a marriage bed to this damnation, to be secluded eternally, eternally, eternally from the sight of God? Especially for us, for as the perpetual loss of that is most heavy, with which we have been best acquainted, and to which we have been most accustomed; so shall this damnation, which consists in the loss of the sight and presence of God, be heavier to us than others . . .

Thus the chief torment of Hell is the *privation of good*: the experience of being irrevocably and permanently cut off from the God whose perfect being the soul has, however momentarily, glimpsed through prayer on earth and directly experienced at the moment of its judgment after death. Now Hell as privation bears the same relationship to Hell as vindictive punishment as life imprisonment does to hanging: the soul is permanently isolated, and the punishment is its knowledge of being cut off from the one thing which would complete its being, union with God. It is, in other words, punished by the knowledge of its own frozen potential. Donne relegated the sulphur and pitchforks, the wailing and gnashing of teeth, to second place; the modern tendency is to drop them altogether, leaving a notion of Hell which would have struck a thirteenth-century monk as blasphemously refined – Hell as state of mind, not as place. It could very well be argued that punishment by privation was always the fundamental idea of Hell; and that the paraphernalia of major and minor demons, smoking pits, boiling rivers, cauldrons, spits, red-hot stakes, pincers, groans and lamentation was simply an incrustation on this idea. Its function was to make Hell concrete. The idea that the pain of sin is loss of the vision of God is, by its nature, difficult to grasp. Only by dint of great metaphysical effort can a man take the idea that it might be supremely unpleasant to be deprived of an experience which he has never in fact had; and only a miniscule fraction of Christians, at any time in the history of the Church, have even so much as claimed to have had direct experience of God. This is one of the traditional problems associated with the writing down of mystical revelation: language will not carry the ineffable experience and so mystics have repeatedly been forced to write metaphorically: thus St Teresa of Avila, for instance, employed sexual metaphors of astounding concreteness to describe her visitation by the angel.

But everyone has suffered physical pain. The prospect of being tortured is therefore much closer to one's sense of *possible* experience than the much more abstract prospect of losing the vision of God. Since life on earth is tolerable without this vision, the sinner could reasonably assume that life after death would be tolerable without it too. The tortures of Hell are the grotesque and terrible metaphor which seals this exit from moral responsibility. It is tempting to speculate that the image of Hell could only retain its obsessive force as long as punishment by torture was identified with justice, whether papal or princely. When Damiens, the would-be assassin of Louis xv, was first tortured for eight months and then, disfigured beyond recognition, was executed, the crowd watched with delight while his right hand was cut off, bubbling oil and lead were poured into his cuts, and four horses, each yoked to a limb, slowly tore him asunder; the *bourreau* had disarticulated his joints with a knife, not to end his sufferings out of pity but to allow the spectacle to be completed before dusk cheated the audience of its climax. It is probable that hardly a member of the crowd, except a few radically-inclined *philosophes*, thought that justice had been anything other than served by their entertainment. And as long as you were aware that the Inquisition, the King, the Signoria or the Council of Three could, and at the least provocation would, punish your crimes with unspeakable torments, you could without difficulty regard the same torments administered forever by the wrath of God as both just and inevitable. For centuries torture was a normal and unquestioned technique for the operation of law. There is little evidence that even the most sensitive Florentine neo-Platonist objected to the judicious use of the rack or the axe. The justice of the republic, conducted by its torturers in the cellars of Palazzo Vecchio, reinforced and was in turn reinforced by the draconic modes of God's justice which ground inexorably on, several thousand feet further down, in the bowels of the Inferno.

But once mass torture presents itself as a perversion of justice to a wide audience, belief in Hell becomes correspondingly more difficult. The last fifty years of European history have witnessed both an unprecedented degree of revulsion from torture on the part of educated men and a vastly expanded use of torture by totalitarian states. If you believe that Hitler was a monster for murdering six million people and torturing millions of others, you are likely to have difficulties with a God who, according to the sixteenth-century theologian Drexelius, managed to cram 100,000,000,000 burnt, flayed and gutted souls into the space of one cubic German mile. The idea of Hell has shifted its position: no longer the metaphor of ultimate justice, it has become the image of total injustice. It may be no accident that (as we shall see later) the imagery of Hell, especially as personified in the figure of Satan, shifted so far into the realm of *aesthetics* during the radical years of the nineteenth century, thanks to the Satanists and Decadents.

Hell, by their implication, is an antidote to vulgarity. Its terrors exist to produce an unexpected *frisson* for poets and painters; and so they are, in reality, neutralised. The theologians of the Middle Ages and the witch-hunters of the fifteenth and sixteenth centuries would not have been impressed by so easy a resolution of aggression. It would have seemed as perversely unrealistic to them as the modern collapse of Satan into a trademark for pepper would, no doubt, have seemed to Baudelaire.

But any study of the history of images of Hell in art must begin by recognising that, for the greater part of its history, belief in Hell was absolute, concrete and specific. The tortures may have begun (as I have suggested) as a convenient metaphor for a state of deprived consciousness which could not, in its nature, have been accessible to a wide audience; but to the painters who covered their walls and panels with Last Judgments, Infernos and Comings of Antichrist during the Middle Ages and the Renaissance, the literal truth of the doctrine that, in a place of smoke and fire, Satan and his minions tortured sinners, seems to have gone unquestioned. And so it did for the audience at whom their visions of Hell were didactically aimed. It is extremely perilous to treat the imagery of Hell as if it were an effusion of the artist's subconscious. In studying the history of that imagery, we are confronted with many recurrent forms, each of which carries a specific load of allegorical or directly symbolic meaning. In short, the art of Hell has what Surrealism does not possess: an iconography rooted in a complex of set and consciously articulated beliefs. This is not to deny that Hell gave painters a rich chance to vent their own sado-masochistic obsessions. But in the end the comparison of recurrent forms with their religious environment may tell us more about the art of Hell than any amount of rhetorical speculation, *à la française*, on the Ids of Ghiselbertus, Taddeo di Bartolo or Hieronymus Bosch.

part 2

Heaven

Faire is the heav'n
Where happy soules have place
In full enjoyment of felicitie;
Whence they doe still behold the glorious face
Of the divine, Eternall Majestie;

Yet farre more faire be those bright Cherubins
Which all with wings are overdight.
And those eternall burning Seraphins
Which from their faces dart out fiery light,

Yet fairer than they both and much more bright,
Be th' Angels and Archangels
Which attend on God's owne person without
    rest or end

These then in faire each other farre excelling
As to the Highest they approach more neare,
Yet is that Highest farre beyond all telling
Fairer than all the rest which there appeare.

Though all their beauties joynd together were;
How then can mortall tongue hope to express
The image of such endlesse perfectnesse?

Edmund Spenser
1552–99

chapter 2

A Garden Enclosed

Our word Paradise comes from the Old Persian *pairidaēza*, which originally meant a circular walled enclosure and came to be applied to royal parks. The Persian went into Hebrew as *pardēs*, meaning, again, a park or garden. (It is used in this sense only three times in the Old Testament, of which the most important is the famous verse from the *Song of Solomon*: 'A garden enclosed is my sister, my spouse; a garden locked, a fountain sealed.')

In Greek, the word became *paradeisos* and kept its reference to parks and gardens. It was first used by Xenophon to describe the park, or vivarium, where King Cyrus kept the animals he hunted[1].

At this stage, 'paradise' did not mean an abstract state imagined in terms of angels and metaphysical ecstasy. Paradise was a place; it had concrete attributes, pleasures, inhabitants; often it was given a geographical location on earth. When Heaven is under discussion, it is useful to distinguish between this Garden of Eden and the alternative convention of supramundane bliss symbolised as a clustering of saints and angels around the Godhead, with no clear location in space. In legend and literature the two visions of Heaven interweave and sometimes become quite inextricable. Christian art however tended to preserve them intact, at a slight distance from one another.

It is natural that our ideas of the earthly Paradise should be coloured by the way we think about gardens today. However, we are heirs to a taste for artificial wildernesses and picturesque, ruin-laden landscape which comes from Romanticism. As a result, gardens are not the epigrams of order for us that they were for a classical or mediaeval man. The idea that gardens ought to have an air of untamed nature is modern and it does not occur in antiquity. Then, gardens were attractive precisely because they were formal: they were images, executed in grass, flowers and vegetables, of the power which consciousness had over brute nature in all its spontaneous irrationality. Gardens became ideal symbols of order, for in them nature is subdued and made to conform to a humanised, rational scheme which is not its own. The thicket, the dark wood and the bramble surrender themselves, in a metaphor enclosed by a few yards of garden wall, to the parterre, the vine and the incense-bearing shrub. Each burrowing root and tumescent pod is watched. The formal garden represents a victory over each element in turn. Air, by the delicate perfume of flowers and herbs; water, by the conduit and the *chasse d'eau*; earth, by cultivation; fire, by the shade of tree and trellis. And its purpose is to make the most

Fra Angelico: the blessed in Heaven, outside the walls of the Celestial City. Detail from *The Last Judgment*, Museo di S. Marco, Florence.

agreeable environment that human beings can imagine for themselves – a place without extremes, where nothing menaces, and the myth of the Golden Age seems not too far away. Man presents himself with another metaphor of that harmony which is expressed in his own body. Moreover, the enclosed garden is a microcosm of innocence. It is a feminine image, suggesting passive repose and uterine protection: mind cushioned by an amniotic fluid of pleasure. All aggression ceases, because desire is satisfied almost before it can take form as action. After Adam and Eve ate the fruit of the Tree of Knowledge, God 'drove out the man; and at the east of the Garden of Eden he placed the cherubim, and a flaming sword which turned every way, to guard the way to the tree of life' [*Genesis* III, 24]. The notion of Paradise is saturated in nostalgia: this is the innocence our ancestors lost for us, at the close of a period over whose vanishing we had no control.

Hence, inevitably, the durability· of Paradise as a recurrent dream (pp. 25–7). At the end of the earth, on an island or a mountain, separated from the rest of the world by an impassable wall, a mountain of ice, dense and perpetual fog or a curtain of fire, there is a green garden full of flowers, nightingales, fruits and exotic perfumes, irrigated by rivers of water, oil, honey, claret or mead, where neither winter nor summer reach: an endless springtime, an enclave of youth, its pavilions and temples glittering with gold and precious stones (p. 46). This vision of the peaceable kingdom is at least as old as the *Epic of Gilgamesh*, and it permeates the mythology of numerous societies and cults – western Christianity is merely the latest – between some of which there was, and could have been, no traffic. Obviously, the most celebrated account of Paradise is given in *Genesis*. But Christian art owes as much to classical ideas of Paradise and its associations as it does to the Old Testament, partly because the revival of interest in antiquity during the Middle Ages and the Renaissance carried with it a resurgence of the myth of the Golden Age; and so we may conveniently begin by sketching Paradise as envisaged by classical writers – since, if Zeuxis, Apelles, Melanthius and other painters in antiquity ever depicted their ideal garden, neither the pictures nor any description of them have survived.

In the fourth book of the *Odyssey*, Menelaus, disguised as a seal, traps Proteus (the Old Man of the Sea) and wrings prophecies from him. 'And now, King Menelaus,' he intones,

hear your own destiny. You will not meet your fate and die in Argos where the horses graze. Instead, the immortals will send you to the Elysian plain at the world's end, to join red-haired Rhadamanthus in the land where living is made easiest for mankind, where no snow falls, no strong winds blow and there is never any rain, but day after day the West Wind's tuneful breeze comes in from Ocean to refresh its folk. That is how the Gods will deal with Helen's husband and recognise in you the son-in-law of Zeus.

Note the ingredients; they will recur. Elysium is at the world's end – very remote, but still on earth, and hence capable of being reached and in a place other than the abode of the Olympian gods. This may be the first appearance of the earthly Paradise in classical literature; later it was to be developed into the myth of Paradise as a place in the East, situated in the fabulous and distant lands of India, Ethiopia or China. Elysian weather is mild, without extremes of heat or cold; a fit climate for the exposition of marmoreal physique by nude Homeric heroes, caught in their endless and aesthetic Now. Life is effortless there. Moreover, access to Elysium is token of the favour of the gods. Menelaus goes there by right of privilege. He married Helen and became the son-in-law of Zeus. For Elysium is not a part of Hades; to it go heroes who have been exempted from death, whereas Hades is filled only by the dead, virtuous and wicked alike, mingled in a grey monotony. Hades is connected with the root of the Christian Hell and Limbo; but in Homer's Elysium, with its throng of undying nobles and warriors rewarded by the fat of the land, one may detect a primitive hint of the promise of Heaven: 'The righteous shall enter into eternal life.'

Hesiod's description of life on the 'isles of the blessed' may have been written as early as 800 BC, and it is close to Homer's. But now the idea of a Golden Age is introduced. This tenacious myth was the classical world's equivalent to Christian belief in the primal innocence of man, destroyed by the sin of Adam and Eve. The Golden Age's character, according to Hesiod, was of noble (not brutishly rustic) simplicity. Under the benign influence of Kronos, youngest son of Heaven and the father of Zeus, Hades and Poseidon, heroes stalked about in Elysium, living

like gods, without sorrow of heart, remote and free from toil and grief; miserable age did not touch them, but with arms and legs which never failed they made merry with feasting beyond the reach of evils. When they died, it was as though they were overcome with sleep, and they had all good things; for the fruitful earth, unforced, bore them fruit abundantly . . .

This way of life, Hesiod went on, is granted to 'men who do true justice'; this is the first suggestion that Elysium is a divinely-given reward for virtue (as distinct from a nepotic privilege for being related to Zeus). It was echoed by Pindar. Ovid on the other hand, did not think one could get back to the garden, past the flaming cherub; he saw the Golden Age through an exquisitely tinted Claude glass of nostalgia; it was an epoch gone forever, succeeded by the ages of Silver, Bronze and – last and miserably – of Iron, 'whose base vein let loose all evil'. The Golden Age was an epoch of 'soft' primitivism, when men were naturally good. Ovid's description of it reads like a classical version of the millennium offered to the nineteenth-century proletariat by Kropotkin or Proudhon:

In the beginning was the Golden Age, when men of their own accord, without threat of punishment, without laws, maintained good faith and did what was right. There were no penalties to be afraid of, no bronze tablets were erected, carrying threats of legal action; no crowd of wrong-doers, anxious for mercy, trembled before the face of their judge; indeed, there were no judges, men lived securely without them.

People were happy at home and so they did not travel. Thus there were no wars.

. . . the earth itself, without compulsion, untouched by the hoe, un-furrowed by any plough, produced all things spontaneously, and men were content with foods that grew without cultivation. They gathered arbutus berries and mountain strawberries, wild cherries and blackberries that cling to thorny bramble bushes: or acorns, fallen from Jupiter's spread-ing oak. It was a time of everlasting spring, when peaceful zephyrs, with their warm breath, caressed the flowers that sprung up unplanted. In time the earth, though untilled, produced corn too, and fields that never grew fallow whitened with heavy ears of grain. Then there flowed rivers of milk and rivers of nectar, and golden honey dripped from the green holm-oak. [*Metamorphoses*, Book 1]

The Garden of Love

It is to this classical background that a painting of the Golden Age like Lucas Cranach's owes part of its existence (p. 90). A garden is set in a peaceful landscape of rocks, castles and villages, with a lake stretching away to the horizon. The light is mild and diffused but a sundial on the tower of a little pavilion set in the garden wall points to noon. Below it, surmounting a trough into which water trickles from a satyr's mask, is an em-blematic figure of Justice, holding up a pair of evenly balanced scales; while on the roof of the pavilion, an owl – the bird of Wisdom – perches. The trees are globed with apples, peaches and pomegranates. Deer, lions, rabbits and a fox disport them-selves on the thick, flowery grass. And so do a dozen nude men and women, frolicking, sharing a bunch of grapes, splashing in the ornamental pool, or dancing in a ring round one of the fruit trees.

So far, everything (except the northern Renaissance architec-ture of the fountain and wall, and the presence of a military castle on the hill) accords perfectly with Ovid's description of the Golden Age. But one important aspect of Cranach's paint-ing does not. This is its erotic content: the Paradise Garden flows with sexuality, whether in the saucy wiggling of those mock-rustic backsides, the pose of the reclining couple by the pool (which is no less sexy for being a rather uninspired quo-tation from the poses of a river-god and a naiad), the come-hither *oeillades* which the nymphs who dance round the tree are darting at the viewer, or the lusciously gawky sprawl of the girl on the right, with a quintessentially Cranach sprig of vegetation hiding – or pointing to – her pubis. Even the animals in the garden are not, on closer inspection, the expected image of the lion lying down with the lamb in Paradise. The lion is lying down with the lioness; while rabbits do a mating dance, doe and stag nuzzle, and a fox, that familiar mediaeval symbol of lust, looks on.

This Cranach is in fact a luxurious and completely secularised version of one of the most common metamorphoses of Paradise: the Garden of Love. Mediaeval romance literature reverts to this image over and over again. It derives from a classical prototype of the Paradise Garden as abode of Venus, which then (with the biblical sanction of the text from the *Song of Solomon*, about the bride as a secret garden) was almost indefinitely allegorised as a symbol of the Virgin Mary, or the Mystical Marriage of Christ and his Church, or Divine Love: the permutations of the garden were without limit, and we can do no more than sketch them in the barest of outlines.

'*Beatus ille*,' wrote Horace, '*qui procul negotiis | ut prisca gens mortalium, | paterna rura bubus exercet suis*' (blessed is he who, leaving business behind him, works his life out on his ancestral land among the cattle): this austere and natural purity was built into the ideas which Romans, in their more idealistic moments, had about the basis of their own state. The story of Cincinnatus called from his plough to rule Rome was as important to Romans, on its own sentimental level, as the myth of the president born in a log cabin is to Americans today. And there would seem to be little connection between the world of ideal form produced by useful labour which lay at the centre of the Roman poet's ideal landscape garden and the extravagant paraphernalia of hard-to-woo damsels, dangerous bridges, crystal vaults, gold moats and angelic messengers which comes with the Paradise images of mediaeval romances. Yet there was a prototype in classical literature, which came from the landscape of the Golden Age and the country retreats of Augustan poets and was to shape mediaeval paradises. This is the walled garden as precinct of Venus. Its most elaborate description was given by Claudian (*fl.* AD 395–404), in his *Epithalamion for Honorius Augustus*. On Cyprus, he writes, there is a mountain where Venus lives. Its climate is of the Golden Age: 'Frost does not dare to fall on it, nor the rude winds buffet it, nor do clouds veil it'. And:

The mountain's height slopes down into a plain, which is encircled by a golden hedge, guarding its meadows with yellow metal . . . The enclosed country is beautiful, always bright with flowers, though no labouring hand touches it . . . The very leaves live for love and in his season every tree experiences love's power ; palm bends down to mate with palm, poplar sighs its passion for poplar . . .

In this pan-erotic landscape (where even the twin rivers, one of sweet and the other of bitter water, serve as wells in which Cupid dips his arrows, thus functioning as symbols of the *dulce amarum*, the pairing of Love and Death), the central monument, glittering in the distance, is the Palace of Venus. It reflects a

A 15th-century French tapestry showing a pleasure garden with birds and other animals. The peacock in the centre takes pride of place.

51

green radiance caught from the trees around it; Vulcan, the Artificer of Olympus, constructed it from gold and precious stones, with roof-beams of emeralds and columns of hyacinth, an agate floor, jasper door-frames and hyacinth columns. In the courtyard even the grass is perfumed, and the earth oozes and drips suggestively with balsam. As Giamatti pointed out[4],

> [Claudian's] legacy to the Middle Ages was to fix firmly the convention of a natural bower or grove or enclosure dedicated to Venus and her pastimes ... He has crystallised much ancient garden poetry, and he stands at the threshold of the Christian world with the riches of antiquity carefully collected and arranged. It was the task of his beneficiaries to adapt what they could.

To anyone who has spent a little time in Italy, the transformation of Venus into the Virgin Mary is a perfectly familiar process. Even today, the rites of St Venerina are celebrated by the *parrocco* and the citizens of one town in Calabria: and St Venerina is merely a Christianised version of an ancient Venus fertility cult. The cult of the Virgin Mary in Latin countries has never lost its basis in fertility worship. Indeed, it could not have survived so vigorously if it had. Therefore it need not surprise us to see the elements of Claudian's walled bower of Venus transformed by allegory into the enclosed garden wherein, grasping the horn of a submissive unicorn, sits the Virgin Mother of God. The Middle Ages were capable of allegorising almost anything. Their imagery was swift to join the classical pleasaunces to the most celebrated garden in the Old Testament, Solomon's.

The *Song of Solomon* is one of the supreme works of erotic literature and today we are apt to read it simply as such.

I come to the garden, my sister, my bride,
I gather my myrrh with my spice,
I eat my honeycomb with my honey,
I drink my wine with my milk.

Eat, O friends, and drink:
* drink deeply, O lovers!*

I slept, but my heart was awake.
Hark! my beloved is knocking.
'Open to me, my sister, my love,
* my dove, my perfect one;*
for my head is wet with dew,
* my locks with the drops of the night.'*
I had put off my garment,
* how could I put it on?*
I had bathed my feet,
* how could I soil them?*
My beloved put his hand to the latch,
* and my heart was thrilled within me.*
I arose to open to my beloved,

and my hands dripped with myrrh,
 my fingers with liquid myrrh,
 upon the handles of the bolt.
I opened to my beloved,
 but my beloved had turned and gone . . .
I adjure you, O daughters of Jerusalem,
 if you find my beloved,
that you tell him
 I am sick with love.   *[Song of Solomon* v, 1–8]

Here, in a sexual image whose precision and directness may be without parallel in ancient literature, the garden merges with the body of Solomon's virgin bride, and its locked gate becomes her vagina. However, the Fathers of the early Church were at some pains to interpret the *Song of Solomon* as an unexceptionably chaste allegory of the future relations of Christ with his Church. Thus the bride's beloved, touching the gate as her aromatic fluids stream over its bolt, developed into the famous image of Christ knocking at the door of the world and appealing to the faithful to accept his doctrines. Even passages like this could be allegorised, and were:

You are stately as a palm tree
 and your breasts are like its clusters.
I say I will climb the palm tree
 and lay hold of its branches.
O may your breasts be like clusters of the vine,
 and the scent of your breath like apples,
and your kisses like the best wine
 that goes down smoothly
 gliding over lips and teeth.   *[*VII, 7–9]

This was taken to mean that Christ would cling to his Church and by firmly gripping its 'branches' prevent them from being buffeted or broken by the winds of heresy. In brief, it was a prediction of papal infallibility. It has often been said that this frenzy for discovering secondary and tertiary levels in the *Song of Solomon,* whilst ignoring its primary one, was forced upon interpreters by the inherent puritanism of the Catholic Church. But this is not really sufficient explanation. The habit of seeing the whole world, let alone the works of art and poetry that existed in it, as an allegory was endemic to mediaeval culture. The universe was experienced as a symbol and not simply as a collection of objects. It symbolised the motions of God's mind. Thus, to take only one of an infinity of possible examples, here is Hugh of St Victor, reflecting on the 'meaning' of a dove in the thirteenth century:

The dove has two wings even as the Christian has two ways of life, the active and the contemplative. The blue feathers of its wings are

53

opposite Mary surrounded by emblems of the Litany of the Virgin. Each image is derived from the *Song of Solomon*, after that erotic poem was Christianised: Tower of David, Chosen Vessel, Well of Water, rose, lily, City of God, Enclosed Garden. Reliquary cover, 17th century, French.

top The Annunciation in the Enclosed Garden. Note the elements from the *Song of Solomon*: locked gate, fountain, Tower of David and so forth. German tapestry, late 15th century, Berlin. **above** Another tapestry of the *hortus conclusus*, German, dated 1554. Note the ritual sacrifice of the unicorn by Adam and Eve: it symbolises Christ offering his redeeming blood for mankind.

thoughts of heaven; the uncertain shades of the body, the changing colours that recall an unquiet sea, symbolise the ocean of human passions in which the Church is sailing. Why are the dove's eyes this beautiful golden colour? Because yellow, the colour of ripe fruit, is the colour too of experience and maturity, and the yellow eyes of the dove are looks full of wisdom which the Church casts on the future. The dove, moreover, has red feet, for the Church moves through the world with her feet in the blood of the martyrs.

If doves could not wear the colours that serve them for mating display, identification and camouflage without demonstrating God's plan for Catholicism, what chance had the protagonists in the *Song of Solomon?* The very presence of so lavishly praised a garden in the Bible would have seemed evidence of its allegorical purpose.

And so Solomon's bride became the Virgin Mary, and the great canticle of sensuality was interpreted as a paean of praise either to the Mystical Marriage of God with Mary or to the marriage of Christ with his Church (p. 54). When Claudian's garden sacred to Venus was transferred into a Christian context and 'moralised' it was fused with the allegorised Garden of Love in the *Song of Solomon.* The result was a specifically religious symbol: the Virgin in her *hortus conclusus*, signifying her Immaculate Conception.

In paintings and tapestries – for the most celebrated representations of the Virgin's *hortus conclusus* generally occur in the latter – there is a complicated and on the whole fixed iconographical scheme for symbolising the Immaculate Conception in this way. The central figure is of course Mary (p. 55). She sits on the ground – a flowery meadow, girdled by a wall – and holds the horn of a unicorn, which has come up to lay its head in her lap.

The reason for the unicorn's presence was given by Honorius of Autun, in the *Speculum de Mysteriis Ecclesiae* or 'Mirror of the Mysteries of the Church':

The very fierce animal with only one horn is called Unicorn. *In order to catch it, a virgin is put in a field; the animal then comes to her and is caught, because it lies down in her lap. Christ is represented by this animal, and his invincible strength by its horn. He, who lay down in the womb of the Virgin, has been caught by the hunters; that is to say, he was found in human shape by those who loved him.*

There is certain fitness in representing the moment of Christ's conception by a beast whose tapered, phallic weapon is pointed at Mary's womb. (Nevertheless, the unicorn can mean not Christ himself but chastity in general. It is used in this sense in some images of St Justine of Padua, for instance; she was a child martyr, and a unicorn crouches at her feet. This fits the unicorn's reputation for tireless speed when pursued, so that it became an ideally chaste beast, and as such a suitable emblem.)

When the unicorn submits to the virgin, the hunters catch it. This was adapted into an elegantly complete allegory. The hunters become Adam and Eve (p. 55). Adam plunges a spear into the unicorn's heart, just as the centurion, Longinus, pierced the heart of Christ in his last agony on the cross. Blood gushes out, in a heraldic arc, and falls into a chalice held by Eve below. A scroll, issuing from Adam's mouth – for artists who depicted the *hortus conclusus* were apt to label every symbol in the garden as meticulously as botanists tie a ticket to each shrub – proclaims that this is he who was wounded for our sins. Adam and Eve, by rejecting the command of God and eating the apple in their original earthly paradise of Eden, consigned all the human race to the state of original sin, which could only be washed away by the sacrifical blood of Christ at his crucifixion. Now, in the new Paradise reconstituted as another enclosed garden, the primordial couple enact the sacrifice which their own weakness had made necessary. The unicorn, then, becomes a symbol of the Eucharist. The fact that this beast could take on at least three different, though related, shades of meaning in one tapestry may account for the presence of a more customary symbol of divine insemination – the Holy Ghost in the form of a dove, flying down to Mary from a cloud and closely followed

Domenico Veneziano: *The Annunciation*, Fitzwilliam Museum, Cambridge. Many paintings of this theme kept allusions to the *hortus conclusus* of Solomon's canticle: here, the closed gate at the end of the arbour – on which the perspective lines converge – is an emblem of Mary's virginity.

by the infant Jesus, who bears a cross over one shoulder.

Outside the garden wall stands the Archangel Gabriel, sent by God to announce her conception to Mary. He is never seen inside the garden, since the objects enclosed by the walls are nearly all attributes of the Virgin herself. He extends his trumpet, greeting Mary with the traditional words – 'Hail Mary, full of grace, the Lord is with thee . . .' He holds a sceptre, and on a leash four hounds, emblematic of the strengths which Christ will pre-eminently radiate: *Veritas, Judicia, Pax, Misericordia* – truth, justice, peace and mercy. And this triumphant annunciation is given at a closed gate to the garden – the *porta clausa* of Solomon's canticle. Soon it will open; the lover has returned to claim the bride. Such is the probable meaning of the closed

The Master of Flémalle and assistants: *Madonna and Child with Saints in the Enclosed Garden*. Flemish, second half of 15th century, National Gallery of Art, Washington. One emblem remains here from Solomon's canticle: the Tower of David, seen on the right.

door at the end of the arbour, whose latch is the vanishing point of the perspective in Domenico Veneziano's *Annunciation* (p. 57).

Several images within the garden walls derive from the *Song of Solomon*. A rose-bush alludes to charity, a lily symbolises purity, and both recall Solomon's verse: 'I am a rose of Sharon, a lily of the valleys'. Fruit and flower burgeon across every square inch of the embroidered green precinct, for

Your shoots are an orchard of pomegranates
  with all choicest fruits,
  henna with nard,
nard and saffron, calamus and cinnamon,
  with all trees of frankincense,
  myrrh and aloes,
  with all chief spices . . .   *[Song of Solomon IV, 13–14]*

The Virgin is endowed with the attributes of Solomon's sister-bride. 'Your neck is like the tower of David, / built for an arsenal, / whereon hang a thousand bucklers, all of them shields of warriors' (IV, 4); and behind Mary is a Gothic tower, hung with heraldic scutcheons which, a scroll tells us, is 'the tower of David which was equipped with a thousand shields'. A fountain spurts forth three jets of water, recalling Solomon's praise of his bride as 'a fountain sealed'. Its three spouts may represent the theological virtues – Faith, Hope and Charity, from which all good actions flow. The fountain itself, of course, is another of the extensions of the bride's body, summed up by the garden as a whole. It is the *Fons Signatus*, one of the names of praise in the doxology of the Virgin, and it is echoed by a stone well outside the garden wall, from which a copious stream gushes: 'a well of living water / and flowing streams from Lebanon'. The contrast between the living spring outside and the sealed fountain within is another link in the chain of metaphors in which the Paradise Garden was bound: spontaneous life outside the walls, but in Paradise a totally controlled, harmonious, self-abnegating consciousness.

Other symbols cluster about the Virgin in the *hortus conclusus*. The descending dove of the Holy Ghost fulfills Solomon's promise that, in his garden, with winter past,

The flowers appear on the earth,
  the time of singing has come,
and the voice of the turtledove
  is heard in our land.   *[II, 12]*

A pelican wounds her breast to feed her chicks with blood – a familiar image of Christ's sacrifice on the Cross. In another part of the garden is an altar. Twelve rods stand on it. The middle one sprouts with almond-blossom. *Virga Aaron:* this is Aaron's rod, which burst into flower at God's command *[Numbers XVII, 1 ff.]* while the rods of the other eleven tribes of Israel remained dry, to indicate that God had chosen Aaron of the tribe of Levi

School of Schongauer: *The Virgin and Child*, late 15th century, National Gallery, London. The wall of the garden has become a rustic plaited fence.

opposite *The Expulsion from the Garden*, miniature from the Bedford Book of Hours, French, c. 1423, British Museum. Inside the walled garden, whose gate is guarded by the armed cherub, Adam and Eve eat the apple. Note the octagonal Gothic building surmounting the well from which the Four Rivers of Paradise issue to irrigate the quarters of the world. **overleaf** Hieronymus Bosch: *The Garden of Earthly Delights ;* Prado, Madrid.

Heraldic nature is completely secularised in the frescoes by an unknown follower of Simone Martini in the Papal Palace at Avignon, c. 1340. Yet traces of the myth of the Paradise Garden remain.

as his high priest. On his descendants devolved the responsibility of (among other things) tending the Ark of the Covenant. Mary was said to come from the tribe of Levi; her role as mother of Christ conferred on her an immediate association with the Ark of the Covenant, so that the blossoming rod turned into yet another of her attributes.

In short, the mediaeval image of the Virgin in the *hortus conclusus* presents us with an exceptionally complex structure of symbols, deriving from the Old Testament and especially from the *Song of Solomon*. Some of them were dropped by artists who were less preoccupied with Annunciation symbolism than the mediaeval tapestry-designers: for instance, the *Madonna and Child with Saints in the Enclosed Garden* (p. 58), by the Master of

Coute nir ceigr̃ aua adam et porta en puadie creestre et trit eue de son cou̇ff et seur deffent le fruit

Restoration after Leonardo da Vinci and assistants: ceiling fresco on the Sala dell'Asse, Sforza Castle, Milan. Much of the effect of this intricate illusionistic ceiling of painted branches depends on its associations with bowers in Eden and, more directly, with the Venus-gardens of classical antiquity.

opposite Francesco Traini: detail of *The Triumph of Death*, Camposanto, Pisa. Note the hexagonal font, the Tree of Death and the Horseman of the Apocalypse.

Flémalle and his assistants, omits all the Virgin's 'attributes' except the garden wall itself, and David's tower.

In the ravishing little *quattrocento* Paradise Garden in Cologne, which is one of the last paintings of the enclosed garden still to retain a specific religious significance, one may detect vestiges of the *Song of Songs*, if only in the fountain of pure water, the shrubs and the presence of the infant Christ, plucking at a zither. Kenneth Clark found in this painting 'the elements of late mediaeval landscape in their most perfect form', and, once their limpid integration has been experienced, it is hard to demur. So perfect is the illusion of an ideal universe that one feels one need only smell the enamelled paint surface to catch, across the fading of half a millennium, a breath of lily or calamus.

The *hortus conclusus* of the Annunciation calls to mind the *Dame à la Licorne* in the Cluny Museum (pp. 66–7), exquisitely posed on a raft of grass and wild flowers which is separated by the merest border of wall from the stippled background field of blossoms and rabbits; here, the unicorn is less an image of Christ than a heraldic summing-up of wildness and natural mystery. And more than a century and a half before this virgin was woven, the earthly Paradise had been thoroughly secularised – though not of course denuded of its magic as an image of nature con-

left and opposite Two panels from the 16th-century cycle of tapestries, *La Dame à la Licorne*. Musée de Cluny, Paris. The image of the Virgin Mary with the sacred unicorn is fused with that of the ideal Lady in mediaeval romance poetry.

trolled and amenable – in the frescoes which, in the 1340s, an unknown follower of Simone Martini painted in the Tour de la Garderobe in the Papal Palace at Avignon (p. 60).

But these are the secular end of the earthly Paradise myth, and the artists who painted them were not, perhaps, under quite the same stringent need to allegorise the original vision of the Garden of Venus into a Garden of the Virgin. Nevertheless, as Giamatti points out, there was a certain embarrassment when it came to reconciling one's vision of the enchanted *secular* garden with the prototype of the earthly Paradise in Eden to which it referred. These Gardens of Love 'are condemned as false in spite of (or perhaps partly because of) their metaphorical relationship with the earthly Paradise. They are condemned, as the Garden of the Rose is, by the laws of Christianity.' The *Romance of the Rose* makes it quite clear that, delightful as the first '*parevis terrestre*' may be, and close as its appearance is to Eden's, it is nevertheless not the true Paradise. The amorous lady in the garden, by the Fountain of Narcissus (p. 68), is closer to Venus than to Mary; and all the features of the garden, its birds which 'sang a song as if they were angelic spirits', its two streams issuing from the fountain, its silvery sand and profusion of greenery and fruit, are only deceptive promises of Eden, just as the rose-bush itself, guarded by a briar hedge, may be a parody of the Tree of Life which grows in Paradise. The pagan attraction of Venus-gardens was not dead yet; and through the example of such works as the *Romance of the Rose* it was to exert significant influence on Renaissance visions of the earthly Paradise. Before examining these, it will be useful to go back to the biblical origins of the Eden myth and see how they were preserved in those works of art which were neither allegories of the Annunciation in a *hortus conclusus* nor illustrations of mediaeval courtly love.

66

The Garden of Love, in its secular form. **left** The amorous lady by the Fountain of Narcissus, from a 15th-century manuscript of the *Romance of the Rose*, Pierpont Morgan Library, New York. **above** Lovers in an enclosed garden by a fountain. 15th-century French manuscript illumination.

The Garden of Eden

The description of Eden in *Genesis* is remarkably laconic.

And the Lord God planted a garden in Eden, in the east; and there he put the man whom he had formed. And out of the ground the Lord God made to grow every tree that is pleasant to the sight and good for food, the tree of life also in the midst of the garden, and the tree of the knowledge of good and evil.

A river flowed out of Eden to water the garden, and there it divided and became four rivers. The name of the first is Pishon; it is the one which flows around the whole land of Havilah, where there is gold; and the gold of that land is good; bdellium and onyx stone are there. The name of the second river is Gihon; it is the one which flows around the whole land of Cush. And the name of the third river is Tigris, which flows east of Assyria. And the fourth river is the Euphrates.

[*Genesis* II, 8–14]

There is no symbol more widely diffused in art and literature than the tree, and it always seems to retain, in however modified a form, one fundamental meaning: the life of the universe. Its intricate, unchanging vegetable functions, the rise of water from its roots, the ooze of sap through its limbs, the diffusion of gas by its leaves, give a tree the aspect of a microcosm – a complete world, self-contained, absorbed in its own processes. The life around it suggests a world too: birds that perch in it, insects that infest it, the worms and moles burrowing under its roots and the creatures that shelter beneath its arms. Its growth cycles – flower and fruit, ripening and decay, the shedding of leaves and bark, even the yearly rings in which it builds its trunk – suggest the cyclical change and regeneration of the universe, the motions of its planets and the turning of Fortune's wheel. Trees are usually benevolent symbols (except in Hell, in such images as the Wood of the Suicides [*Inf.* XIII] and the general symbolism attached to dark woods and forest-fears by mediaeval and Renaissance artists); they are nicely balanced between masculinity (robust trunk, vertical growth, penetration into earth and sky) and femininity (shelter, fruitfulness). Moreover, in growing upwards from the ground, they link the three regions of the Underworld, Earth and Heaven – an aspect which was to be of great importance to Christian symbolism when the 'Tree of Life' was equated with the crucifix, on which Christ died in order to restore the balance of these three worlds. Two types of this idea are the garden precinct, enclosed by a wall of plaited rushes, in which a tree, representing Hope, grows (left); and the image of the flowering cross on which Christ hangs, also walled in like a secret garden, with extravagantly fruiting branches from which the elect pluck the grapes and apples of salvation.

Two images of the Tree of Life: **top** 'The Tree of Hope', growing in an enclosed garden. **above** an 11th-century tympanum from the parish church of Stoke-sub-Hamden, Somerset.

69

Because Christ's sacrifice enabled man to recover from his original sin and enter Heaven, the Cross itself was sometimes depicted as a form of the Tree of Life, flowering and fruiting. **opposite** *Crucifixion* by Dürer, Musée des Beaux-Arts, Rennes. **below** Miniature of Crucifixion, Morgan Library, New York.

above The Old Man of the Mountain with his adepts, in the artificial paradise of hashish-eaters. Miniature from 15th-century MS of Marco Polo's travels, Bibliothèque Nationale, Paris.

The Tree of Life occurs in innumerable descriptions of Paradise other than the Old Testament's. It is inherited from eastern mythology. In ancient Persia the tree was called Gaokerena; from it sprouted a white manna or fruit (the description is not clear) called *haoma*. To eat this was to achieve immortality. It was the food of the gods. Clearly, it was connected with the magical drink of ancient India, mentioned in the *Rig-Veda* before 800 BC:

The heavens above do not equal one half of me.
Have I been drinking soma?
In my glory I have passed beyond the sky and the great earth.
Have I been drinking soma?
I will pick up the earth, and put it here or put it there.
Have I been drinking soma?   [*Rig-Veda* X, 7–9]

Indeed, in the *Vedas*, there are passages which equate the divine drink with a picture of Paradise singularly close to the ecstatic descriptions of the Golden City in Christian tradition:

Eight wheels, nine doors
has the impregnable castle of the gods.
In it resides the golden disc,
celestial and brilliant.

72

opposite top Date-palm flanked by two lions. 12th-century mosaic, Royal Palace, Palermo, **opposite below** Winged Assyrian deities fertilising the ritual palm. British Museum. **right** Assyrian eagle-headed winged figure fertilising the palm. British Museum. **far right** Winged bull with man's head from palace of Assurnasirpal, Assyrian, c. 890 BC. British Museum. **above** Capital with lions flanking a tree, possibly the Tree of Life. 11th century, Musée des Beaux-Arts, Poitiers.

The golden castle, colour of Soma,
which shines from far away, all covered
with glory – the Brahmin enters there,
into this impregnable castle.   *[Atharva-Veda* x, 2, 31–3]

Soma was cannabis – or one of its derivatives. And there are examples which show that hashish or marijuana was connected with visions of the earthly Paradise, especially in the east. The most famous of them is Marco Polo's account of the great sheikh, or the Old Man of the Mountain, who constructed

the biggest and most beautiful garden that was ever seen, planted with all the finest fruits in the world and containing the most splendid mansions and palaces that were ever seen, ornamented with gold and with likenesses of all that is beautiful on earth, and also four conduits, one flowing with wine, one with milk, one with honey, and one with water . . . And he gave his men to understand that this garden was Paradise. That was why he had made it after that pattern, because Mahomet assured the Saracens that those who go to Paradise will have beautiful women to their hearts' content to do their bidding and will find there rivers of wine and milk and honey and water.

Into this garden (p. 71) the sheikh put young men to whom he had first given 'draughts that sent them to sleep on the spot'; when they woke, they believed that they had reached the promised land[3]. That the Tree of Life should give food to the blessed and inspire grace in them is thoroughly consonant with the kind of Christian symbolism which, by equating the tree with the cross, turned its fruit into the Eucharist. In the *Book of Enoch*, the narrator is taken through Paradise by the angel Raphael and shown the Tree of Life, 'whose fruit shall be for food to the elect', and the *Apocalypse* of St John describes

the water of life, bright as crystal, flowing from the throne of God and of the Lamb through the middle of the street of the city; also, on either side of the river, the tree of life with its twelve kinds of fruit, yielding its fruit each month; and the leaves of the tree were for the healing of nations.   *[Rev.* xxii, 1–2]

The twelve kinds of fruit, probably, were for the twelve tribes of Israel.

With this biblical and apocryphal sanction the Tree of Life passed into Christian visions of the earthly Paradise. There is scarcely a description of Paradise in mystical or devotional writing between the New Testament and the twelfth century which fails to mention the healing, nourishing tree. As a motif it seems to have passed into Romanesque art from an eastern prototype, the *hom*, or tree flanked by two fabulous beasts (pp. 72–3). Solomon (*1 Kings* vi, 29, 32 and 35) decorated his temple 'with carvings of cherubim, palm trees and open flowers; he overlaid them with gold, and spread gold upon the cherubim and upon the palm trees'. One authority[4] persuasively suggests that these temple cherubim were the winged creatures of Assyrian art, 'who are represented frequently in the symbolic

Piero della Francesca: *The Death and
Burial of Adam*, S. Francesco,
Arezzo. c. 1452.

gesture of fertilising the ritual palm' (pp. 72–3). And one need
only compare the appearance of the great Assyrian colossi in the
British Museum (p. 73), formed of a man's head, an eagle's
wings, the body of a lion and the legs of a bull, with the description given in the Old Testament of the cherubim who dance
attendance on God, to see how possible this relationship is:

*As for the likeness of their faces, each had the face of a man in front ;
the four had the face of a lion on the right side, the four had the face of
an ox on the left side, and the four had the face of an eagle on the back.*
[*Ezekiel* 1, 10]

If Ezekiel's cherubim come from his memory of monumental
Assyrian bulls, there may be an interesting connection between
the palm-trees and cherubim carved in Solomon's temple and the
Tree of Life in Eden, because '. . . at the east of the garden of
Eden, [God] placed the cherubim, and a flaming sword which
turned every way, to guard the way to the tree of life' [*Genesis* III,
24]. In any event, whether the Tree of Life was a palm or not
(and what more natural choice for the magical tree that bestradd-
led the source of the rivers of Paradise than the palm which
grows in oases?), it was so firmly established as one of the attributes of Paradise by the Middle Ages that Thomas Aquinas
could write of its existence as one of the few knowable facts
about the *paradisus terrestris*. Aquinas was echoed by a parade of
mediaeval writers, from Vincent of Beauvais to Brunetto Latini.

And the idea that it prefigured the Cross appears as early as the third century AD, in the *Legend of Seth* : here, the leafless Tree of Life produces three seeds, each of which grows, in turn, into another tree. Eventually these three trees are felled, hewn, and nailed together by the Romans to make the cross on which Jesus died. This legend is the source of another, used by Piero della Francesca in his fresco cycle of the *Legend of the True Cross*, in which the tree of the cross sprouted from Adam's buried corpse (p. 75).

The other normal use of the Tree of Life was as symbol of the Church. Here, another aspect of trees than their woodenness could be exploited: their profusion and the number of creatures that nested in them. Thus in the *Vision of Tundale*, perhaps the most famous of all mediaeval visions of Heaven and Hell and certainly the most elaborate, the narrator enters the earthly Paradise, passes by the Fountain of Youth, crosses walls of silver and of gold, and finds himself in a realm where (in a curious anticipation of the water-organs in sixteenth-century Italian gardens, or the artificial birds that hooted by the throne of the Byzantine emperor) musical automata play tunes and souls chant with them. Inspired by these warbling ancestors of the steam calliope, Tundale presses onwards to find the Tree of Life: an immense growth of indeterminate species, laden with every kind of fruit, flower, herb and aromatic spice, and the perch of countless birds. The birds are souls, and saints, martyrs

Romanesque fresco, c. 1125, from Church of the Holy Cross, Maderuelo, Spain. Prado, Madrid. On left, the Tree of Life; at right, Adam and Eve at the Tree of Knowledge.

76

The Creation of Adam, the Creation of Eve and, at right, Eve tempting the reluctant Adam to eat from the Tree of Knowledge. Bas-relief by Wiligelmo, façade of Modena Cathedral, c. 1100.

and desert fathers live in golden hutches beneath the branches of the tree. It is an admirable image of the all-inclusive Church, and certainly many of the Trees of Life which appear in Gothic and Romanesque decoration, with their interlaced boughs and myriad fruits, were intended in this sense.

Despite the constant flow of literary references to it, the Tree of Life is not found in art as often as its counterpart in Paradise, the Tree of Knowledge of Good and Evil. There is a scriptural basis for this discrepancy, since God is not recorded as having shown the Tree of Life to Adam and Eve whereas the Tree of Knowledge, as everyone knows, was the hinge on which the fate of this first couple turned. 'You may freely eat,' said God, 'of every tree of the garden; but of the tree of the knowledge of good and evil you shall not eat, for in the day that you eat of it you shall die.' Whereon, in that conversation which consigned us all to a world of acne, prudery, political upheaval and tax,

[. . . the serpent] said to the woman, 'Did God say, "You shall not eat of any tree in the garden"?' And the woman said to the serpent, 'We may eat of the fruit of the trees of the garden; but God said, "You shall not eat of the fruit of the tree which is in the midst of the garden, neither shall you touch it, lest you die."' But the serpent said to the woman, 'You will not die. For God knows that when you eat of it your eyes will be opened, and you will be like God, knowing good and evil.' So when the woman saw that the tree was good for food, and that

77

it was a delight to the eyes, and that the tree was to be desired to make one wise, she took of its fruit and ate ; and she also gave some to her husband, and he ate. Then the eyes of both were opened, and they saw that they were naked . . .   [*Genesis* III, 1–7]

By eating that infinitely desirable fruit, Adam and Eve had completed the first stage in a rebellion against God, by becoming *like* God: the primal sin of pride. They had raised themselves above the lotophagous simplicities of the earthly Paradise:

Then the Lord God said : 'Behold, the man has become like one of us, knowing good and evil ; and now, lest he put forth his hand and take also of the tree of life, and eat, and live for ever' – therefore the Lord God sent him forth from the garden of Eden . . .   [*Genesis* III, 22–3]

So specific is the Bible account that one would not expect the scene of Adam and Eve at the Tree of Knowledge to vary, iconographically, from artist to artist or even from period to period. Nor does it. Eve may be the awkward, slabsided nude, flat feet rooted to the soil, that Wiligelmo carved at Modena at the beginning of the twelfth century (p. 77), or the ripe crea-

above left *Adam and Eve*, engraving by Marcantonio Raimondi after Raphael. **right** Hugo van der Goes (1440–82): *The Temptation*. Kunsthistorisches Museum, Vienna.

'Like a naiad weaving through sea-growths'; a Romanesque carving of Eve in Paradise from the lintel of Autun Cathedral. French, 12th century.

ture who throws out the long, rich curve of her hip, like a promise of transfiguration, to Adam, in Marcantonio's sixteenth-century engraving after a lost original by Raphael (opposite, left). Hugo van der Goes may stand her beneath the tree, filled with shy confidence yet touched, at the moment she feels the fruit, by a premonition of shame (opposite, right); or, like a naiad glimpsed weaving through sea-growths, she may undulate across a lintel at Autun (above), plucking the apple as she goes. Adam may be the slender, vulnerable figure which Hieronymus Bosch painted in the left wing of his *Haywain* (p. 81), or the expressively stringy quotation from a battle sarcophagus in Pol de Limbourg's image (p. 80) of the Fall, or the resplendent nude who stretches out his arm to the tree and the serpent on the Sistine Chapel ceiling (p. 81). The devil hardly changes; whether all reptile or a hybrid of human torso and serpent's tail, he remains the archetypal snake-in-the-grass – one important exception to the usual method, in other biblical scenes, of painting him as a fearsome amalgam based on the classical satyr. (The serpent coiled round the tree gave rise to the habit of depicting the devil whom Mary crushes underfoot as a snake or dragon. The

80

Versions of Adam: **right** detail from
The Haywain (1500–2), by
Hieronymus Bosch; **opposite** *The
Expulsion from Paradise*, by Pol de
Limbourg, from the *Très Riches
Heures du Duc de Berry*, 1410, Musée
Condé, Chantilly; **above** *The
Temptation and Expulsion*, by
Michelangelo; Sistine Chapel, Rome,
1509–10.

mother of Man is led astray by the serpent but the mother of God vanquishes him in the end. It is tempting to presume that the association of Eve and the serpent reinforced another customary use of the snake as devil in Christian art: the serpent or dragon who, having a virgin in his power, is speared by St George.)

The Garden of Earthly Delights

Of all the great visions of the earthly Paradise in Christian art, the one that seems, at first sight, closest to the spirit of *Genesis* and of later visionary literature is the left wing of Hieronymus Bosch's triptych, *The Garden of Earthly Delights* (pp. 62–3). In the foreground of a rolling green parkland, God the Father raises Eve into life with an effortless, flowing gesture. Eve's skin is translucent and new-minted as a pearl; her hair cascades down her back, a stippled blonde mandorla. The vagaries of erotic taste in the last four hundred years have not altered the attractiveness of her compact little body – though one needs to allow for the bulbous Gothic paunch, which, though not to us, was a primary characteristic of sexual attractiveness in fifteenth-century Flanders. Her pose is derived from the classical nereid – she is in fact the exact northern counterpart of Lorenzo Maitani's fourteenth-century Eve on the façade of Orvieto Cathedral (opposite, top), 'floating,' as Kenneth Clark put it, 'into new life' – and one is apt to share the surprise of Adam, bolt-upright and pop-eyed on the shaven lawn of Paradise, staring at this proof of God's benevolence. All around, birds and animals frisk, hop, prowl and graze. In this vision of the Peaceable Kingdom, with all species living together in one garden immediately after the Creation, Bosch was able (instead of inventing a zoo of hybrid monsters) to deploy, with some pride, his scope of reading about the zoological marvels of what, in the fifteenth century, the real world was thought to be. In some cases, he was surprisingly erudite. His spotted came-leopard, or giraffe, is a more accurate rendering of the African animal than one usually finds in zoological illustrations a century later. Wild boar and duck he would have seen, and perhaps, in some travelling circus, an elephant; the flying fish in the fore-ground pool is real, and the unicorn and narwhal, though fabu-lous, conform to familiar prototypes. Not even the hybrid reptiles and birds that cluster round the little pond are alarm-ing; the birds, in particular, have the metallic, jewelled elegance one associates with Fabergé eggs. On a rock to the right, the Tree of Knowledge of Good and Evil grows, a date-palm, with a black snake coiled about its trunk. To the left, immediately behind Adam, is a queer tree with fleshy lobed branches and palmate, lance-shaped leaves. Wilhelm Fraenger has shown[5] that this derives from a woodcut of the 'Tree of the Sun and Moon' in a German edition of the travels of Sir John de Mande-ville, that stay-at-home compiler of eastern marvels filched

The age of the image of a serpent tempting its victim with an apple can be gauged by comparing any Christian use of the symbol with its pre-Christian appearance in Egypt. **above** The snake, a phallic image, was suited to express the uncontrolled libido suggested by temptation.

Lorenzo Maitani: *The Creation of Eve*,
Orvieto Cathedral, 14th century.
Compare Maitani's Eve with
Hieronymus Bosch's (p. 62). **right**
Lorenzo Maitani: *The Temptation*.
Note, behind the Tree of Knowledge,
the fountain of Paradise, with the
Four Rivers issuing from it.

opposite Adam and Eve, miniature
from a 15th-century book of hours.
French, Bibliothèque de Châlons-sur-
Marne.

from Pliny, Megasthenes, Ctesias and others (above). This tree, according to Mandeville, grows in the earthly Paradise, somewhere in the east, and it seems to be yet another form of the familiar Tree of Life: there can be little doubt that Bosch intended it as such. It may be worth noting, as a sidelong glance, the odd resemblance between Mandeville's and Bosch's tree and an illustration, in an early Dioscorides ms. from Constantinople, of the cannabis plant; but to use this as evidence of a link between the soma-growing Trees of Life in eastern mythology and the imagery of a northern Renaissance painter would be tendentious.

Several writers on Bosch have discovered, in this crystalline and idyllic vision of the earthly Paradise, signs of 'unnaturalness and corruption'. 'Eve,' writes Charles de Tolnay severely, 'is already an image of temptation, and the first look that Adam is giving her is a first step towards sin. This is seen in the fauna and flora: a lion is devouring a deer, a wild boar is pursuing a strange beast...[6]'. Tolnay's assumption is that the *Garden of Earthly Delights* triptych is to be read serially, from left to right: incipient sin with Adam lusting after Eve, sin rampant in the complex lubricities of the central panel, and sin punished in the right-hand panel of Hell. Yet, considering that few unions be-

opposite left Adam and Eve in Paradise. Woodcut from Schedel's *Nuremberg Chronicle*, 1493.
Compare the exotic tree on the far right of this illustration with the Tree of Life in Bosch's *Garden of Earthly Delights* **opposite**. Note also the rivers of Paradise issuing from an aperture in the garden wall.

God shows Death to Adam and Eve, after their original sin. Miniature from 15th-century French MS of St Augustine's *De Civitate Dei*, Bibliothèque Ste Geneviève, Paris. The rivers are the Pison, the Geon, the Tigris and the Euphrates.

tween a man and a woman can ever have been as thoroughly sanctioned by God as Adam's with Eve in their primal innocence, de Tolnay's distress at the look on Adam's face is surely misplaced. Unless one is to fly in the face of the *Genesis* narrative and assume that God did not mean our ancestors to make love at all, it is more reasonable to take Bosch's earthly Paradise as a moral contrast, not an *hors-d'oeuvre*, to the Garden of Lust. As for the pugnacious animals, there is nothing in *Genesis* to suggest that God intended carnivores to eat grass rather than meat. Shift the angle of view a little, and Bosch's enchanting cat (opposite), padding off into the shrubbery with a rat dangling from its jaws, could just as convincingly be read as a symbol of Virtue triumphing over Vice. There is every reason to suppose that Bosch, whose power of detailed zoological observation was in its way almost as acute as Leonardo's, would have seen that animals, in the unimpeded course of their natural activities, do eat other animals, and that this is part of God's plan. Paradise would only be disturbed if they turned on man himself, thus upsetting the hierarchy of organisms set by God at the moment of creation.

The image which dominates Bosch's painting is, however, the

fountain. Tier after tier it rises into the limpid air of Paradise, a tower of knife-edged forms of leaf, shell and carapace, fossilised in pink spiracles of horn. It is as if the flamboyant border decorations of a Gothic Book of Hours had detached themselves from the vellum and become solid. An owl perches in a hole in its spherical base, looking as incongruous as the fragment of organic matter one sees behind the crystal window of an elaborate *trecento* reliquary. (It is not possible to tell what meaning, if any, this owl has. Tolnay *[ibid.]* saw it as the worm in the apple, 'the bird of misfortune'. However, owls in classical times were symbols of wisdom, and in mediaeval art they became attributes of Christ, who died 'To give light to those who sit in darkness and the shadow of death' *[Luke* I, 79*]*. As with so many of Bosch's images, you pays your money and you takes your choice.) Of all Bosch's images, this fountain is among the dozen or so which most excite the post-Freudian sensibilities of modern critics. 'It is pink, tumescent, phallic, streaming with pearly liquid. Only a sluggish subconscious could ignore it[7].' But the significance of this fountain to Bosch – and, no doubt, to his contemporaries – was thoroughly conscious. It is the Fountain of Life; and as such it is the result of a long development of the imagery of water in Paradise.

Water as Grace

If one lives in a city with plumbing, it is difficult to recapture the feelings which, in the Middle Ages and the Renaissance, fountains tended to provoke. For city-dwellers, water is not an element; it is something clear and tasteless that appears when you turn a tap or flush a lavatory, useful for boiling peas or wetting the toothbrush; it is only dimly related to the stuff that floods towns or sinks ships. In Florence, after the 1966 flood, it was interesting to see the reactions of Italian friends to the other, the alien water which had gutted the city. It might have been a totally different substance to the fluid that normally came out of pipes. For a few weeks in Italy, water became an element again: an unpredictable substance, appalling in its force, which demanded a vast spending of ingenuity and work to control it. All the water-fears of primitive man stared back from the swollen Arno, just as the pleasure of controlled water was brought home by the daily arrival of the tanker of *acqua potabile* in Piazza Signoria, precious stuff, almost sacramental, hoarded in flasks.

Technology has insulated us from the symbolic power of water. This was not of course the case five or six hundred years ago. To take water from a rain-filled reservoir or an underground spring; to direct its course through a network of lead pipes, buried underground; to cause it, at last, to fling its glittering plume twenty feet into the air, or slide in a veil from a shell held by a nymph, or trickle from the lips of a satyr – what more articulate triumph over nature could be imagined? The fountain

Abraham in Paradise with the elect clustered in his bosom. At each corner are the Four Rivers, depicted as variations on classical river-gods with urns of water.

causes water, which as a rule had to be laboriously windlassed up from a well, to bubble out of the ground as if by magic, an apparition, a benison, the very metaphor of abounding grace. And so the fountain emphasises both the power of consciousness over hostile elements in the world and the positive, life-giving aspect of water itself (pp. 62–3).

Water as grace: this is the meaning of the Four Rivers of Paradise mentioned in *Genesis*. They are the Tigris, the Euphrates, the Pison and the Geon. They rise in the centre of Eden, issue from its boundaries, and irrigate the four quarters of the world. The Pison and the Geon corresponded, it seemed, to the Nile and the Ganges, and a good deal of ingenuity was expended by early writers on the geographical problems involved in this. If the rivers encircled the earth (as Flavius Josephus, in the first century AD, thought), how did they come from the centre of the – flat – world? Pomponius Mela[8] and the Venerable Bede[9] concluded that they disappeared underground before they left Paradise, passing beneath one another like tube tunnels so as not to mix their waters. This meant a tortuous course. One school of thought held that the rivers flowed to the ocean, dived along its bed and came up at the other side miraculously pure and saltless. Philostorgius[10] found the whole business a little obscure but had no doubt that their direction of flow was complicated:

[The Nile], then, if one may conjecture, takes its rise in Paradise, and before reaching any inhabited region, its waters are absorbed by the sand, whence it makes its way secretly into the Indian Sea, and there takes a sort of circular course – for what man knows anything accurately concerning this matter? – and then passing under all the intervening continent, makes its hidden passage into the Red Sea, on the other side of which it eventually appears again beneath the mountain which is called after the Moon. There it is said to form two great fountains, situated at no great distance from each other, and throwing their waters up to a great height from below. The river then falls down a steep ridge of cliffs and passes through Aethiopia into Egypt.

Leaving aside the speculations about circular courses and hidden passages under the Red Sea, the last part of Philostorgius' account is fairly accurate. The Blue Nile does rise in the northern highlands of Ethiopia, from the southern end of Lake Tana; and a few miles away it plunges over the Tisisat Falls – as steep a ridge of cliffs as any traveller could wish to see – into the long gorge which cuts through Ethiopia and releases its waters into the flatlands of Egypt.

The *Vision of St Paul* (3rd century AD) mentions the Tigris, the Euphrates, the Geon and the Pison. Since the Pseudo-Paul said they were composed respectively of wine, milk, oil and honey, it was well that they did not mix; the emulsion might have distressed all but the most intent souls. In any case, whatever happened to the rivers after they issued from their source (traditionally, beneath the Tree of Life), they became an important symbol in Christian art. In Romanesque and Gothic painting and sculpture, the rivers were usually personified as four men with water-jugs. This was a Christian adaptation of the classical river-god (p. 86). A suggestive link between river-gods and the river-figures of Paradise is provided by Christian mosaics in North Africa, where the vase-bearers recline in the posture of classical gods; the earliest of these can be ascribed to the third century. A Limoges plaque of the twelfth century shows four figures – clockwise from top left, Geon, Pison, Euphrates and Tigris – emptying their water-jars, around a small central *tondo* in which the Lamb, symbol of Christ, stands. Since being washed in the blood of the Lamb is a basic metaphor of conversion to Christianity, we may see in this plaque one of the earliest sculptural examples of what was to become the chief use of the rivers of Paradise: a symbol of baptism.

This is made explicit in the figures of the Four Rivers on the early thirteenth-century font at Hildesheim. The font, with its contents of baptismal water, rests on their shoulders as they grip their water-jugs; since the rivers support the font, it is implied that the holy water comes from the rivers of Paradise. They are to the baptismal font what the underground stream or the conduit is to the secular fountain: for, as its very name implies, the font is a symbolic fountain.

The characteristic shape of fonts is polygonal. This is also the shape of the fountain in the tapestry of the *Hortus Conclusus* (p. 55), and it recurs in innumerable paintings; for instance, the fountain which occupies so prominent a place in the foreground of the Van Eyck brothers' *Adoration of the Lamb* (p. 90). A choir of angels surrounds the sacrificial lamb on the altar; below them, in the realm of earth, the faithful and the clergy chant their doxologies before the eight-sided fountain into which, from a metal shaft surmounted by an angel of salvation, the waters of baptism pour. So new-minted is this image, so caught in its perpetual springtime of flowered meadow and crisp red robes, that one is not apt to suppose that any of its images has an ancient history – except, of course, the lamb; but the octagonal fountain unquestionably does. It goes back to the symbolism involved in Mesopotamia and ancient Greek attempts to square the circle.

It has often been pointed out[11] that the square, with its firm symmetry, its solidity and definition, was a fundamental symbol of material things and thus of the earth and its stable characteristics – four seasons, four elements of earth, fire, water and air, four points of the compass. The circle, on the other hand, is the 'perfect form', serene, without angles, self-enclosed; angels and planets trace out its path; it is free from gravity, with no resting-point. It is the perfect symbol of Heaven and it was so incessantly used as such that one need adduce no examples here.

Now it was a habit of the ancient Greeks – and of the mediaeval schoolmen and Renaissance neo-Platonists who followed

Giovanni Bellini: *The Virgin in the Meadow*, National Gallery, London. Although the scene is ostensibly in open country, the picture is in fact virtually a *hortus conclusus*, and the well, for example, an echo of the fountain.

Hubert and Jan van Eyck: *The Mystic Adoration of the Lamb*. The *Allerheiligenbilder* or All Saints' Picture here finds a new expression. Note also the octagonal fountain, reminiscent of the *hortus conclusus*.

Lucas Cranach: *The Golden Age*. Here, in ironical relationship to the ideal Garden of Eden, the *hortus conclusus* has become a garden of fleshly love.

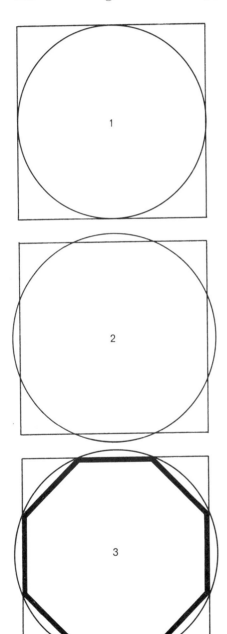

them – to regard geometry not as a pure science but as a symbolic activity. Pythagoras' attempts to develop a theory of numbers is an early example of this, and Leonardo's efforts to relate the ideal proportions of the human body to the square and the circle a late one. And there is no doubt whatever that the quest for a geometrical method of squaring the circle – that is, of inscribing, with ruler and compasses only, a circle and a square which would be of exactly equal area – was infused with symbolic intention. The completed figure, earth-square exactly conforming to the area of the Heaven-circle, would signify the fusion of the divine and the mundane, of essence and existence.

But how to do it? It was never done. At least, not by geometrical methods. An accurate slide-rule can give you, by calculations involving Π and x^2, a circle area within a fraction of a thousandth of a unit of the area of a square. But the obsessive search for a *geometrical* method of squaring the circle, in which mathematicians and alchemists (for whom it was a task second only in importance to the discovery of the philosopher's stone) absorbed themselves for centuries, could result in nothing more than a series of approximations. Of these, the most commonly represented was the octagon. If one inscribes a circle ·in a square, the difference between their areas will obviously be that of the curved triangles left over at the corners (1).

The solution must be to have the circle bulge outside the mid-points of the sides of the square, so that the bits of circle sticking out of the square will exactly cancel out the bits of the square's corners which stick out of the circle (2).

There is no way of constructing this circle so that the four cut-off corners of the square precisely equal in area the four portions of the circle which overlap the square. But the figure remained infinitely tantalising. And if one joins up all the internal lines, there appears a figure which contains, so to speak, the essence of both square and circle, reduced to an apparently equal area. It is an octagon (3).

This geometry may seem to have wandered some distance from the rivers of Paradise. Not so; for the octagon, as a symbol of the union square and circle and of the merging of their identities in a 'higher synthesis', was of all forms the most fit to symbolise the union between God in Heaven and the human soul on earth which grace alone made possible. And the chief way by which this grace was transmitted was through the sacrament of baptism, the purging of original sin from the soul by immersion in water. Hence the octagonal font (p. 94); and on a grander scale the octagonal plan of baptisteries. The Baptistery in Florence is one of the purest examples of this kind of symbol-form (p. 95). Its entrances, with their sumptuous bronze doors, correspond to the traditional exit-points of the rivers of Paradise at the cardinal points of the compass.

But the traces of the Four Rivers welling from their common source at the centre of Eden were not confined to religious art

above Antonio Vivarini: *The Fountain of Love*. National Gallery of Victoria, Melbourne.

The Fountain of Life in Paradise. **opposite left** Hieronymus Bosch: *Paradise*, left wing of diptych in the Ducal Palace, Venice, 1500–4. Water drips from a circular basin into a square receptacle, symbolising the passage of grace from Heaven to Earth. **opposite** Hieronymus Bosch: left wing of *The Last Judgment*, Bruges, 1508–9?.

and architecture. They determined the plan of innumerable secular gardens and courtyards. The courtyard after all is one of the types of the enclosed garden – an enclave, insulated from street noises and traffic by four walls: a cloister of peace. The typical layout of mediaeval and Renaissance courtyards and cloisters (pp. 94–5) involves a square plan, with a fountain or well at the middle and four paths leading away from the fountain to the sides of the enclosure. It may not be fanciful to see in this time-hallowed architectural prototype, which is still one of the most deeply soothing and pleasant ways of articulating a space ever devised by builders, a precise reflection of the layout of Paradise. At the centre, the fountain; flowing from it, the Rivers, which are symbolised by the paths, different in texture and material from the lawn or ornamental paving which covers the four unwalked-on segments of the courtyard.

The courtyard with its fountain is an ideal symbol of refreshment. Silence, sunlight, and water tinkling in the basin – no wonder that the fountain of baptismal water so readily became the *fons iuventutis*, the Fountain of Youth. It is touching to reflect that the unhappy Ponce de Leon, hacking his way through the

The design of baptismal fonts and even courtyards was affected by the symbolism of the Fountain of Life in Paradise, transmitting the waters of God's grace to earth. **upper left** Luca di Giovanni's octagonal font in Orvieto Cathedral derives its plan from the idea of a Heaven-circle fusing with an Earth-square. The fountain in the centre of formal Renaissance courtyards recalls the Fountain of Life in the centre of the enclosed garden **opposite.** The four paths radiating from it to the centres of the arcades refer to the Four Rivers of Paradise, as in the large cloister of S. Martino in Naples **left.**

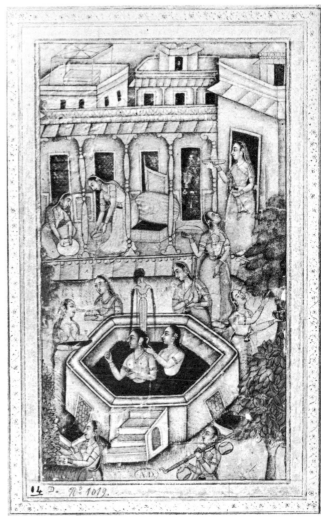

Its associations with baptismal grace made the octagonal or hexagonal plan a norm for baptisteries, such as S. Giovanni, Florence **upper left**. Here, the doors by Ghiberti and Pisano correspond to the exit-points of the Four Rivers. However, the polygonal fountain did not only exist in a Christian context, as an Indian miniature shows **above**.

creepers of the New World, probably expected that the Fountain of Youth which lay forever in the next glade of the rain forest looked like a Vivarini (p. 93). The soul in Paradise is refreshed by the Four Rivers and lives in perpetual youth; the sixteenth-century duke, lugging his accidie-dried brain round a formal garden, finds consolation in its *giochi d'acqua*. It is all much of a piece with the constant references to fountains in the Bible. God is 'the fountain of living waters' [*Jer*. II, 13]. 'On the last day of the feast, the great day, Jesus stood up and proclaimed, "If any one thirst, let him come to me and drink. He who believes in me, as the scripture has said, 'Out of his belly shall flow fountains of living water'"' [*John* VII, 37–8]. The fountain may even stand directly for sexual potency and fecundity: this, according to biblical exegesis since the eighteenth century, is what God meant when he expressed to the Jews his wish 'Let thy fountains be dispersed abroad' [*Prov*. V, 16]. It might be fanciful to connect this text too closely with the Mannerist fountain-sculptors' fondness for urinating cherubs, but it is interesting to see that the Freudian connection between fountain and penis had some biblical sanction, however slight. Nevertheless, the penis is the greatest solvent of complexity known to symbolism, and having

'For Paradise . . . means nothing other than a most pleasant garden, abundant with all pleasing and delightful things.' Lorenzo de' Medici. **above** Sandro Botticelli: *La Primavera*, Uffizi, Florence, 1477–8. **opposite** Benozzo Gozzoli's vision of Paradise as a Tuscan landscape; fresco, Palazzo Riccardi, Florence.

observed some of the ramifications of the Fountain of Life we may feel that it is a crass oversimplification to treat the fountain in Bosch's garden as merely a phallic symbol.

The earliest Fountain of Life in Bosch's work probably occurs in the Venice *Earthly Paradise* (p. 92). It stands on top of a knoll like a diminutive castle; from the square cistern at the base an ornate round basin rises on a pedestal – the circle of the heavens surmounting the square of earth, with water, as grace, falling from the upper into the lower receptacle. But the architectural orthodoxy of this fountain – you might expect to find it in any fourteenth-century courtyard – pales beside the weird elaboration of the fountain-cum-gazebo-cum-watchtower in the left wing of the Bruges *Last Judgment* (p. 92). We are in the earthly Paradise, though an odder one than Bosch's customary vision of rolling lawn and fruit-trees; the distance has the flat, vapour-saturated look of a world in the throes of evolving from mud, but in Paradise all is crystal, horn, shiny veined petals and slender bodies. The fountain is like a confectioner's fantasy in three storeys with Gothic lacery piped on. Gargoyles spit jets of water from the first storey into the pool which surrounds its base; and from each of the four corners of this cistern a stream flows out through the garden. Clearly, Bosch has retained the Four Rivers and incorporated them with the Fountain of Life; and to make the point explicit, the healing powers of the water are stressed by a tiny figure on the right, up to his waist in one of the streams, washing himself clean of sin. The fancifulness of this fountain leads naturally on to the fabulous structures of lobster-claw and onyx which, like petrified carnivorous flowers, dominate the *Garden of Earthly Delights* in Bosch's great Prado triptych (pp. 62–3). It is infinitely tantalising to make guesses at the relationship Bosch was implying between this central panel and the *Earthly Paradise* hinged on its left (p. 92). Probably the most attractive is that Bosch, in the Garden of Lust, intended a parallel on the social plane to the state of absolute harmony between man, nature and the beasts which is the centre of the earthly Paradise. The Garden of Lusts is Blake's Garden of Love, except that the chapel has not yet been built on the green and the priests in their black robes have not yet found a way in. It is an exquisitely elaborate dream of the perfectly integrated society achieved through collective sexuality: 'better to murder an Infant in its Cradle than nurse unacted desires'. Or is it? We do not know; it is the most enigmatic work of genius in the Renaissance, perhaps in the entire history of art; and, as Panofsky remarked,

In spite of all the ingenious, erudite and in part extremely useful research devoted to the task of 'decoding Jerome Bosch', I cannot help feeling that the real secret of his magnificent nightmares and daydreams has still to be disclosed. We have bored a few holes through the door of the locked room ; but somehow we do not seem to have discovered the key.

A Secular Paradise

With the revival of interest in antiquity for its own sake – as distinct from the survival of antique gods and motifs in a 'moralised' form which characterised the classical revivals in Europe between the tenth and fourteenth centuries – the dream of the earthly Paradise in art returned to a secular context. The result was that the iconography of *Genesis* and the mediaeval visions dropped away; fountains are pagan though they may refer back to Christian prototypes; Adam and Eve are not so often met with and the Tree of Life, the Tree of Knowledge and the Four Rivers are not insisted on. Instead, painters concentrate on Paradise as the *locus amoenus* of Latin poetry. The spirit of their picture, and of the Renaissance Paradise, was captured by Lorenzo the Magnificent in a commentary on his own sonnets:

For 'Paradise', whoever might wish to define it narrowly, means nothing other than a most pleasant garden, abundant with all pleasing and delightful things, of trees, apples, flowers, vivid running waters, song of birds, and in effect all the amenities dreamed of by the heart of man; and by this one can affirm that Paradise was where there was a beautiful woman, for here was a copy of every amenity and sweetness that a kind heart might desire.

In the Paradise Lorenzo describes in his *Selve d'Amore* (The Woods of Love), elements of the mediaeval Eden remain – because they are the very things that the Middle Ages retained from the classical gardens and Venus-bowers, and *Il Magnifico*, steeped in Graeco-Roman literature as in the writings of Poliziano and the neo-Platonist speculations of Ficino, had gone back to their source in the Golden Age. Predators (wolf, lion, bear) frolic with the sheep and cows; peacocks spread their fans for man, parrots and finches perch tamely on his shoulder; and the Virgin in her *hortus conclusus* has turned into a Botticelli nymph in the Garden of Venus, in the spring, *la primavera quando Flora di fiori adorna il mondo* – 'when Flora adorns the world with flowers'. The profound allegorical subtleties of Botticelli's *Primavera* (p. 96), embedded as they are in a matrix of almost unbelievable formal perfection, express the dream of the secular Paradise as no other picture has: and though the flattened space (as in a mediaeval tapestry), the thousand flowers, the interlaced grove of trees, and the ecstatic flow, gathering and release of the Graces' draperies locate the image in the transfigured air of Paradise, Botticelli's pagan Eden is made *accessible* by that character of his art which Pater described; a concern

with men and women, in their mixed and uncertain condition, always attractive, clothed sometimes by passion with a character of loveliness and energy, but saddened perpetually by the shadow upon them of the great things from which they shrink. His morality is all sympathy; and it is this sympathy . . . which makes him, visionary as he is, so forcible a realist.

99

Ever since Virgil hailed the reign of Augustus, the recognition of the new ruler as a sign of the Golden Age's prompt return has been a familiar habit of court poets. Colley Cibber and William McGonagall were as prone to this *tic* as Virgil and Poliziano; and yet there can be no period in which the conviction that one lived in the best of all possible worlds so infused poetry and the visual arts as the Italian *quattrocento*, especially in Florence under Lorenzo. (Nevertheless, one should be slower to deduce from this that Lorenzo's was the Golden Age than nineteenth-century writers were. We do not, after all, necessarily believe that Josef Stalin was a benevolent *pater patriae* because Stalinist writers and painters proclaimed it so often and so emphatically.) To show Paradise, all Benozzo Gozzoli had to do was paint the kind of landscape that one can still see in the Val di Pesa on a spring morning (p. 97). The angels and saints in the Van Eycks' *Adoration of the Lamb* convince one of the spirituality of the landscape. Not here: the landscape is actual, and it feeds humanity back into the two groups of angels which stand in it, chanting like choristers in a Tuscan village. But there was never a real landscape more like the ideal Paradise than this Florentine vista, with its grape-trellises and rose-bushes, its umbrella-pines and cypresses, its muscular fold and clench of hill-flanks around distant castles and villas, and the leaf-greens and purplish browns which drift towards the eye through the thin, lucid air. And Giovanni Bellini's *Madonna of the Meadow* is, in effect, an image of the Virgin's walled garden minus the wall (p. 89). For by now the wall is no longer necessary; there is no terrifying dark wood in which a garden need be enclosed; the Virgin's rapt meditation and the light sleep of the Child in her lap are protected by the universal benevolence of nature, a grace suffusing all things. But some of the elements of the *hortus conclusus* remain. The Tower of David has become a castle on the hill, with martello towers, chalky in the candid air; the *fons signatus*, a rustic well with a pole on a pivot for drawing up the water; and on the left, the pelican of the Church flaps and stiffens to fight off the serpent of evil.

Poussin and Watteau

The continuity between classical Arcadia and Christian Paradise may enable us to mention, in the latter context, the great Arcadians of the seventeenth and eighteenth century: Poussin and Watteau. Poussin inherited the Renaissance vision of actual landscape as Paradise and transmuted it back through its classical origins into the setting of the Golden Age, the vales of Arcady. But what was actual in Gozzoli or Bellini was, in Poussin, nostalgic. None of his paintings shows this more clearly than his second version of *Et in Arcadia Ego* (opposite). As Panofsky demonstrated in a masterly study[12], Poussin's theme of the tomb in Arcadia is a development of a more threatening image used by, among others, Guercino. Guercino has two innocent shep-

opposite above Stoic acceptance of death, and nostalgia for the vanished Golden Age, in Poussin's *Et in Arcadia Ego*, c. 1635–6, Louvre Paris. The presence of death in Arcady was more threateningly put in Guercino's earlier painting of a similar theme **below**. 1621–3, Galleria Corsini, Rome.

herds gazing at a mouldy skull atop a grave-slab in the middle of an Arcadian dell (p. 101); here, the words *Et in Arcadia Ego* remind us that 'I [death] exist even in Arcadia'. It is, in short, a *memento mori*. But in Poussin's case,

> . . . *we can observe a radical break with the mediaeval, moralising tradition. The element of drama and surprise has disappeared . . . Instead of being checked in their progress by an unexpected and terrifying phenomenon, [the Arcadians] are absorbed in calm discussion and pensive contemplation . . .*
>
> *Here, then, we have a basic change in interpretation. The Arcadians are not so much warned of an implacable future as they are immersed in mellow meditation on a beautiful past* [13].

With Poussin it is not death that speaks from the tomb, but a ghost, one of the *lares et penates* of the spot, wistfully reminding the living that he too was once alive and enjoying himself in Arcadia. It is like the voice that gentlemen on the Grand Tour imagined addressing them from the marble ruins of the Forum: dignified and profoundly nostalgic, patiently insisting that the present is worse than the past.

By the middle of the seventeenth century, nearly all the conviction about innocence and ideal states of being on earth which mediaeval artists gave to the walled garden, and the Renaissance to actual landscape, had been channelled into the neo-classical image of Arcadia. There, in the hands of Poussin's less gifted followers, it stiffened and became an academic convention. And it was left to one genius in the eighteenth century to reanimate the form. This was Jean-Antoine Watteau, and he did it by endowing the Arcadians with a most poignant psychological tension. There is a figure which recurs in Watteau's paintings: a woman with turned back, in a long dress of heavy silk, which falls in stiff, prismatic columns to the grass or the marble pavement. Watteau seems to have experienced the same fascination with this person, this shape, as Ingres did with the smooth nude back of the *Baigneuse de Valpincon* (and perhaps for the same reason, as an image at once remote and self-contained yet strangely consoling). She appears in the *Enseigne de Gersaint*, the *Assemblée dans un Parc*, the *Bal* (opposite); the unheeding statue in the background of *Le Mezzetin* is her marble sister. She is the still point past which the gestures of lovers, the notes of a lute, everything that is evanescent in the *fête champêtre*, flow; her silence holds them in existence and it is because of this that the space between her and her dancing partner in the *Bal* is as tense as the gap between God's finger and Adam's on the Sistine ceiling.

'If one asks what this picture [*Assemblée dans un Parc*], what all Watteau's pictures, are *about*, they are about men and women falling in love, trying to make up a society of love which nothing will disturb.' So Michael Levey[14]; and who would demur? It is Watteau's quest for an image of a society of the elect, living in harmony with an idealised nature – feathery green

Jean-Antoine Watteau (1684–1721),
Le Bal, Dulwich College Picture
Gallery, London. 'It is Watteau's quest
for an image of a society of the elect,
living in harmony with an idealised
nature and united *as a society* by love,
that relates him to the painters of the
earthly Paradise.'

trees, golden light sifting down on a lake – and united *as a society* by love, that relates him to the painters of the earthly Paradise. We need not be surprised that, after Watteau, artists could produce nothing better, in the way of Paradise Gardens, than the whimsical primitivism of Hicks' *The Peaceable Kingdom*. There was nothing left for them to say.

The Ape in Eden

Lavater once remarked that 'Sin and the destruction of order are the same' – a belief which is central to Christian moral theology, and to the visions of Heaven and Hell that came out of it. And that is fundamentally why the Paradise myth lasted. Paradise epitomises our dream of order: natural organisation, with no aggression, no frictions, no tensions of any kind, is the reward of virtue, the concrete evidence of it. We came from innocence, lost it, and may – with luck and God's mercy – get back to it, in the walled garden with its herbs and flowers, its birds and soft-eyed giraffes, its golden pavilions and streams of healing water.

About twenty years ago, a vast deposit of fossilised bones was found in a cave of the Makapan valley, in South Africa[15]. They dated from the Villafranchian era – about 500,000 BC. They were of every species: hyena, porcupine, deer, horse, monkey, rhinoceros, baboon, pig. The cave had been the home of a colony of carnivorous anthropoid apes, the Australopithecines. Observation and statistical analysis of the bones in the cave showed two things, that the other animals had been eaten by the meat-fed, prehistoric apes and that *Australopithecus* was a weapon-user. Instead of scavenging from other predators' kills, he had gone up to his victim and, as bone analysis repeatedly showed, killed him with the knobbly distal end of an antelope's legbone.

Now the traditional view of human evolution is that, from a line of progressively more intelligent apes, *Homo sapiens* sprang with his big brain; and this superior intellect enabled him to invent the first weapon. In other words, man as a species preceded what anthropologists so euphemistically call 'the tool'. If the conclusions drawn from the Makapan cave, and from other African sites, are to be believed – and the weight of evidence for them is immense – what happened was exactly the reverse. The weapon, wielded by an ape, invented man; it gave *Australopithecus* the edge of survival over other species. We are Cain's progeny, not Abel's; and our vision of our first ancestor loping about the greensward of the Garden of Eden, sniffing flowers, eating berries and innocently chucking the docile lion under its chin, must give way to a murderous, cannibalistic ape, grunting with pleasure as he bashed in the skulls of unsuspecting relatives. The Paradise Garden has long been recognised as a myth. But what it stood for remained intact: the idea of the primal innocence of man, the idea that human beings, if left to their own devices without the malevolent artifices of king and capitalist to pervert them, will stop being aggressive and display their 'natural' propensity for living in harmony, still lives on. In the eighteenth century it made possible Rousseau's theory of politics. In the nineteenth and twentieth, it fortified Bakunin and Kropotkin, and nourished the Marxist fantasy of the withering-away of the state once the dictatorship of the proletariat has been achieved. However, it may be that the oafish, grenade-festooned corporal, kicking in the teeth of a Vietnamese adolescent, is closer to Adam than Adam ever was. The myth of primal innocence persists; but there may be nothing to regain in Paradise, because there was never anything to lose – except a metaphor of ideal consciousness which for more than two thousand years has endured as one of the most consoling figures of speech ever produced by mankind.

left Masolino (ca. 1383– after 1432?): *A Pope with St Mathias*, National Gallery, London. St Anselm, Archbishop of Canterbury, held that the scars and attributes of martyrs would shine gloriously in Heaven.

opposite above Fra Angelico (fl. 1417–55): *Christ Glorified in the Court of Heaven*, National Gallery, London. **below** *The Coronation of the Virgin* by Andrea Orcagna, National Gallery, London.

chapter 3

The Heavenly Mansions

The Body Glorious

Everyone agrees that Heaven will be pleasant; but what will the soul – especially when it is united with its glorified body after the Final Judgment – actually feel? St Anselm, Archbishop of Canterbury, who was born at Aosta in 1033, carefully listed the qualities of the transfigured bodies of the elect. There were seven: beauty, agility, strength, penetrability, health, delight and perpetuity.

On the beauty of the saved souls, Anselm remarked – with curious but, when you think of it, consistent logic – that 'There shall be none blind, lame or defective; but such defects shall remain as would redound to the glory of the elect'. The scars of martyrs in particular will shine 'with an especial and transcendent glory'. One may presumably also imagine choirs of desert fathers with brilliantly luminous eczemoid rashes; though whether the eyes which St Lucy (who tore them out to send on a dish to an importunate chaser of her maidenhead) is customarily depicted holding will glitter like carbuncles is open to speculation. But a soul new to the company of martyrs need not be put off by the myriad shining nail-holes, burns, missing skins, wheel-marks, empty flapping abdominal cavities, amputated tongues and (in the case of St Agatha, who had them torn off and so carries them on a platter as her attribute) lost but fluorescent breasts. Everyone in Heaven, martyrs included, will have the gift of health. They will suffer 'no pain, discomfort or unease'. To this will be added agility – the ability to move rapidly from one point to another; all points being taken as equidistant from the centre, God – and strength. 'A glorified body,' St Anselm thought, 'would be so strong that it could move the entire earth.' (Which is reasonable, since even in the much inferior ecstasies of mystical experience which God gave to living mortals, he permitted St Peter of Alacantra to pluck out an entire pine-tree by its roots and carry it up with him into the air, where he hovered, for several hours, clutching it to his breast until one of his disciples persuaded him to land.) The gift of penetrability is not what one might think, but rather the ability to pass through solid matter, as Jesus Christ walked through a closed door in order to appear to the Apostles after the Resurrection. (This gift may have its uses in Eden, where solid matter abounds; it is difficult to see its advantages in Heaven, which is the domain of pure aetherial spirit.) The gift of perpetuity is simply the result of eternal life: 'The just shall live for ever'. No wonder, then, that the soul, conscious of these great privileges, will be suffused with the seventh and last gift, that of delight. 'All the whole glorified

opposite Christ enthroned, a section of the Pala d'oro, St Mark's, Venice.

109

body will be filled with abundance of every kind of comfort – the eyes, the ears, the nose, the mouth, the hands, the throat, the lungs, the heart, the stomach, the back, the bones, the marrow...'

One is hard put to imagine a modern theologian dotting the i's of heavenly bliss with such apparently zany attention to detail. But St Anselm's vision of Heaven is, like all mortal descriptions of the Last Things, a metaphor; if we do not accept it, it is largely because we have lost the inherent symbolizing faculty of mediaeval thought, and not because the saint was deluded. Moreover, his description is based on a theory of the cosmos which, though universally held in the eleventh century, is discredited today.

Without understanding this theory, we cannot easily comprehend the significance the Celestial Paradise had for mediaeval and Renaissance artists.

The Mediaeval Theory of the Cosmos

The earth was at the centre of the universe. Around it revolved a series of concentric spheres, like a nest of ivory Chinese balls, one outside the other. These are Dante's famous *rote*, the Heavenly Wheels. As you move out into space from the earth, you encounter, first, a girdle of fire; which, once crossed (it corresponds roughly to the Van Allen radiation belt of modern science) leads you to the Sphere of the Moon. The other planetary spheres, in outward order, are:

2. The Sphere of Mercury
3. The Sphere of Venus
4. The Sphere of the Sun
5. The Sphere of Mars
6. The Sphere of Jupiter
7. The Sphere of Saturn

The eighth Sphere is that of the Zodiac, the fixed stars, which rotate in an unchanging pattern – like the band of numbers of a spinning roulette wheel. The ninth is the Sphere of the *Primum Mobile*. This contains no stars, planets or other heavenly bodies. It is the source of all motion in the universe; its energies keep the stars in their courses and the planets spinning. Beyond the *Primum Mobile* is the Empyrean, eternal, infinite, without dimension or measurable location. It is here that God and the saints dwell (p. 112). Since each of the nine spheres, from Moon to *Primum Mobile*, rotates around the earth as a centre once every twenty-four hours, it follows that the remoter spheres – which have a great circumference – must move faster than the nearer ones, just as the rim of a wheel moves faster than a point near its hub. The Empyrean, however, does not move at all. It is perfectly still and tranquil; from it, the will of God emanates, and is (so to speak) transmitted through the *Primum Mobile*, converted into energy and motion, and then conveyed to every

opposite Angels crowning the transfigured souls in Heaven, by Luca Signorelli (c. 1441–1523). Orvieto Cathedral (detail).

111

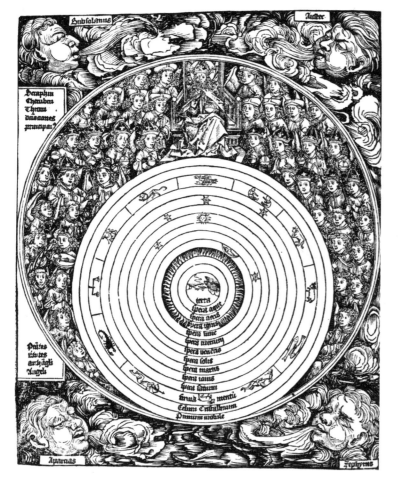

The mediaeval cosmos: diagram from Schedel's *Nuremberg Chronicle*, 1493. The universe was thought to consist of concentric 'spheres', of which there were ten main ones. First, the earth, with its girdles of water, air and fire. Next, the seven spheres of the planets, followed by the 'firmament' – where the Zodiac revolved – which was separated by the 'crystal heaven' from the *Primum Mobile*, the source of universal movement. Beyond the *Primum Mobile* was the Empyrean, seen here crowded with God and his saints.

sphere and individual component detail of the universe.

Now the crucial point about this cosmogony, which the Middle Ages inherited from Ptolemy, is that these concentric heavenly spheres represent an ascending scale of perfection. Earth, being the lowest, the central point, and the slowest-moving of all the heavenly bodies, is the worst of all: a dull clod of clay, populated by creeping things and fallen men. Everything terrestrial fades, decays, changes, dies. But Christianity took over from Aristotle the idea that the 'substance' of the heavens was imperishable and perfect; that it was not subject to age or rot, and, being complete, had no capacity for change.

And so a line drawn between earth and the Empyrean, across the planetary heavens, the Zodiac and the *Primum Mobile*, represented 'a journey from corruption to perfection'. The further from earth, the better.

This scale of perfection was not confined to astronomy. It was echoed in the mediaeval idea of the 'natural order' of created things. From earthworm to angel, a chain of existence, lower form leading to higher, was forged; each creature could

In mediaeval eyes, gold and jewelry were not simply units of economic power; they symbolised the light and glories of Heaven. **above** The Basle Antependium, German, 11th century. Musée de Cluny, Paris.

function as an allegory of God's mind, of a desirable virtue, or of some aspect of God's actions, because God had implanted it in the world as part of a linked sequence which led back to him. The world itself was nothing other than God's thinking process made concrete. Aristotle had remarked that[16] 'the relationship between bodies is that the upper one stands to that which lies under it as form to matter', but now, as one author put it[17],

Aristotle's Ladder of Nature turned into a hierarchy, the continuous scale of beings into a 'chain of command'. The more complex creatures were 'higher', not just in a bald zoological sense, but because, in the divine government of the world, they were the 'superiors' of the 'lower' creatures – set in authority, and having dominion over them. Human beings had a 'divine right' to slaughter or domesticate the brute beasts; and the higher animals in turn were entitled to subjugate the lower ones; and so on down the scale . . . The whole point of the doctrine now lay in its ethical and theological content.

It is significant, in that theological framework, that the nine spheres from Moon to *Primum Mobile* are exactly paralleled by the nine orders of angelic being, which, in ascending order, may be tabled thus:

1. Sphere of the Moon	Angels
2. Sphere of Mercury	Archangels
3. Sphere of Venus	Principalities
4. Sphere of the Sun	Powers
5. Sphere of Mars	Virtues
6. Sphere of Jupiter	Dominations
7. Sphere of Saturn	Thrones
8. Sphere of the Zodiac	Cherubs
9. *Primum Mobile*	Seraphs

This was brought into the *Paradiso* by Dante, who in Canto XXVIII sees the light of God as a tiny, burning point, surrounded by nine dazzling concentric rings. These make up the angelic hierarchy, with the seraphs, closest to God, as the ring nearest the centre, and so on to the angels on the extreme circumference. 'From this Point', Beatrice informs him, 'hang the heavens and all nature.' The seraphs control the *Primum Mobile*, transmitting to it the force of God's love which sustains its motion; the cherubs keep the Zodiac spinning, and so forth. Each angelic type is a love-conductor, transmitting to its unique sphere 'the love that moves the sun and the other stars' [*Paradiso* XXXIII, 145]. (Dante observes that the order of the angels apparently contradicts that of the spheres. The seraphs are *closest* to the centre and move the fastest of all. The sphere of the *Primum Mobile*, however, which they control, is in cosmology the *furthest* from the centre. Beatrice, however, points out that what counts in the angels' rotation round God is not the circumference of their circles, but the amount of virtue they contain. As the seraphs are the most exalted of all, they are fit to control the *Primum Mobile*: 'It follows that the sphere, which as it goes / turns all the world along, must correspond / to this, the inmost, which most loves and knows' [*Paradiso* XXVIII, 61–78].)

The medium whereby God transmits the energy and motion of his love to the universe, by means of his angels, is light: *luce intelletual, piena d'amore* – the light of the intellect, filled with love. Light belongs to the intellect in a double sense. First, it is the supreme attribute of God, whose wisdom is the fount and model of all human understanding Secondly, most knowledge is gained by using one's eyes – reading and looking – and only light makes this possible. This gave the sun great significance in Christian iconography – it is the physical source of light (which, in mediaeval theory, it merely reflected in a dull and dim way from the actual light which God radiated from the Empyrean), and hence it could be taken to stand for Christ, who descended to earth in order to shed the benefits of God's intellect on men. Consequently, the attributes of classical sun-gods – Apollo, Helios, Mithras – could be grafted, in art, on to Christ himself. This was convenient for Renaissance painters who, seeking a concordance between antiquity and Christianity, were able to project their sacred themes through a language of form, pose and prototype sanctioned by its origins in Graeco-Roman art.

The Radiance of Heaven

Since the light of God was an essential feature of Heaven in literary and theological accounts, one would expect to see an equivalent for it in art. And indeed, this was found. It was gold.

The symbolism of sacred gold may have entered western art from Byzantium. There are some animals, like the mink, whose short life is assured by the beauty of their coats. What is to the mink a natural part of its body becomes, for the trapper and the consumer, a rarity of great value; and so the mink dies. A like fate befell the icons and mosaics of Constantinople when, in 1204, the Fourth Crusade sacked the city – an act of grotesque political treachery with few parallels in history. One of the few literate Crusaders, Robert de Clari, left us his account of the looting, and the slack-jawed greed of the provincial gapes from every line: *rich, rich, rich*:

[In the palace of Blachernae] there were fully twenty chapels and at least two hundred chambers, or three hundred, all connected with one another and all made of gold mosaic. And this palace was so rich and so noble that no one could describe it to you or recount its great nobility and richness. In this palace of Blachernae there was found a very great treasure, for one found there the rich crowns which had belonged to former emperors and the rich ornaments of gold and the rich cloth of silk and gold and the rich imperial robes and the rich precious stones and so many other riches that no one could number the great treasure of gold and silver that was found in the palaces and many other places in the city ... the master altar [of Hagia Sophia] was so rich that it was beyond price, for the table of the altar was made of gold and precious stones broken up and crushed all together, which a rich emperor had made. This table was fully fourteen feet long. Around the altar were columns of silver supporting a canopy over the altar which mas made just like a church spire and it was all of solid silver and so rich that no one could tell the money it was worth.

The altar was broken up, the canopy melted, the golden tesserae torn from the walls and the reliquaries stolen; illuminated manuscripts were destroyed and icons reduced to splinters by Crusaders who wanted their thin layer of gold leaf. Rarely have the profit-motive and the impulse towards symbol-making collided with such drastic results. By which I do not intend to suggest that the Byzantines were as indifferent to the negotiable value of the gold on their churches, mosaics and icons as the hairy Frankish thugs who ripped it off were to its symbolic value. Gold and jewels would not have been selected as divine attributes if they had not been costly, precious and rare. Yet probably a gold tile would have cost no more than one of the blue tesserae on Christ's robe in the eleventh-century mosaics

LIBERTAS · ECCLESIASTICA

OPVS · CARO
LI · CRIVELLI
VENETI

· 1486 ·

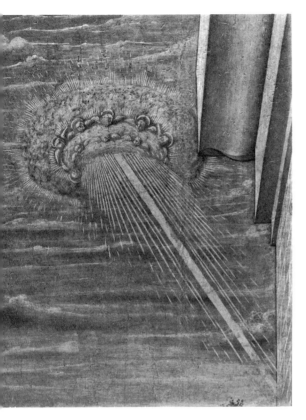

opposite Carlo Crivelli: *The Annunciation*, National Gallery, London. **above** detail showing the fiery rings of angels around the point of divine light from which the beam descends to Mary.

which survive in Hagia Sophia, Istanbul. Whatever one's guess at the convertible value of that uneven wall of lambent gold-faced cubes, their effect has very little to do with economics. Christ, flanked by the Emperor Constantine Monomachos and the Empress Zoë, sits against a spaceless void of light. His majestic form inhabits Yeats' Byzantium:

O sages standing in God's holy fire
As in the gold mosaic of a wall,
Come from the holy fire, perne in a gyre,
And be the singing-masters of my soul.
Consume my heart away; sick with desire
And fastened to a dying animal
It knows not what it is; and gather me
Into the artifice of eternity.

Once out of nature I shall never take
My bodily form from any natural thing,
But such a form as Grecian goldsmiths make
Of hammered gold and gold enamelling
To keep a drowsy Emperor awake;
Or set upon a golden bough to sing
To lords and ladies of Byzantium
Of what is past, and passing, and to come.

Yeats' poetic intuition seized what art critics can only express in halting prose: gold is a symbol of transcendence, the stuff of Heaven. The early Middle Ages have left us few documents which reveal anything specific about the use of gold in art. One lucky exception is the treatise on the administration, rebuilding and redecoration of the Abbey of St Denis, by the Abbot Suger[18]. Suger's writings reveal him as a man gripped – in Panofsky's charming phrase – by 'the unselfish rapacity of the modern museum director'[19].

One merry but notable miracle which the Lord granted us [while making the great golden crucifix for St Denis] we do not wish to pass over in silence. For when I was in difficulty for want of gems and could not sufficiently provide myself with more – for their scarcity makes them them very expensive – then, lo and behold, monks from three abbeys of two Orders – that is from Cîteaux and another abbey of the same Order, and from Fontevrault – entered our little chamber adjacent to the church and offered us for sale an abundance of gems such as we had not hoped to find in ten years, hyacinths, sapphires, rubies, emeralds, topazes . . . Freed from the worry of searching for gems, [we] thanked God and gave four hundred pounds for the lot, though they were worth much more.

One might imagine, from this isolated passage, that Suger's rapacity was fully equal to that of the caricature priests, hands dripping with gold and diamonds, who bob up in the pamphlets of the Loyal Orange Lodge. But no. One theme recurs above all others in Suger's writings: that the riches of his new-minted abbey are to be interpreted spiritually, and their purpose is to work as a metaphor of that moment when the soul confronts

117

the incomparably greater splendours of God in Heaven.

One of Suger's projects was the casting of a set of bronze doors for the main portal of St Denis. They were finished in 1140, and depicted the Passion and Ascension of Christ. Sheathed in gold, 'at great cost and much expenditure', the doors bore a Latin inscription in gilt copper letters. It was written by Suger:

Whoever thou art, if thou seekest to extol the glory of these doors,
Marvel not at the gold and the expense, but at the craftsmanship of the
work.
Bright is the noble work; but, being nobly bright, the work
Should brighten the minds, so that they may travel, through the true lights,
To the True Light where Christ is the true door.
In what manner it be inherent in this world the golden door defines:
The dull mind rises to truth through that which is material,
And, in seeing this light, is resurrected from its former submersion.

The precious metal is not there to tickle greed. It is aimed directly at the spirit, exciting it to rise up along the pipeline of correspondences implicit in the mediaeval universe: the contemplation of gold shifts into the contemplation of light, and the earthly light reflected from those gleaming mediaeval figures on Suger's portal turns, by analogy, into the supramundane light of God's grace, will and love which emanates from the core of the Empyrean, from Heaven. Suger was no Volpone. We do not catch him gloating

Good morning to the Day, and this my Gold!
Open the Shrine, that I may see my Saint –

– even though Ben Jonson's sardonic transformation of Volpone's coffer into a reliquary would have had no point without the link between gold and God which the efforts of artists and church patrons had fixed before the sixteenth century. Suger's gold is not God. It is a means to understanding him (p. 108):

Thus, when – out of my delight in the beauty of the house of God –
the loveliness of the many-coloured gems has called me away from external
cares, and worthy meditation has induced me to reflect, transferring
that which is material to that which is immaterial, on the diversity of
the sacred virtues: then it seems to me that I see myself dwelling, as
it were, in some strange region of the universe which neither exists
entirely in the slime of the earth nor entirely in the purity of Heaven;
and that, by the grace of God, I can be transported from this inferior
to that higher world in an anagogical manner.

Panofsky has shown how Suger's connection between the gleam of precious stones and gold and the radiance of Heaven derives from the neo-Platonic theories of John the Scot and the Pseudo-Dionysius, alias Dionysius the Areopagite, alias (or so it was believed in Suger's day; so passionately, in fact, that Abelard was thrown out of the abbey for doubting it) the same

School of Duccio (fl. 1278–1319):
Maestà with Attendant Angels. Sienese,
National Gallery, London.

119

St Denis after whom the abbey was named. But even without their example, the Scriptures abound in texts which link gold with God and Heaven. '. . . If the Almighty is your gold, and your precious silver; then you will delight yourself in the Almighty, and lift up your face to God' *[Job* XXII, 25–6*]*.

It is true that St Paul preached at Athens that 'Being then God's offspring, we ought not to think that the Deity is like gold, or silver, or stone, as representation by the arts of man' *[Acts* XVII, 29*]*. This was one of the texts used by Cromwell's followers to justify their destruction of ecclesiastical plate and works of art. Curiously, however, this text is embedded in the very sermon which converted the man whom Suger believed to be the founder of his abbey: 'But some men joined [Paul] and believed, among them Dionysius the Areopagite . . .' *[Acts* XVII, 34*]*. One can imagine Suger asking himself whether it was likely that Dionysius, with his notions of gold, radiance and God, would have been converted if St Paul had meant his sermon to be a diatribe against symbolism. Even today, knowing that the works of the Areopagite were really written by a nameless Syrian more than four centuries after Paul's death, we may prefer to think about the promise of the Celestial City in the *Book of Revelations;* Jerusalem transfigured, with streets of gold, 'having the glory of God, its radiance like a most rare jewel, like a jasper, clear as crystal' *[Rev.* XXI, 11*]*. For the link in art between gold and Heaven is indissoluble. It pervades Byzantine mosaic; and there is hardly an altarpiece painted anywhere in Europe between the twelfth and fifteenth centuries which does not possess a ground of gold leaf, against which the figures of Mary, angels and saints perform their stately ritual of divine praise (pp. 119, 134–5).

For gold, as well as signifying divine light, also suggested eternity. It is the incorruptible metal. It does not oxidise or decay or tarnish. A prehistoric Irish torque or the mask of Agammemnon, buried for thousands of years, come gleaming out of the ground, while wood and bone vanish into dust and a bronze spear is fretted to a green thread. What better substance to reflect the unchanging glory of God?

opposite Giovanni di Paolo (active 1420, d. 1482): *The Baptism of Christ*, National Gallery, London. God appears above the Jordan in a glory – a sunburst of light.

The Mandorla

God, the source of all its light, sits at the centre of Heaven, surrounded by choirs of angels and saints. He is sometimes (though rarely) shown seated on an ornate throne; but this device is generally reserved for the Virgin Mary. God's customary attribute is an aureole, a glory or a mandorla.

These three words, which refer to what seem to be much the same things – a circular or egg-shaped burst of light around God's figure – are not interchangeable and ought not to be mixed up. An aureole is a 'solid' disk of light, with defined edges, around a form (p. 133). A glory is a burst of light-rays, emanat-

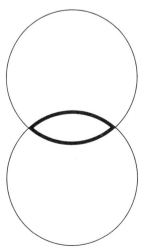

ing from a source behind the form, like a conventional sunburst (above). The mandorla, however, is a vehicle of ascension. It usually takes the form of a round or elliptical frame, with pointed ends and often an elaborately decorated border, in which the Godhead stands or sits.

A mandorla is produced when two circles intersect (left). Cirlot, in a fundamentally sound but rather strained note on the symbolism of mandorlas[20], holds the view that the two circles represented the earth and the sky, and so the shape was by nature horizontal. But, he adds,

in order that, for the puposes of iconography, the mandorla might be drawn vertically, the two circles have come to be regarded as the left [matter] and the right [spirit]. The zone of existence symbolised by the

121

Two ways of ascension. **left** The
Virgin supported in an elliptical
mandorla, with winged cherubs.
Detail from Carlo Crivelli: *The
Apparition of the Virgin to St Francis*,
National Gallery, London. **right** 'The
soles of his transfigured feet' – Christ
disappearing in the cloud, at the
moment of his ascension. Note that
the cloud resembles a horizontal
mandorla.

123

mandorla . . . embraces the opposing poles of dualism. Hence it is also
a symbol of the perpetual sacrifice that regenerates creative force through
the dual streams of ascent and descent . . .   *[Ibid.]*

These are, of course, very attractive associations for a form so closely connected with the transfigured Christ, risen from earth to Heaven. Nevertheless to test the hypothesis a look at those factors which Cirlot brushes aside as 'purposes of iconography' might not go amiss[21].

The use of the mandorla in Christian art stems from a biblical text [*Acts* i, 9] describing the Ascension of Christ. 'And when he had said this, as they were looking on, he was lifted up, and a cloud took him out of their sight.'

The idea of a god appearing in or being absorbed by a cloud was by no means new when this was written. Virgil has Pallas Athene appear on the ramparts of blazing Troy, 'the storm-cloud lurid about her' [*Aeneid* ii, 588 ff.]; Juno descends 'from the heights of heaven, cloud-enshrouded, riding upon the storm' [*ibid.* x, 632 ff.]. And there are enough references to gods who manifest themselves in clouds, aureoles of light and bursts of radiance scattered throughout the writings of Homer, Ovid and other classical authors to show quite conclusively that the Graeco-Roman world had an established tradition of this image – inherited, perhaps, from eastern sources. Being an attribute of gods, their means of transport between earth and Heaven, the cloud took on the lustre appropriate to heavenly bodies. It was a symbol of apotheosis and glory – this is the sense in which the text from the *Acts of the Apostles* just quoted describes the cloud on which Jesus went to Heaven. But it had a second aspect: that of a protective device. Thus, after his mother Aphrodite finishes her speech to Aeneas, she vanishes, enwrapped in 'night's thick darkness' [*Aeneid* ii, 621]. It may be worth noting that the god's cloud, glowing or opaque, has shown itself to be an exceptionally durable myth. Every day thousands of people glue their eyes to telescopes and the tracking-screens of home-made radar devices in an effort to detect flying saucers. Science-fiction constantly deals in force-fields which human beings or extra-terrestrials generate around themselves to repel attack. Saucers generate a luminous egg-shaped aureole around themselves, or so innumerable reports claim. Indeed, what is a flying saucer but a kind of horizontal mandorla, round in plan but elliptical when seen edge-on, in which incomprehensibly powerful and technologically advanced beings descend from outer space – for which, read Heaven – and take off from earth? Thumbing through the American publications devoted to saucer lore, one still periodically hits on the hoary belief of saucer enthusiasts that Christ's cloud was really a space-ship in which beings from a planet of some distant sun took him away, as friend or specimen, to regions far removed from ours.

A 16th-century painting of the Ascension of Christ.

The mandorla as aura of holiness. *Abraham and the Three Angels*, mosaic, c. 352–366, Sta Maria Maggiore, Rome.

The mandorla represents both Christ's cloud and the glowing light which Christ's body has received as a sign of his position at the light-emanating centre of the Empyrean. It is also a means of transport. As such it clearly differs from the nimbus or halo, which stays with the wearer wherever he goes but does not cause his motion. There was another convention, apart from the mandorla, which Christian artists found for representing the Ascension (though when one looks at it one can see why mandorlas were accepted as the more dignified and popular choice). It was to depict Christ ascending vertically into the sky, showing the soles of his transfigured feet to a group of thunderstruck Apostles (pp. 123–5). Moreover, the upper half of Christ's body was out of the frame, so that he looked like some hero of a Victorian pantomime dangling impotently in mid-air while stagehands struggle with a stuck pulley. Sometimes Christ is seen disappearing through a cloud which looks like a horizontal mandorla, and may refer back to one, but which looks like a giant smoke-ring when read in illusionistic space (p. 123); it is the ascension cloud and he rises through it with the majestic deliberation of a rocket lifting from its pad. Such an image could not have the decorum which Europe expected of its sacred art; nor even the fidelity to biblical text. Today, Eliot's rude line about Christ's 'unoffending

The mandorla as protective shield. *The Stoning of Moses*, mosaic, Sta Maria Maggiore, Rome.

feet' springs to mind whenever one looks at such a picture.

Two of the earliest mandorlas in Christian art are in the fifth-century mosaics of Santa Maria Maggiore, Rome. In the first, Abraham is confronted by the three angels (opposite). A transparent, oval mandorla surrounds the middle angel and slightly overlaps his companions. We can surmise that this shape is meant only to indicate light and holiness – the 'aura of sanctity' got by living so close to God. But in the second mosaic (above), the mandorla which envelops Moses and his companions acts as a protective shield against the hostile crowd on the left. It is the descendant of the murky clouds in which Homeric gods were apt to veil themselves from human eyes, and the ancestor of science-fiction's Invisibility Machine. The crowd fling stones at Moses, but they bounce off the mandorla; and its physical boundary is marked by a wiry black line. The foot of one of Moses' companions sticks out through this boundary as he scrambles into the mandorla's field of safety.

Not only then does the mandorla act as a shield and look like one but it may also derive from one. The Romans had a funerary motif called the *imago clipeata*. It consisted of a medallion portrait, the strong man imaged on his own shield, carried aloft by flying *putti* (pp. 128–9). This was adapted by Byzantine art; the

127

portrait went, the air of glorification and transfiguration stayed. One of the sixth-century mosaics in San Vitale, Ravenna, shows two flying angels holding up a *tondo* which contains a crucifix (above). Presumably this began with some memory of a Roman sarcophagus. An early use of the mandorla as a throne of ascension is found on a seventh-century pilgrim flask at Monza. It was not unusual to see emblems of the Passion, instead of Christ himself, thus glorified. The oddest example of this I have seen is by a French miniaturist, *c.* 1375: the subject is Christ as the Man of Sorrows, and on the left one of his wounds (opposite, above) is seen, a pointed ellipse of flesh slit down the middle, surrounded by a mandorla-frame. Much later, and by direct reference to classical sources rather than by any lingering memories of Byzantine art, Renaissance artists adopted the *imago clipeata* for its original purpose of praising the illustrious dead – a good example being Antonio Rossellino's medallion portrait of Neri Capponi in Florence, borne up by *putti* (opposite, far right).

That these medallions, tondos and mandorlas must have been heavy because angels were employed to carry them may seem a rather obvious point. Yet it has some interest, because sometimes mandorlas are depicted as if they and Christ were heavy,

The development of the mandorla. **upper left** Late Roman sarcophagus of a Christian prince, with emblem carried aloft by two angels, Archaeological Museum, Instanbul. **left** Angels supporting *tondo* with crucifix. Mosaic, 6th century AD, S. Vitale, Ravenna. **opposite right** Christ as Man of Sorrows, and glorification of Holy Wound. French miniature, c. 1375: Morgan Library, New York. **opposite far right** The Renaissance reverts to the classical *imago clipeata*. Antonio Rossellino, sarcophagus of Neri Capponi, Florence, pre–1457. **right** Unknown 13th-century mosaicist: Christ enthroned and supported by angels. Façade of S. Frediano, Lucca.

NERIO CAPONIO GINI FILIO C VI PRECLARO AC DE R P FLO DOMI
FORIS QVE OPTIME MERITO GINVS PATRI PIENT PONI PROCVRAVIT
VIX AN LX VIIII MEN IIII DI XXI

sometimes not; and the difference may slightly affect the degree of spiritualisation which we read into the image. The heavy, angel-borne mandorla tends to become a solid throne; the light mandorla a nimbus. An ivory plaque in the Museo Nazionale, Florence, depicts Christ being carried up to Heaven by two angels who are gripping the sides of an elliptical, pillow-like cloud; starbursts, suggesting light breaking through an opaque and possibly dense substance, twinkle on its surface. The façade mosaic of Christ in Glory on San Frediano in Lucca, by an unknown master of the thirteenth century, reverts, in its Byzantinising style, to the angels carrying the tondo in San Vitale, and like them alludes to a sarcophagus prototype. But here, Christ is actually seated on a throne, which is heavy, solid, draped with patterned stuffs and cushioned with a bolster; the mandorla which the angels grip has four rippling bands which grow lighter in tone and brighter in colour towards the outside (p. 129). These may refer to the elements of the world on which God is casting his blessing: earth, water, air, fire.

A later tendency was to do away with the mandorla and keep the supporting angels, as in a miniature of Christ enthroned between two seraphim, by the fourteenth-century Trinity Master (right). Later, the angels fluttered into a mandorla-like shape around the Godhead; one can see this happening in Orcagna's Strozzi Altarpiece (top), though the rim of the mandorla is still visible behind the crowd of chubby seraphs. The profusion of little winged angels can sometimes remind one of nothing so much as the pigeons at feeding-time in Piazza San Marco, although one eighteenth-century traveller compared the effect to 'a damn'd overdressed Italian salad with too many radishes'.

Finally, out of the demands of Renaissance naturalism, it became imperative to give these highly-modelled and plastic figures of God and the Virgin hovering in the sky some more credible reason for staying up. The convention thus arose of the cloud as aerial platform (opposite). The difference between the symbolic and the naturalistic mode may be neatly summed up in the two famous *Agonies in the Garden*, by Andrea Mantegna and Giovanni Bellini. The *putto* which appears to Bellini's Christ simply hovers unsupported in the sky, holding up a chalice (p. 132). Mantegna's obsession with weight, density and structure made him stand his apparitions on a platform of solid-looking cloud (p. 137). And he did this even though, in another respect, he stressed the *subjectivity* of Christ's vision of the angels. Seen from the spectator's angel, these *putti* lean forward at an impossible angle; you expect them to fall off the cloud. They are designed to look erect and real from Christ's eyeline only.

The 'weightless' mandorla also survived at least until the end of the *quattrocento*. It is the decorated ring at whose centre God the Father, as Creator of All Things, glares imperiously

top Detail from the Strozzi Altarpiece by Orcagna, 1354–7, Sta Maria Novella, Florence. **above** Christ enthroned by seraphim, miniature from the *Petites Heures du Duc de Berry* by the Trinity Master, Bibliothèque Nationale, Paris. **opposite** Peselino (active 1422–57): *The Trinity with Saints*.

131

down from the roof of the Florence Baptistery (p. 137); it is the glittering gold almond (*mandorla*, by the way, is Italian for almond) from which Christ punches holes in the hands and feet of St Francis, as with a celestial laser, in Sassetta's *Stigmatisation* (p. 140); or it is the sublime disk of gold, surrounded by pulsing zigzags and trails of light, wherein the Virgin and Child stand glorified above Pisanello's *St George and the Hermit* (p. 141). Michelangelo – deliberately, I think – allowed a memory of the mandorla to survive in God's billowing oval mantle, through whose curve the finger goes out to Adam (p. 141).

The Pantocrator in the Baptistery (p. 137) sits on a segment of a circle interlocking with the mandorla to produce a horizontal almond shape, divided into bands. This is a common motif and represents the universe – each concentric band being one of the planetary spheres, while the decorated band on which God sits is the *Primum Mobile* and the free space above becomes the Empyrean. God is sometimes seen, as in Giovanni di Paolo's *Creation*, spinning the universe in his hand like a marvellous rainbow disk, or holding it up so that it sits on his palm, as in a mediaeval French miniature (p. 138). Can this figure be a classicising memory of Apollo in his incarnation as *Sol iustitiae*? Albrecht Dürer might have recognised it (p. 138).

The Halo and the Nimbus

Whereas the mandorla is the exclusive property of Christ, the Father and the Virgin Mary, haloes and nimbuses belong to

opposite The halo as mark of closeness to God: gold caught from the light of Heaven. Icon in St Catherine's Monastery, Sinai, 5th–6th century. **overleaf** Two kinds of 'All Saints' Picture', showing the population of Heaven. **above** Tintoretto: *Paradise*, Louvre, Paris. Note the diminishing rings of angels and saints around the seat of God in the upper part. **below** Duccio da Buoninsegna: *The Virgin in Majesty*, 1308–11. Museo dell'Opera del Duomo, Siena.

below Giovanni Bellini (1429–1507): *The Agony in the Garden*, National Gallery, London.

everyone in Heaven, irrespective of individual status.

In Aristophanes' *Lysistrata*, a police officer swore an oath by 'the goddess with the shining disk'; which prompted a gloss from a nineteenth-century Hellenist to the effect that, in Athens, a plate was set behind the heads of statues of gods which stood in the open air, to protect them from bird-droppings. Archaeology, I understand, has discredited this as a possible origin of the halo in Christian art. Nonetheless, it cannot be said that haloes have fared well in the twentieth century. They are little more than a cartoonist's cliché of pompous rectitude, fit material for Jacques Prévert:

The Last Supper
They are at table
They do not eat
Or touch their plates :
And their plates stand up straight
Vertically behind their heads.

Yet the halo played an important role in the imagery of Heaven; its original vitality as a symbol came, in part, from its extreme antiquity. Haloes were not invented by Christian artists. The haloes one sees behind the heads of divinities and god-kings, incised on Mesopotamian seals, conclusively establish their existence as a symbol-form before 3000 BC.[22]

Its use in the east was quite as extensive as in the west and examples need not be multiplied. In classical times however Virgil had some interesting passages in which light, as the refulgence of a god, as the physical sign of vatic inspiration or Heaven-sent courage, crackles around the heads of hero or priestess:

The Latians saw from far, with dazzled eyes,
The radiant crest that seemed in flames to rise,
And dart diffusive fires around the field,
And the keen glittering of the golden shield.

[*Aeneid* x]

. . . when fair Lavinia fed the fire
Beside the gods, and stood beside her sire,
[Strange to relate !] the flames, involved in smoke
Of incense, from the sacred altar broke,
Caught her dishevelled hair, and rich attire ;
Her crown and jewels crackled in the fire :
From thence the fuming trail began to spread,
And lambent glories danced about her head.
This new portent the seer with wonder views,
Then pausing, thus his prophecy renews :
'The nymph who scatters flaming fires around
Shall shine with honour, shall herself be crowned,
But, caused by her irrevocable fate,
War shall the country waste, and change the state.'

[*Ibid.*]

opposite Cimabue: *The Virgin with Child and Angels*, Uffizi, Florence. **above** Trinity Master: *Petites Heures du Duc de Berry*. Jean de Berry before the Lord. God holding up the disk of the Universe, Bibliothèque Nationale, Paris. **top** Albrecht Dürer: Apollo holding the sun-disk, 1501, British Museum, London.

139

right Michelangelo: *The Creation of Adam*, from the ceiling of the Sistine Chapel, Rome, 1510. God's billowing cloak is a far but distinct reference back to the idea of the mandorla surrounding God.

Pisanello (1397/9–1455/6): *St Anthony and St George*, National Gallery, London.

opposite Sassetta (1392?–1450): *The Stigmatisation of St Francis*, National Gallery, London.

The halo, or nimbus, occurs in art whenever a culture has, in its mythology or in its theory of the cosmos, the conviction that gods inhabit the upper air. Thus it was an attribute of Apollo. For space is the sphere of fire; sun and stars blaze there; it is a world of sublime and burning essences, an unthinkable purity of light, and all beings which share it take on the radiance of their environment – like the girl in *Paradiso*:

Cunizza fui chiamata, e qui refulgo
perchè mi vinse il lume d'esta stella

[*Paradiso* IX, 32–3]

(Cunizza I was called, and I glitter here because the light of this star overwhelmed me.)

Saints and angels, then, can be recognised by the halo, envelope or effulgence of light which they carry with them, caught from the undiminishing fire of God's love in its transmitted form as light. This is a Christian extension of the older symbolic practice by which certain pagan gods were thought able to transmit their power, or the marks of it, to heroes[23]. Thus the halo was a sign of God's approval and so, *par excellence*, of the saint or the angel.

More than a hundred and fifty kinds of Christian halo have been listed – solid disk, pierced disk, fiery, cross in circle, pierced cross in disk, sunburst, *rayonnant*, and so on. It is unnecessary, for our purposes, to go into them in detail. Certain types of halo differ in iconographic meaning: for instance, a cross within a circle is usually – if not quite always – reserved for Christ. But the basic shapes of halo are round, square and triangular. Elementary number-symbolism is involved here. The circle, as we have seen, is an archetypal symbol of Heaven; circular haloes are therefore appropriate to God, the saints and the angels. But in many paintings the donor who commissioned the panel is included with the saints and angels, adoring the Virgin or lamenting Christ's death on Golgotha. He could not be put on equal terms with the holy ones, but equally he might have been offended if made to seem too blatant an intruder. The elegant solution to this problem was to use a *square* halo for the donor and round ones for the saints. The patron had his halo, the saints kept their superiority, and everyone was happy; for, as we saw earlier in connection with the fountains of Paradise, the square symbolises earth and terrestrial life as distinct from the circle's Heaven. The triangular halo is reserved for God; with its three sides enclosing one figure it symbolises the existence of three persons in one God.

Torcello Cathedral: 12th-century mosaic. Detail showing thrones.

The Heavenly Hierarchy

In Heaven, the Virgin Mary usually sits on a throne, within the mandorla (opposite) or on its own, standing in clear space, as in the great *Maestà* by Duccio (pp. 134–5); a figure in

142

The Virgin and Christ enthroned in Heaven from *The Last Judgment* by Francesco Traini, Camposanto, Pisa. Note Christ's gesture of reprobation as he turns towards the damned souls below on his left.

costly lapis-lazuli, her gown, webbed with gold in the fold, falling on a piece of furniture so elaborate that it is better thought of as architecture: indeed, this may be the throne's underlying significance. In Cimabue's hands it becomes an incomparably precious structure, wrought out tessera by tessera in mosaic and marble, gilded, polished, every vein in the tiny flakes of inlaid stone judged against its russet or creamy neighbour. The eight angels who attend the Madonna caress its surface with gestures of shy delight, as if unprepared for the existence of such splendour; so might one see an art student touching the flank of Orcagna's tabernacle in the gloom of Orsanmichele, to assure himself that it is not only for the eyes. Evangelists stand in the vaults beneath the throne, protected as by the arches of a piazza. For such is Cimabue's throne: a metaphor of the New Jerusalem, the Golden City, rising tier upon tier to ensconce the couple who are the means of its renewal and transfiguration.

Mediaeval and Renaissance painters were generally prepared to accept the divison of angels into the ninefold hierarchy which the Pseudo-Dionysius and Aquinas had set out. But in practice the types were not closely differentiated – perhaps because one soon runs out of permutations and combinations of wings and albs. However, some were.

Seraphim, the highest angelic beings, were depicted with six wings (p. 14): two pointing above the head, two down to the feet, and two spread out to fly. Sometimes they hold a scroll in their right hand; in Byzantine images made for the Greek Orthodox rite, this may be replaced with a small fan.

Cherubim often consist of a head with no body, and two wings sprouting from it. They are among the most often-painted angels in art, thanks to their undeniably decorative appearance, but it is difficult to see why they acquired the form they did. Could it have been through some conflation with Hypnos, the god of sleep, or Hermes, with his winged helmet? Probably not; there is nothing in the theological character of cherubim to suggest that they have much in common with either, since according to the Pseudo-Dionysius their characteristic is 'the power of beholding God, their receptivity to the highest gift of light'. From this we may perhaps surmise that the cherub is bodiless because he does not need a body; all he requires to do his job is eyes, a mind and wings; hence the winged head. But not all cherubim are bodiless, and presumably the cherub whom God set to guard the way to Eden could not have been, unless he held the flaming sword in his teeth.

The thrones afford a remarkable illustration of the Pseudo-Dionysius' effect on iconography. He described them as 'winged wheels' revolving round God: 'for the Divine fiery wheels truly revolve, by reason of their ceaseless movement, around the highest Good Itself, and they are granted revelations because to them the holy hidden mysteries are made clear . . .' (There is quite a lot more of this; after the Pseudo-Dionysius, the most verbose sermon is like a teleprinter message.) The thrones were customarily depicted to the letter of Dionysius' text. They appear as wheels of fire – the fire symbolises love – with wings around their rims. The hub of the wheel is sometimes studded with eyes, to signify the thrones' ability to see clearly into the heart of holy mysteries (pp. 14, 142).

Dominations, virtues and powers seem to run to pattern: flowing white albs, golden cinctures[24], a rod or sceptre of gold in the right hand – to denote their justice as the ministers of God's bureacracy – and sometimes in the left hand a seal.

Principalities, archangels and angels, being the warriors and factotums of Heaven, are dressed accordingly in functional military garb. They – and especially the Archangels Michael and Gabriel – are the most commonly represented of all. But as soon as one is acquainted with any range of Renaissance paintings, it becomes clear that artists were either only vaguely aware of these theoretical differences of dress between the lower layers of the hierarchy or chose simply to disregard them. Gabriel, who with Michael is one of the two archangels mentioned by name in the Old Testament, is the angel of the Annunciation and was incessantly painted: but usually wearing the flowing garments which mediaeval iconographers thought proper to dominations, virtues and powers, as in the *Annunciation* by Leonardo (opposite, top). The Archangel Michael, chief angel of repentance, righteousness, mercy and sanctification, was appointed the guardian angel of policemen by Pius XII in 1950[25]; but his main role is that of slaying the serpent which is the devil – a job not unlike painting the Sydney Harbour Bridge, since the devil never dies and is never in fact vanquished. It was St Michael who threw the rebel angels down to Hell; Bruegel painted him doing so, with the angels changing into grotesque monsters at the instant of their descent from grace (opposite, below). One of Michael's portraits is arguably the most beautiful picture of an angel in western art, Piero della Francesca's (p. 147). This is no insipid harp-fingerer, but a Tuscan curlywig transformed, by number and rhythm, into a shape as satisfying and solidly pure as a Doric column: a buttress of the Lord.

The 'All Saints' Picture'

When all these elements meet in one picture (including the saints. But I do not propose to attempt a description of each saint in the Christian calendar. There are several thousand of them, and among these at least six hundred are distinguished by specific attributes when they are painted – the wheel for St Catherine, a pair of breasts on a plate for St Agatha, a pot of ointment for the Magdalen, a lion and a red hat for St Jerome – and so on. The reader is referred to any one of the several standard dictionaries of Christian iconography) the result is a pictorial type which dates from the ninth century but does

The Archangels Gabriel and Michael: **above** Luca Signorelli, Orvieto Cathedral. **opposite top** The Archangel Gabriel announces Mary's pregnancy in Leonardo da Vinci's *Annunciation*, 1472–5, Uffizi, Florence. **opposite bottom** The archangel Michael, at the centre of Bruegel's *Fall of the Rebel Angels*, hacks the monsters down into Hell, 1562, Musées Royaux des Beaux-Arts, Brussels.

not exist earlier: the comprehensive image which is called, in German, an *Allerheiligenbild* or 'All Saints' Picture'[26].

The biblical context of the All Saints' Picture is two verses in *Revelations*.

Then I looked, and I heard around the throne and the living creatures and the elders the voice of many angels, numbering myriads of myriads and thousands of thousands, saying with a loud voice: 'Worthy is the Lamb who was slain, to receive power and wealth and wisdom and might and honour and glory and blessing!' And I heard every creature in heaven and on earth and under the earth and in the sea, and all therein, saying 'To him who sits upon the throne and to the Lamb be blessing and honour and glory and might for ever and ever! . . .'   [*Rev.* v, 11–3]

After this I looked, and behold, a great multitude which no man could number, from every nation, from all tribes and tongues and peoples, standing before the throne and before the Lamb, clothed in white robes, with palm branches in their hands, and crying out with a loud voice . . . And all the angels stood around the throne and round the elders and the four living creatures, and they fell on their faces and worshipped God . . . Then one of the elders addressed me, saying, 'Who are these, clothed in white robes, and whence have they come?' I said to him, 'Sir, you know.' And he said to me, 'These are who have come out of the great tribulation; they have washed their robes and made them white in the blood of the Lamb.'   [*Rev.* VII, 9–14]

The Feast of All Saints was instituted in 835 and, as Panofsky has shown, an iconography based on *Revelations* grew to match it, a typical painting of this kind being a miniature from a tenth-century sacramentary at Göttingen (p. 150), with its choirs of the blessed virgins, martyrs, Church fathers, prophets, confessors and apostles. In its developed form, which it achieved by the thirteenth century, the All Saints' Picture was the most complete metaphor of celestial order ever devised by art. Against the long slow blaze of unfurling gold in the background of Duccio's *Maestà* (pp. 134–5), the successive choirs of saints and angels rise, in nobly ordered and impassive ranks, around the Virgin's throne; each quillet of hierarchy is set down, but with such unobtrusive grace that you are plucked out of the Museo dell'Opere del Duomo and find yourself, for a moment, in the core of Heaven, from which all order and light emanates and where everything connects, *cum pondere et mensura*, with weight and measure, in a grave dance before the Lord. This is illusion perfected – the illusion of a controllable and controlled universe. And even in the light-drenched extravagance of Baroque art – the *trasparente* in Toledo Cathedral, say, or the ceiling of the Gesù (p. 151) – the All Saints' Picture still carries that profound sense of well-being, achieved through a metaphor of the final integration between maker and product in the Celestial Paradise.

However, this brilliant means of suggesting apotheosis by dissolving ceiling, dome and wall into a painted infinity also had its secular uses. And when we are confronted by Joseph II

The Archangel Michael, in moulded leather cuirass and shoulder-armour, stands victorious over the devil-serpent. Piero della Francesca, 1470, National Gallery, London.

The vision of the city of God: **left** Miniature from a 15th-century MS of St Augustine's *De Civitate Dei*. Bibliothèque Ste Geneviève, Paris. **opposite** The inclusive vision of Heaven. Nardo di Cione, fresco in Sta Maria Novella, Florence.

of Austria being received into Elysium by a troupe of ladies in elegant hats or, at Göttweig, Troger's fresco of Francis of Lorraine complacently displaying his chubby torso and potato nose from the driving seat of Apollo's chariot, while the rays of Helios stream from his wig, we can only wonder what Dante or the Pseudo-Dionysus would have said about so fleshy an Empyrean.

right The All Saints' Picture, transformed by the infinite space of Baroque ceiling-painting. Baciccio, main vault of the church of the Gesù, 1668–83, Rome: *The Triumph of the Name of Jesus.*

left The All Saints' Picture, miniature from a 10th-century codex, Göttingen, University Library: saints, confessors, virgins and angels adoring the Lamb, indicated by St John the Baptist.

part 3

Hell

The Statue	*Pentiti, scellerato!*
Giovanni	*No, vecchio infatuato!*
The Statue	*Pentiti!*
Giovanni	*No!*
The Statue	*Si!*
Giovanni	*No!*
The Statue	*Ah, tempo piu non v'e!*
Giovanni	*Da quel tremore insolito* *Sento assalir gli spiriti!* *Donde escono quei vortici* *Di fuoco pien d'orror?*

(Mozart, *Don Giovanni*, 1787)

Hell, as subject for art, has not recovered from the shattering blow Baudelaire dealt it – unintentionally, perhaps? – in such lines as these from *Le Voyage* :

Ô Mort, vieux capitaine, il est temps! levons l'ancre!
Ce pays nous ennuie, ô Mort! Appareillons!
Si le ciel et la mer sont noirs comme de l'encre,
Nos coeurs que tu connais sont remplis de rayons!

Verse-nous ton poison pour qu'il nous réconforte!
Nous voulons, tant ce feu nous brûle le cerveau,
Plonger au fond du gouffre, Enfer ou Ciel, qu'importe?
Au fond de l'Inconnu pour trouver du nouveau!

It is the classical cry of the *avant-garde* and could look well carved on a sandstone slab in the foyer of the Museum of Modern Art in New York, facing the marble list of Rockefellers and Sculls who, in our century, have made Baudelaire's gulf less vertiginous by padding its sides with cheques. However, the attitude of Baudelaire (and of the nineteenth-century Satanists generally) to Hell would have profoundly startled an artist of, say, the thirteenth century. For Baudelaire, Hell is where you find new shapes, which may be terrifying – within the limits which art imposes on fear – but are valuable mainly *because they are an antidote to vulgarity*. To a Christian artist of the Middle Ages this would have seemed an impossible dilution of Hell. If Hell is to be esteemed as a corrective to the vulgarities of bourgeois taste, it exists *as* taste: as aesthetics rather than ethics. And this moves Hell (from any orthodox Christian viewpoint) out on to the rim of life, beyond vital concerns. Mario Praz has shown[1] the ideas which interwove to form the aesthetic Hell of nineteenth-century literature: the cult of the beautiful Lucifer, reincarnated as a Byronic demon-lover; a revival of interest in Sade, the myth of the Fatal Woman, a neurasthenic obsession with cross and self-mortification, poppy and silk. The Satanism of most nineteenth-century writers who preached it had the same relation to the traditional Hell of Christianity as the bird in long patent-leather boots at a Chelsea pub has to sado-masochism.

And so it may not be only a difference of quality in the paintings that makes us respond in a different way to Gustave Moreau's vaporous demon-Liliths or Aubrey Beardsley's decorative Satanism than to the figure of Satan in Francesco Traini's fresco in the Camposanto at Pisa (opposite). Do we not

The horned Satan, surrounded by his victims and minor demons. Francesco Traini, detail of fresco, Camposanto, Pisa.

155

tend to recognise that the aesthetic Satanism of the nineteenth century was too easy a solution to aggression: that it posed a fake question and got a fake answer? John Berger once remarked, on Delacroix, that the peculiar falsity of the Romantics' view of war lay in their habit of believing that you could stop it and start it like a film. The Satanists thought the same about Hell. Its mouth would open at the wave of a brush. It would emit a set of images which could give the audience a pleasant (but safe) *frisson* of surprise, disgust or perverse pleasure; and then Hell would obediently close. Leviathan as tame crocodile, performing for a seated audience. The aesthetics of evil are, inevitably, a luxury. The recognition of evil is a moral necessity; and here Traini's Satan inevitably wins, for he is the appalling, deformed personification of aggression: a force which may be controlled by God, but which once unleashed cannot be ridden by man. He is a central fact of moral existence, whereas the nineteenth-century Satan is little more than a metaphor of aesthetic revolt.

The Imagery of Hell

Hell is chaos; and the difficulty of painting it resides in the problem of finding a form for chaos. When theologians spoke of the chaos of the Pit they did not mean it in the sense of undifferentiated matter awaiting form – the 'primordial substance' of Plato and the Pythagoreans. The chaos of Hell is active, malevolent, aggressive. It confronts order. It is the other half of a dualistic universe.

We have seen that artists, when dealing with the theme of Heaven, were able to use the formal harmony of their paintings as a metaphor, in itself, of the perfect relationship between the soul and God. The painting became a microcosm of Heaven, aesthetic clarity echoing the clarity of the transfigured soul in its union with the divine essence. This analogy between form and subject could not be pursued in Hell. To paint Chaos in a chaotic manner would merely produce an illegible picture. And so the problem was to discover a form for the Pit without depriving Hell of its terrible and negative formlessness.

It goes almost without saying that random configurations, in painting, have no power to frighten. Even supposing that a mediaeval or a Renaissance artist had been able to think of a chance blot as a work of art complete in itself, it is unlikely that he would ever have attributed much emotional capacity to it. (That Leonardo advised painters to seek chance inspiration in puddles and stains, or that Piero di Cosimo visited the Florence hospital to draw ideas from the marks of spittle on the walls of its wards, does not mean that either of them regarded these chance patterns as works of art in themselves.) We may be pleased or not by the cracked, muddy, ragged surface of a Fautrier or by the whiplash rococo of an action painting by Jackson Pollock. What is certain is that neither will be frighten-

156

ing in its own right because neither offers enough clues to build up the set of expectations which will culminate in a sense of fear.

Artists and poets were therefore driven to another solution for depicting Hell. They evolved a set of images which were, to a surprising degree, stable. They were the negative images to Heaven's reality, doubling it, parodying it, like hallucinatory reflections in black water. The Trees of Life and Knowledge, as well as the aromatic shrubs of Paradise, found their counterpart in the dark woods at Hell-Gate and the Wood of the Suicides. The stinking lakes and rivers of Hell correspond to the healing waters of the Four Rivers of Eden; the geysers and volcanoes to the Fountain of Life. The hierarchy of demons inverts that of angels. Out of this system of correspondances and analogies rose a terrifying world, complete in itself, with its own ruler, laws, ecology, population, substances and weather. Thus Hell took shape. The first question to be settled, then, was where Hell might be in relation to Earth and the Universe in general.

The shore of Lake Avernus, in Italy, was supposed in classical times to be the entrance to Hell. Here a follower of Bruegel the Younger, perhaps Jan Mandyn, turns Aeneas' arrival there with the Cumaean sibyl into a scene of Piranesian grandeur. Palazzo Doria, Rome.

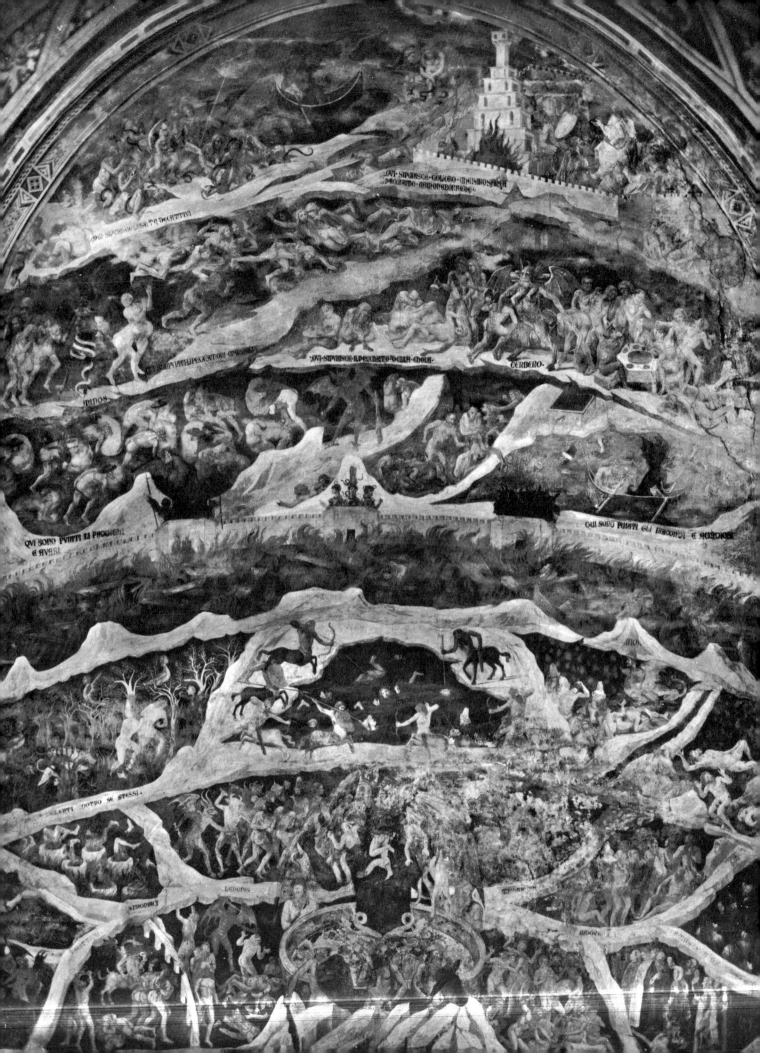

chapter 4

The Map of the Pit

The Subterranean Theory of Hell

The poets of classical antiquity agreed that Hades was under the earth. There were good reasons for thinking so – notably the identification, mentioned in the last chapter, between the gods of the Underworld and the fertility gods. That the soul, loosed from the body, should return to the domain of the spirits which, under the soil, controlled physical growth of crops and animals, had an immediate attraction both as myth and symbol. Homer's souls merely go on a long flat journey to Hades, which is another country; but references to *descent* into Hell are common elsewhere in Greek and Roman literature. Their basic form is that of Virgil's account of Aeneas visiting the Underworld.

Some actual places were thought to be entrances to the Underworld. One was Lake Avernus, a deep, extinct volcanic crater near Puteoli in southern Italy. The district round Lake Avernus is dormant today but it was known for its volcanic activity in ancient times; the miasma of sulphurous gas which rose from the verges of the lake was reputed to choke birds flying over it so that they fell dead into the water. It was from a cave on Lake Avernus that Aeneas, after his encounter with the Sibyl, descended into Hades (p. 157); and so the lake bequeathed its name to one of the best-known tags about Hell – *Facilis descensus Averni*, the slippery slope to damnation. Not only Virgil, but Strabo, Lucretius and Livy thought it the vestibule of the Underworld, and certainly on a gloomy day the sulphur-whiffs, sticky heat and impenetrably dark, tangled woods on the shores of Avernus recall its classical reputation. Another and equally celebrated entrance to Hell is at Taenarus, near Marmari, in the southern Peleponnese – a cave approachable only by sea, 'one of the ventilation holes of the Underworld' as Apuleius called it, into which Psyche descended to procure from Pluto the casket which would restore Aphrodite's beauty. There are of course local legends attaching to half the sulphur-springs and caves in Italy; here Orpheus descended, here Christ went down into Limbo; Christian and pagan myths, inextricably mixed together, flock like bats to dark places.

Nothing could be more natural than the identification of Hades with volcanic areas; the rumble of an earth tremor, the jet of steam from a geyser, the unnatural fetid warmth of a deep tufa cave, all announced the presence of subterranean life. And the instinctive line of symbolic thinking which places evil in an inferior place and good in a superior one need hardly be stressed. Not all pre-Christian myths placed Hell below the earth. Amenthe, the Hell of Egyptian mythology, lay on the earth's surface,

Nardo di Cione: *The Inferno*, Fresco, Sta Maria Novella, Florence. The only major fresco of Hell which minutely followed Dante's programme in the *Divine Comedy*.

159

beyond the sea, in the west; but even here one may note that the identification of Hell with the place where the sun goes down – as in Homer's account – implies both the idea of descent and that of darkness.

The Old Testament contains many references to a subterranean Hell:

But you are brought down to Sheol, to the depths of the Pit. Those who see you will stare at you, and ponder over you : Is this the man who made the earth tremble, who shook kingdoms, who made the world like a desert and overthrew its cities, who did not let his prisoners go home?
[*Isaiah* XIV, 15]

Ezekiel (XXXI, 16, 17, 27) places Hell in a pit, and *Proverbs* (IX, 18) mentions the foolish man who 'does not know that the dead are there, that her guests are in the depths of Sheol'.

Amos (IX, 2) implies the distance between Heaven and Hell; the Lord, cursing the people of Israel, declares that 'Though they dig into Sheol, from there shall my hand take them; though they climb up to Heaven, from there I shall bring them down.'

Quite apart from the immense weight of biblical and classical precedents for putting Hell in the bowels of the earth, the idea of a subterranean Hell in mediaeval Christian legend was reinforced by the cosmological belief of the time: that of a universe which revolved around the earth as its centre. Plato, in *Phaedo*, located his Underworld, in the usual Greek way, beneath the surface. And Plato's geocentric theory of the sun and planets dominated mediaeval thought. Around the earth revolved the successive spheres of the planets, growing more 'sublime' with their increasing distance from the earth until, in the seventh and last sphere, one reached the Empyrean, the domain of pure spiritual existence, inhabited by essences of which the physical realities of earth were only a gross shadow. The closer it got to the earth-centre of the universe, the coarser and grosser reality became. What was more natural than to assume that Hell, the most grotesque and least ideal of all realities, the caricature-house of nature, should be at the furthest possible remove from the ideal circumference of the universe: at the centre of the earth?

This sophisticated argument could only stand up as long as earth was the centre. It took Christianity a little time to adjust its idea of the site of Hell to the impact of Copernicus' theory that the earth went round the sun, along with the other planets. A reconciliation was tried by Tobias Swinden, in *An Enquiry into the Nature and Place of Hell*, published in 1714. Hell, Swinden argued, was in the sun (p. 163). Some reasons for this were self-evident – the sun was very hot, and demonstrably much hotter than the centre of the earth, so that God's design of infinite punishment by fire would be better served in the sun than anywhere else. But the sun was also very large and so could accommodate the huge numbers of damned souls which, Swinden felt, could not possibly fit into the centre of the earth.

opposite El Greco: *The Dream of Philip II*, c. 1580, Escorial. This compound of eschatological nightmares derives from Christian visionary literature of the 12th and 13th centuries. Note the jaws of Leviathan on the right, stuffed with sinners; and the figures crossing the narrow Bridge of Judgment above the burning lake.

160

opposite Zane (John) of Climax: *The Ladder of Judgment*, stretching between earth and Heaven. As the virtuous ascend it, the wicked are dragged from its rungs by demons and fall into Hell. 7th century, St Catherine's Monastery, Sinai.

He was offended by the pawky conservatism of the Jesuit Drexelius, with his Hell a mere cubic mile in size, stuffed with no more than 100,000,000,000 souls: a 'poor and mean estimate':

The number he [Drexelius] calleth a prodigious stupendous number, and a place of such dimensions, he says, is capable of receiving such a number of men. But alas! How infinitely short is that computation to those multitudes who, as many, are set in opposition by Christ to the few saints, yet these no man can number . . .

If the sun is the centre, it must be further from the Empyrean than earth; and so further from Heaven. This made it a better site for Hell. Moreover, since the Empyrean was the highest, and the sun the lowest created place in the universe, a Hell placed in the sun would be best fitted to receive Lucifer and the rebel angels, whose revolt against God and consequent fall happened before the creation of the world. Why let them fall only part of the way, no further than earth? Such a notion was an offence to the divine sense of symmetry. Finally, the diabolic associations of the sun were proved, for Swinden, by the 'early and almost universal idolatry' given to it by pagans. Here we catch a trace of the traditional Christian shift from classical god into demon; any false deity, including Apollo, could be equated with Satan or Antichrist. (And there is, indeed, an interesting parallel between the refulgent Lucifer and the Sun-God Apollo.)

Swinden's theory of Hell in the sun may have been influenced

Hell located in the sun. This attempt to reconcile the doctrine of Hell with the theory of a sun-centred universe was made by Tobias Swinden in 1714.

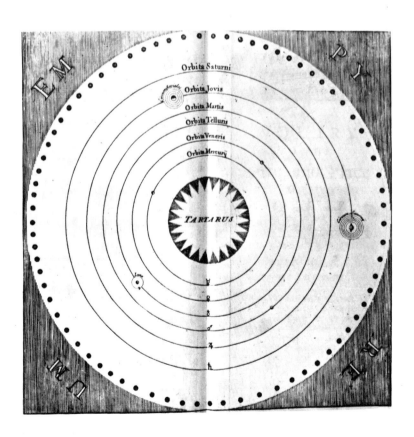

by Aristotle, who mentioned[2] certain Pythagorean philosophers who placed the sphere of fire in the sun and even referred to it as 'Jupiter's Prison'. But the solar Hell had no real chance of popularity. The sun, as symbol, was too pregnant with benevolent and heroic associations to carry the evil load necessary for its acceptance as the site of Hell. The sun is the supreme heroic and godly symbol; it represented the eye of God to the religions of India (as Varuna), Egypt (as Ra), Persia (as Ahuramazda), Islam (as Allah) and, in its familiar character of Helios-Apollo, of Greece. Sol as benefactor, as noble lion, as chariot, as incarnation of virility and wisdom; but never as anti-world. Even when sunlight is divested of its symbolic trappings and considered as physical pleasure, it is hard to believe that the most iron-laced Puritan, basking in July, could have been persuaded that he was being warmed by the glow of burning buggers.

And so it is the subterranean theory of Hell which dominates Christian eschatology, whether Hell is considered literally as a closed space in the middle of the earth, or, for flat-earthers, as a hemisphere under the disk of earth which doubled the arc of the heavens above, or as a vast gulf or pit, open to the sky, in some unknown region of the globe. And gradually, through the heritage of classical, Oriental, Egyptian and Islamic myths, fortified by the visions of early Christian and mediaeval monks, saints, desert fathers and hysterics, Hell came to acquire a detailed and highly typified set of contents.

The Bridge of Judgment

One of these is the Bridge of Judgment. It first appears in ancient Persian mythology as the Kinvad Bridge, which spans the gulf between earth and Heaven. Immeasurably far below its frail arch lie the stinking marshes and fire-pits of Hell. Every soul must cross it; and the bridge judges them all. For the holy man, it widens and becomes smooth, so that he has no trouble going over it. For the bad it becomes impassably narrow –

like the edge of a razor. And he who is righteous passes over the bridge . . . [but] he who is of the wicked, as he places a footstep on the bridge, on account of affliction and its sharpness, falls from the middle of the bridge, and rolls over head-foremost[3].

Sometimes the soul meets its *doppelgänger* coming in the opposite direction:

. . . But when the vices outweigh the virtues, a dark and fearful image, featured with ugliness, and exhaling a noisome smell, meets the condemned soul and cries: 'I am thy evil spirit; bad myself, thy crimes have made me worse.' Then the culprit staggers on his uncertain foothold, is hurled from the dizzy causeway, and precipitated into the gulf which yawns horribly below[4].

The Mahommedan equivalent for the Bridge of Judgment was

called *al Sirat*, and it is precisely the same as the Persian bridge.

Not surprisingly, this dramatic image passed intact into Christian visions of Hell. (It does not occur in either the Old or the New Testaments. In fact, the word 'bridge' does not appear in the Bible at all. But there is a relationship between the Bridge of Judgment and Jacob's Ladder, which we will come to presently.) It first appears in the *Dialogues* of St Gregory, written in the late sixth century[5]. The Hell-traveller, a soldier who had been at the point of death and miraculously recovered, tells how his soul was brought within sight of Hell:

He saw a bridge, under which ran a black and smoky river, that had a filthy and intolerable smell; but on the further side there were pleasant green meadows full of sweet flowers, in which also there were divers companies of men apparelled in white ... Now those that desired to pass over the aforesaid bridge, were subject to this manner of trial: if any that was wicked attempted to go over, down he fell into that dark and stinking river; but those that were just and not hindered by sin, securely and easily passed over ...

In the early eighth century, St Boniface described how, in his vision of Hell, the traveller – known as the Monk of Wenlock – saw a river of pitch spanned by a wobbly timber plank. Some souls crossed it without difficulty. Others fell into the boiling slime, where they stuck, some up to their necks, others to their waists or to their knees, and so on, in proportion to the gravity of their sins. Eventually they all came out, guilt burnt away, and entered the Celestial City on the other side. The pitch river, in this case, is Purgatory. But in later visions it is always firmly associated with Hell. Thus the *Vision of Tundale* (twelfth century) describes two bridges in Hell. The first is of wood,

... an immensely long plank which ran from one mountain-peak to another like a bridge, above the valley. It was a thousand paces long and no more than a single foot wide. No one except the elect could cross this bridge. He saw many people fall from it, and only one man, a priest, managed to cross it. But he was a priest on a pilgrimage, carrying his palm ... and he set off before all the others, quite without fear ...

The second bridge is still more difficult. It spans a 'wide boiling marsh', in which monsters lurk (p. 161).

The bridge was exceedingly narrow and long. Its length stretched for two thousand yards, which was the breadth of the swamp. And it would be true to say that this bridge was no more than one palm wide. Thus it was even longer and narrower than the one we mentioned above. And it was studded with iron nails, very sharp ...

The *Vision of Tundale* was the best-known of all mediaeval visions. Before the end of the fifteenth century it had been disseminated all over Europe, with translations in Italian,

165

German, Dutch and French. (It even existed in Gaelic and Old Norse. Probably it was originally written in Latin.) It is most likely that Hieronymus Bosch read it – a version, in Dutch, was actually published in his home-town of 's-Hertogenbosch in 1484, and an earlier edition in Antwerp – and certainly it was known to his contemporary imitators. A painting of Hell by one of them in the Museo Lazaro in Madrid is inscribed, at bottom left, *Visio Tondaly*. Just above this incription can be seen the Irish knight, Tundale, dreaming his vision, accompanied in reverie by the angel who, in the narrative, was his guide and guardian. Around the picture, a wierd panorama of allegorical punishments unfolds; a naked man (perhaps a gambler?) sits on a die and is tormented by two freaks; souls wallow in a great vat of liquid, into which the nose of a Mask of Hell dribbles, instead of mucus, gold coins; gluttons are force-fed and hacked to pieces by demons. Some of these images are transcribed directly from Tundale's vision – the punishment of the gluttons, for instance; others seem to be free inventions, or quotations

Hell, by a 16th-century follower of Bosch, Herri met der Bles (or Il Civetta). Despite its appearance to post-Freudian eyes, this is in no sense a surrealist painting; each image carries a specific allegorical weight. The bag-pipe on the right, for instance, is a symbol of vain speech; below it, the figure dragged across a die by a bird-beaked demon is suffering the punishment reserved for gamblers and wastrels. Note the *pons asinorum*, or Bridge of Fools, in the middle ground.

166

Pieter Huys: *The Temptation* of
St Anthony, Louvre. The apparition
of monsters to this saint was a
favourite theme for demonic imagery.

from Bosch himself. The woman in the bed, tormented by
monsters, is one of the latter, and it comes from a fragment
of an early altarpiece wing now in New York. Despite such
variations from the text of Tundale's narative, we can be
reasonably sure that a bridge with a tower on it, silhouetted as
a ruinous, gapped arch against Hell's sulphurous light, is the
Bridge of Judgment. There are innumerable images in Bosch's
own paintings which coincide with those of the *Vision of
Tundale*. In the background of the Hell panel of the *Garden
of Earthly Delights*, a thin plank is seen, stretched between two
black and dreadful buildings on the horizon; it spans the burning mud of the lake of Hell, and the single figure tottering in
mid-span, holding a long rod or spear, is probably a transformed
reference to the lone priest carrying a palm who in Tundale's
account crossed the wooden bridge. On the nearer side of
the lake Bosch introduces a second bridge, this time of stone;
a motley gaggle of demons and damned, riding on pigs and
asses, is crossing it. Here, the Bridge of Judgment would

seem to be fused with the proverbial *pons asinorum*, or Bridge of Fools; and it is probably in this light that one should interpret other bridges painted in Hell by such followers of Bosch as Jan Mandyn (opposite) and Herri met der Bles (p. 166). In Pieter Huys' *Universal Judgment* the bridge actually becomes a sword-blade, across which fiends are harrying souls into the open visor of a giant helmet. This motif of the sword-bridge also appears in mediaeval romance literature and illumination, where it became a test imposed on the good knight as he seeks the garden or castle, through peril and adversity; it is a common feature of Arthurian legends (above).

The Ladder of Salvation

The Ladder of Salvation is a variant on the Bridge of Judgment, but – unlike it – has a biblical origin in the Old Testament.

> *[Jacob] dreamed that there was a ladder set up on the earth, and the*

French MS illumination, early 15th century: the trials of the Knight. At left, he crosses a sword-blade bridge above a perilous river; centre, he vanquishes lions in the forest; right, the arrival at the Citadel.

top of it reached heaven; and behold, the angels of God were ascending and descending on it. And behold, the Lord stood above it . . .

[*Genesis* XXVIII, 12–3]

But in later visions, the ladder is transformed into an obstacle course, like the bridge. The third-century *Vision of Perpetua* speaks of a golden ladder stretching to Heaven from earth, each of whose thousand steps is guarded with hooks and sharp knives. If a wicked man treads on one, the cutters go to work on him and he falls into the clutches of an enormous dragon which lies coiled round the ladder's base. This idea was repeated by later visions, notably the twelfth-century *Vision of Alberic*. On his trip through Hell, Alberic spies a long iron ladder, with teeth on its rungs. Flame and sparks burst from the teeth, and the iron is red-hot; to make the ascent more difficult yet, there is a cauldron of boiling oil and tar beneath the ladder, and its heat rises to sear the climbers – some of whom tumble into the vat.

Ladders were normally used in art as symbols of moral im-

The Temptation of St Anthony, wrongly ascribed to Bruegel, probably by Jan Mandyn. Galleria Barberini, Rome. Note the Bridge of Fools on the extreme right, filled by a procession of devils carrying a head of Pan.

169

provement. The soul's ascent, rung by rung, away from the earth, fitted neatly into the Platonic cosmos with its concentric spheres of perfection, rising from earth to *Primum Mobile*. But quite often the ladder is depicted simply as a trial, with demons and angels flitting about it, the former dragging sinners down into the pit of Hell, the latter keeping the feet of the virtuous on the rungs and directing their eyes to Heaven (p. 162).

The Dark Wood

But there are more ways of getting to Hell than by falling into it. Two traditions interweave in the approaches to Hell. The one we have just considered entered Hebraic lore and then Christianity through Persian, Islamic and other eastern sources. However, Christian art also absorbed the idea of a descent into the bowels of the earth, on foot. Its most famous prototype is Virgil's account of the descent of Aeneas and the Sibyl into the Underworld, in the sixth book of the *Aeneid*:

Obscure they went through dreary shades, that led
Along the waste dominions of the dead.
Thus wander travellers in woods by night,
By the moon's doubtful and malignant light,
When Jove in dusky clouds involves the skies,
And the faint crescent shoots by fits before their eyes.

Many visions of Hell begin with an initiation by fear in a wood. The Hell-traveller loses consciousness; on waking, he finds himself in a dreadful forest, and when he picks his way out of it he is at Hell-Gate. Dante incorporated Virgil's image of the dark wood into the *Inferno*, and made it the first taste of the landscape of Hell:

Nel mezzo del cammin di nostra vita
mi ritrovai per una selva oscura
che la diritta via era smarrita.

Ah quanto a dir qual era e cosa dura
esta selva selvaggia e aspra e forte
che nel pensier rinova la paura!

Here, as so often happens with images in Hell, the Dark Wood has a double aspect. The traveller loses his way in it, and hence, by implication, his conscious will: he is given a foretaste of the freezing of moral action which Hell imposes on its prisoners. At the same time, the reader (as one of Dante's fourteenth-century audience) has raised before him one of the worst phantoms of the mediaeval imagination – the fear of Nature untamed. At the time that the image of the Dark Wood was developed, forests had none of the pleasant overtones with which the Romantic movement endowed them for us. The mediaeval Italian experienced a sharp contrast between the city and the chaos

170

of uncultivated nature for which the Dark Wood was the most vivid symbol. Landscape was wild in the same sense as Hell represented Chaos: it was not a mass of unformed potential but a complete and hostile anti-world, pressing up from the valleys to the town, creeping in on the ploughed fields and terraces, strangling paths in undergrowth, and harbouring apparitions. An extraordinary range of malevolent forces and incidents – from bandits to snakes, from thorn-cuts to death by starvation, from enraged dogs to marauding *condottieri* – were incorporated into mediaeval forest-fears. Nor did they pass with the Middle Ages: Macbeth's declaring

I shall not be afraid of death nor bane
Till Birnam forest come to Dunsinane

and then succumbing to an advancing wood of troops, must have carried some primitive forest-terrors into the minds of an Elizabethan audience; as, even today, they are re-created for children in fairy-stories.

The theme of initiation by trial in the wilderness is common to a great deal of European and eastern literature and art. After Dante, the Dark Wood naturally tended to be an imitation,

Chaos against consciousness: the devil pitted against the warrior and the pilgrim. **below** A peg-legged devil accosts an itinerant monk: drawing by Urs Graf, German, 1512, Basel. **right** The devil captures an infantryman. Urs Graf, 1516, Basel, Kupferstichkabinett. **left** Battle between a soldier and a horned demon, drawing by Martin Schongauer, Uffizi, Florence.

conscious or not, of the forest outside the *Inferno*; thus in the *Hypnerotomachia Poliphili*, a visionary allegory of consciousness written in the sixteenth century, the hero, Polifilo, falls asleep and wakes in a fearsome, almost impassable wood. The prototype is obvious enough in this case, but mediaeval and Renaissance art, especially in northern Europe, abounds in Dark Woods which (unlike Dante's) are given a specifically demonic character as the abode of Satan. The most famous representation of this theme is Dürer's *The Knight, Death and the Devil*. This Faustian metaphor shows, in its most concentrated form, the opposition between articulate consciousness and Chaos which is at the root of the symbolic value western artists discovered in the themes of Heaven and Hell. The knight, the hero on horseback, was for Dürer (as for all Renaissance artists) the epitome of the *uomo di virtù* – intelligence and will imposing themselves on brute nature. The forest is his opposite: tangled, incoherent, strewn with skulls and thorns, it has an animistic 'presence', and Dürer's demon, flop-eared, warty and dewlapped, with its boar's snout and unicorn's horn, shares the life of the place as naturally as a Claudian nymph fits her Arcadian pastures.

The Dark Wood of Hell. On a Romanesque capital from Autun, two winged demons hang their victim from a tree. Cathedral Museum, Autun.

Sometimes, in Hell, the Dark Wood is more than an initiation: it is an actual part of the torture. This symbolism is extremely ancient and probably relates to the fact that forests were among the first places to be given over to the cults of local gods. The demons of the wood could be appeased by offerings, and especially by human sacrifice. Such offerings were suspended from trees. (The gallows, a peculiarly artificial means of killing victims, survives to remind us of these tree-cults.)

The Dark Wood as torture-chamber appears both in the east and in the west. The Tibetan idea of the Last Judgment includes, among the torments of the damned in the Eight Hot Hells – sections of Hell reserved for those who have committed sins of anger – one named *Shal-ma-ri*, or the Hell of the Spiked Tree, on which the dismembered limbs and trunk of the victim are impaled by demons. An early Brahman text, the *Markandeya-Purana*, describes how in one part of Hell the damned encounter a deceptively cool and green forest of trees. This is the *Asi-patravana*, or 'forest with sword-leaves'. If a soul enters it, the leaves bow down and impale him, while myriads of hungry dogs rend his flesh. The comparison with Dante's She-Wolf in the forest, slinking towards her prey, *carca nella sua magrezza*, gaunt with hunger, is significant.

Two vivid parallels in early Christian literature are the *Vision of St Paul* and the *Vision of Alberic*.

Alberic was written early in the twelfth century; though it was given out as the vision of an eight-year-old boy, this (as a Victorian scholar surmised with some asperity) 'was probably done advisedly by the monk or monks who wrote and spread this vision, and who realised that a vision of this nature, vouchsafed to an unsophisticated child, would appear all the more marvellous and convincing to the credulous public'.

The narrator, Alberic, falls into a trance-like sleep which lasts nine days. His soul leaves his body and is carried upwards by a white dove. He is met by St Peter, who, like Virgil to Dante, acts as his guide through Hell. Peter descends with Alberic into the pit and shows him valleys, lakes, and inland seas of boiling oil and pitch. One valley contains a forest of trees with sword-like branches festooned with sinners; adultresses hang by their hair over flames and uncharitable women who refused to nurse orphans swing from trees while snakes crawl on their bodies and suck their breasts dry.

The *Vision of St Paul* is some eight centuries older than *Alberic*. Versions of it are known from the fourth century. There is no evidence whatever that it was written, or even experienced, by St Paul; successive Christian fathers, including Epiphanius and St Augustine, inveighed against it, and it has never formed part of the Scriptural canon of the Church. But manuscripts of the pseudo-Paul's vision were copied in mediaeval Italy and it is not inconceivable that Dante or Giotto might have read it or at least heard of it. In the vision Paul is shown a forest at the gate of Hell. The trees are on fire but they are not consumed; from them, sinners hang by different organs – adulterers by their genitals, the proud by their hair, and so on. It was thus that Giotto depicted the fate of adulterers in his fresco of the Last Judgment in the Arena Chapel at Padua (p. 179).

The theme of the Dark Wood has a third aspect, whose most famous image is the Wood of the Suicides in Dante's *Inferno*. The punishment of suicides is that their souls are turned into withered trees. Harpies nest in the branches of this repulsive grove and Dante finds, to his amazement, when he breaks off a twig, the distressed soul of Piero delle Vigne speaks to him:

Come d'un stizzo verde ch'arse sia
  dall'un de' capi, che dall'altro geme
  e cigola per vente che va via,
si della scheggia rotta usciva inseme
  parole e sangue ; ond'io lascia la cima
  cadere, e stetti come l'uom che teme . . .

(*Inf.* XIII, 40–5: 'As a green brand, set burning at one end, drips from the other and hisses with the escaping air, so from the broken splinter came words and blood together; at which I dropped the twig and stood like a frightened man.')

Here, the trees *are* the souls, not simply their gibbets. But after the Last Judgment, when the souls of the dead are reunited with their bodies, the suicides' bodies will hang on these branches, like the damned in the visions of Paul and Alberic. William Blake's illustration to this passage contains all the essential elements (p. 174): the trees, spiked like alligators' backs,

with harpies sitting in their gloomy branches, flapping their wings and chewing the leaves; Dante stares with astonishment at the shade of Piero delle Vigne who, like an image from Arcimboldo or one of the metamorphic drawings of Tchelitchew, has half-materialised from the trunk. Because it was tied to a universally read and incorrupt text, the image of the Wood of the Suicides did not substantially change throughout centuries of illustrations to Dante: compare, to the Blake, Nardo di Cione's Wood of the Suicides (opposite). The trees are denser and thornier (with their prickly lobes, they look like Italian cacti), but the means of representing the soul of Piero delle Vigne as a pathetic face materialising from the wood is the same.

Dante and Virgil in the Wood of the Suicides. Illustration to *The Inferno*, by William Blake, 1824–7. The face of Piero delle Vigne can be seen emerging from the trunk.

The Mouth of Hell

Today, the Dark Wood has become a smear of pines between one gas station and the next on the Autostrada del Sole; Satan rides through the dreams of a shrinking minority, and a kiosk sells Motta ice-cream on the shores of Lake Avernus. But at least one of Hell's introductory marvels still keeps a fraction of its power, though in a sadly debased form. This is the Mouth of Hell, which still gapes, a red-nosed, gummy, toothy, papier-mâché mask, at the entrances of innumerable Luna Parks and Ghost Trains throughout the western world. Its once horrific features are twisted into an exaggerated grimace of jollity – Pluto as vaudeville ham; but still the audience, jingling their sixpences as they walk under the plaster molars, might sense that a certain basic symbolism is implied: that in walking through the grotesque smile they are passing into another world where magic can happen: the centrifuge inverts the law of gravity, the motorbike riders invite death, the Bumble-Bug whirls and the wavy mirrors throw back squeezed images, the tin ducks perpetually resurrect themselves before the airgun sights and the dusty skeleton jiggles its pelvis, in a fluorescent *memento mori*, from a recess in the Tunnel of Love. However filtered and weakened, the great fun-fairs which survive from the 1920s still present their clientele with the image of a *monde à rebours*, an experience which was built into the nature of Hell; the entrance-mouth testifies to the covered origins of the symbol.

The Mouth of Hell was traditionally represented as the mouth of a huge and malevolent beast, which dragged sinners into its maw. It is not within the scope of this book to go into the origin of this image in detail, but it seems to derive from primitive eastern sea-dragon myths which found their way into the Old Testament as the myth of Leviathan, a gigantic fish or marine serpent which supported the sea on its back – rather as, in Indian mythology, the earth was supported by a giant turtle – and was in turn mixed, successively, with the whale which swallowed Jonah and the horned Beast of the *Apocalypse* of St John. Leviathan as described by Job sounds like a Nile crocodile, and indeed the Hebrew word can mean, impartially, crocodile or Leviathan:

Can you draw out Leviathan with a fishook,
* or press down his tongue with a cord?*
Can you put a rope in his nose, or pierce
* his jaw with a hook?*
Will he make many supplications to you?
Will he speak to you soft words?
Will he make a covenant with you to take
* him for your servant for ever?*
Will you play with him as with a bird,
* or will you put him on leash for*
* your maidens?*
Lay hands on him ;

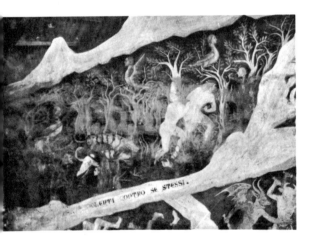

The Wood of the Suicides: detail from *The Inferno* by Nardo di Cione. Sta Maria Novella, Florence.

de beemoth belua tte · l ·

Eemoth eſt belua et aıal quadru
pes dentuı ımmanıtate armatū
et lınguam exerꝛt · habes cornua
aꝛuetuın ſımılıa et eıus caꝛtılago quaſi la
mıne ferꝛece habens teſtıculos ꝛplexos et pe
des aıımnalıs · eıus oſſa ſunt ſıcut fıſtule
erꝛıs · hꝫ autem caudam draꝛonıs atꝛocenı et
longam quaſı cedꝛus Cauda quıdeın lıgat
dentıbꝫ · ꝙ vulnerat · huıc mılle montes her

ıpſo tranſeunte perꝛbıt · ſıgnıfıcat autem
dꝛabolum · quı de excelſıs ad ymıa ꝛuıt · et
pro merıto ſuo ut amımal brutū effectus e
Sıgnıfıcat eaaın antxpm perꝛdıtıoıs fılıum
ın fıne ventuꝛū Quı ınquantū poterꝛıt coo
perꝛante dꝛabolo perꝛdet genus humanū · et
ın nouıſſımo ſcrıptum

think of the battle ; you will not
  do it again !
Behold, the hope of a man is disappointed ;
he is laid low even at the sight of him.
The arrow cannot make him flee ;
  for him slingstones are turned to stubble.
Clubs are counted as stubble ;
  he laughs at the rattle of javelins.
His underparts are like sharp potsherds ;
he spreads himself like a threshing sledge
  on the mire.
He makes the deep boil like a pot ;
he makes the sea like a pot of ointment.
Behind him he leaves a shining wake ;
one would think the deep to be frosted.
Upon earth there is not his like, a
  creature without fear.
He beholds everything that is high ;
he is king over all the sons of pride.   *[*Job XLI*]*

In the last line, Leviathan's future connection with Hell and the forces of evil becomes apparent: like Lucifer, Leviathan is 'king over all the sons of pride' – which later interpreters took to mean the rebel angels who were cast, with their leader, into Hell. This was reinforced by *Revelation's* XIX, 20:

And the beast was captured, and with it the false prophet who in its presence had worked the signs by which he deceived those who had received the mark of the beast and those who worshipped its image. These two were thrown alive into the lake of fire that burns with brimstone.

The association of Antichrist with Leviathan is indicated by a mediaeval illustration in the *Liber Floridus.* Here, Antichrist, with his crown and blasphemous sceptre of power, is triumphantly borne across the waves by Leviathan. The marine monster has some of the attributes which *Revelations* gave to the 'beast rising from the sea' [XIII, 1]: four sharp teeth which have grown into incurving tusks, a head halfway between lion and fish, two horns and a crest, the feet of a lion, wings, and a long, elegantly swirling tail.

A miniature from the Missal of Poitiers shows us how Lucifer-Antichrist's friendship with Leviathan degenerated once the two of them were in Hell. Antichrist is transformed back into his original state, that of Satan; a horrific beast, with the face of an ape-lion and vipers hissing from a hole in his belly, he bestrides Leviathan in an ironic parody of horsemanship, caricaturing the heroic and courtly associations which cling to the image of the knight. Where in the *Liber Floridus* Antichrist controls Leviathan, here he is chained to the brute's jaws, goading it with a stick, but unable to escape it. Leviathan's jaws are

The devil Behemoth riding on Leviathan. 15th-century Apocalypse miniature; Musée Condé, Chantilly. Here, the 'beast from the sea' is a hybrid: lion's head with ram's horns, cloven hoofs, scaly body and serpentine tail. Note the supplementary face Behemoth carries on his chest: it derives from a legendary race of creatures which were believed to inhabit India, which had heads in their breasts but none on their shoulders.

177

open and flame gushes out, so intense that a minor demon recoils.

Once immersed in the lake of burning pitch, Leviathan bobs up again and again in early Christian and mediaeval visions of Hell. This visionary literature, some of it concocted by moralising priests out to terrify their congregation, but part of it without doubt the result of one man's hallucination or mystical experience, is the principal source for mediaeval Hell-painters. In the *Vision of Alberic*, Leviathan presents himself as a twin-headed monster (a variant on three-headed Cerberus) standing 'at the very mouth of the infernal chasm'. He is the entrance to Hell, and 'before one of his mouths was an infinite multitude of souls, whom the monster inhaled like flies, disgorging them again from the other mouth in the form of burning embers'. The *Vision of Tundale*, which is the most elaborately detailed of all English texts relating to Hell, recapitulates this theme: Satan, chained supine on a bed of burning coals, blows out a thousand incinerated souls every time he exhales, while his hands crush sinners and drop them into his furnace bed.

This description in *Tundale* was faithfully copied by Pol de Limbourg in the *Très Riches Heures du Duc de Berry* (p. 183). The miniaturist jibbed at endowing his Satan with the thousand hands with twenty fingers on each which Tundale gave him, but the griddle and coals are there (with forced draught supplied by a pair of demons, each working two bellows), and the unhappy souls, light as ash, whirl upwards on the tornado-spindle of heat which issues from the Adversary's mouth.

Nevertheless, the dominant image – the paradigm of consumption, so to speak – was the mouth of the apocalyptic beast, Leviathan. His identification with Hell-Mouth was complete by the early twelfth century. A miniature of about 1150, in the Psalter of St Swithun's Priory, painted by an artist of the Winchester School (p. 205), depicts the mouth as a generalised image of Hell itself: the monstrous head with its lion eyes and flaming tufts of hair gapes as flat as a kipper, and within the circle of its jaws the sinners, inextricably mixed with their torturers, flounder in pain. A door is hinged to the incisor teeth of the monster (or, more exactly, to the teeth of a pair of dragons which sprout from its lower jaws) and an angel, in the classical posture of Hermes Psychopompos (p. 190), presides with a key in the lock. The same identification of mouth with Hell can be traced in other mediaeval miniatures which show the fate of Antichrist or that of ordinary souls. The motif appears in mediaeval sculpture, whether in decorative form as on an early twelfth-century doorknocker in Durham Cathedral, where Leviathan appears as a lion (p. 182), or, greatly elaborated, in the celebrated York Minster Mouth of Hell (p. 186). Hell could be laconically symbolised by a pair of jaws, to which no body was attached; thus the sinful alewife, carved on a choir-seat in Ludlow Parish Church, is flung to Hell-Mouth (p. 185) while the images of door and jaws are neatly fused in a mediaeval

The fall of Antichrist, dragged by demons into the jaws of Hell. German woodcut, 15th century.

opposite Giotto: *The Last Judgment* (detail); Scrovegni Chapel, Padua.

REGNVM SATANAE ET PAPAE,
2. THESS. 2.

Jn aller Teufel namen sitzt
Alhie der Bapst: offenbart jtzt:
Das er sey der recht widerchrist
So in der schrift verkündigt ist:
Mar. Luth. D.

1545.

Lutheran propaganda woodcut, 1545: the Pope, as Antichrist, consigned to Hell and enthroned between the jaws of Leviathan. Note the beast's fishy eye.

opposite Giusto di Menabuoi: *The Last Judgment* (detail), Viboldone Parish Church.

carving at Conques-en-Rouergue, where Leviathan, whose leonine muzzle is bloated to the semblance of a pig's, stuffs his head through the door to Hell (p. 184). The beast and the entrance are here distinct but their association is obvious.

One of the common motifs of mediaeval and Renaissance Hells was the cauldron in which sinners are boiled; often a devil is depicted dragging a band of souls towards it by means of a chain looped round their reluctant bodies, as on a mid-thirteenth century tympanum at Reims (p. 187). A century later, the cauldron, as a primary image of suffering, was fused with Hell-Mouth, which is turned upside down, with the cauldron rammed into its maw so that it acts as a stove. Almost invariably in such representations the head turns into a lion's, as over the main door of Bourges Cathedral.

Between such relatively straightforward visions as the Hell of the St Swithun's Psalter (p. 205) and the gigantic demono-machies Bosch produced three and a half centuries later, there was of course a vast expansion in the range and complexity of different sins, sinners, demons, torments, topographical features and other images that an artist could fit into one painting of Hell. This meant that some images, once dominant, were slowly push-ed into an ancillary role as part of the general mechanism of damnation. So with the Mouth of Hell. By the middle of the *quattrocento* it had ceased to be the only gateway to the Under-world. Andrea di Firenze's fresco of Christ leading the souls out of Limbo, in the Spanish Chapel of Santa Maria Novella (p. 187) shows the crowd issuing from the mouth of a cave in a hillside; it may be that the oddly-formed rim of the entrance, whose rocks are split and separated to look like teeth, held a reference to the jaws of Hell-Mouth, but if so the metaphor has none of the explicitness of the monster Leviathan in mediaeval art. Andrea's method of showing Hell by cutting away part of the surface of a hollow hill and revealing the activity inside was used by other Florentine, Pisan and Sienese artists of the late

opposite The devil tormented in Hell, by Pol de Limbourg, from the *Très Riches Heures du Duc de Berry*. Satan's role as king of Hell is indicated by his crown. The grid, the bellows and the mouth exhaling clouds of burnt souls are taken from *The Vision of Tundale*, an English text of the 12th century which enjoyed wide currency in Europe. **left** A lion's head as mouth of Hell. Doorknocker from Durham Cathedral, c. 1140.

trecento. In the disgusting anthill thus revealed, with souls and demons pullulating around the winged, three-headed Satan, Leviathan and his gaping mouth shrink into merely one more of the terrors. Francesco Traini's fresco of Hell in the Camposanto at Pisa (p. 189) has a Hell-Mouth at the extreme top right in the first layer of the Inferno, which it shares with simoniacs and heretics; a recumbent figure wearing a turban, presumably a representative of Islam, is being drawn into the open jaws. The same scheme was used by Fra Angelico in his Last Judgment, painted for the Confraternity of St Mark in Florence (pp. 206–7). Again, the mouth is on the right – though it has become softer, with a nasty, fat, flaccid tongue lolling out to engulf the sinners. A demon is flinging a sinner, neck and crop, into it; the heretics are further to the left, with a figure holding a banner; this may be a reference to Dante's vision of the first layer of Hell, just inside the portal, where the souls of vacillators and lukewarm men follow a purposeless ensign:

above Hell, with Leviathan thrusting his snout through its doors. West doorway, Abbey of Conques-en-Rouergue. **opposite** 'And there they shall be tormented night and day, for all ages to come.' The jaws of Hell are linked lions' mouths. English mediaeval MS illumination. **lower right** The Punishment of the Alewife – flung into the jaws of Hell for watering beer. Choirstall carving, Ludlow Parish Church.

opposite Sinners boiling in the cauldron: the York Minster Mouth of Hell. **above** from the façade of Reims Cathedral, a devil loops a chain around all classes of men – king, bishop, priest, merchant – and drags them towards the fire.

below The cave of Hell from which Christ leads the saved souls, in Andrea da Firenze's fresco of *The Descent into Limbo* in the Spanish Chapel at Sta Maria Novella, Florence, retains the appearance of a gaping mouth.

Hermes Psychopompos, or Guide of
Souls, leading the spirits of the
suitors killed by Ulysses to Hades.
Drawing by John Flaxman,
illustrating Pope's translation of the
Odyssey.

E io, che riguardai, vidi una insegna
  che girando correva tanto ratta,
  che d'ogni posa mi parea indegna ;
e dietrole venia si lunga tratta
  di gente, ch' io non averei creduto
  che morte tanta n'avesse disfatta.

(*Inf.* III, 52–7: 'And I looked and saw a whirling banner which
rushed by so fast that it seemed it could never stand still; and
behind it came so long a trail of people that I could not have
thought death had undone so many.')

By the middle of the sixteenth century the jaws of Leviathan
had been changed into a different, but related, symbolic type:
the Mouth of Hell seen as a building, grotto or cave. To observe
this change we need to digress a little, into the classical images
of the 'half-open door' to Hell, and Hermes as shepherd of souls.

The most famous description of the end of the soul in classical
literature is probably Homer's. Ulysses comes back to Ithaca

Francesco Traini, *Hell*. Portion of the fresco cycle of *The Universal Judgment*, Camposanto, Pisa.

and finds his house full of suitors. He slaughters them all, and

Cyllenian Hermes came to summon the souls of the dead men. He held the rod of fine gold with which he enchants the eyes of men at his whim, or wakes those who sleep; with this he stirred them, and they followed gibbering. They were like a swarm of bats in the hollows of a great cave, which hang clinging to one another from the roof, until one falls out of the chain and they all fly about gibbering in confusion. So Hermes the Master-Trickster led them along the mouldering road, and they gibbered as they went. Past the stream of Ocean they went, past the rock of Leucas, past the gates of the Sun and the realm of dreams; and at last they came to the meadow of asphodel where abide the souls of those whose work is done.   [*Odyssey* 24, 1 ff.]

The god manifests himself here (opposite) as Hermes Psychopompos, the Guide of Souls. This is in keeping with the generally subordinate role which Hermes played in Greek (and as Mercury in Roman) mythology. He is the messenger of the

Gods, and especially of Zeus: an intermediary between life and the Underworld. Hermes was traditionally connected with fertility rites, and this related him to the Underworld and its gods because the fertility of the earth's crust was thought to be controlled by Pluto (the god of the Underworld, wealth and fecundity), his wife Persephone, and her mother Demeter.

In art, Hermes Psychopompos appears in two general forms. As a rule, he is seen taking a soul by the hand or arm before leading him down to Hades. But he is sometimes depicted standing just inside or half-way through the door of Hades, which is ajar. There is a carving of Hermes Psychopompos in this pose on a Roman monumental sarcophagus of the third century AD which stands outside the south door of the Baptistery in Florence (above). This sarcophagus was known in the late Middle Ages and it influenced the artist who designed the mosaics on the cupola of the Baptistery itself (opposite). The figure of the angel standing withing the half-open door of

Hermes Psychopompos, standing within the half-open door to Hades, waiting for the souls of the dead. Roman sarcophagus, Baptistery of S. Giovanni, Florence.

Angel conducting the souls of the virtuous to Paradise, with another angel standing inside the half-open door, welcoming a soul. 13th-century mosaic on the cupola of the Baptistery of S. Giovanni, Florence. The angel within the door is adapted from the classical prototype of Hermes Psychopompos.

Giovanni Bellini (?), *Christ's Descent into Limbo*. City Art Gallery, Bristol. Note the broken door of Hell.

Orpheus and Eurydice at the entrance to Hades. 14th-century MS illumination from a 'moralised' edition of Ovid's *Metamorphoses*, Bibliothèque Nationale, Paris. Note the guardian devil at the door to Hell.

opposite The gloomy kingdom of Hades, with Pluto and Persephone enthroned inside the mask of an owl – the bird of night – and Cerberus at their feet. Note the four streams of Lethean water: an inversion of the Four Rivers of Paradise. French MS illumination to Ovid, Bibliothèque Nationale, Paris.

193

Paradise is clearly an adaptation of Hermes behind the door, just as the larger angel, leading the souls of the elect towards the gate, is taken from Hermes in his more common form as guide.

So the Christianising of Hermes and his door as the angel (or cherub) of Paradise standing at the gate is readily established. What of Hell? One parallel jumps to mind at once – the theme of Christ's 'Harrowing of Hell': his descent into Limbo, whence he led forth the souls he had chosen to redeem, thus proving his power over Satan. This scene was so often repeated by artists that one would expect it to develop constant symbolic types. And so it did. One of these was the vanquished demon who is seen writhing beside the collapsed door to Hell and, very often, pinned and crushed beneath it (p. 187), as the triumphantly liberated souls march out of Hell into the sphere of power of Christ's protective mandorla. Obviously, the figure of Christ as leader of souls inherits the prototype of Hermes Psychopompos. But so did the prostrate devil. He could only have been guarding Hell, either outside or just inside its door. The proximity of this type of representation to the original classical myth is neatly

Jerome Cock after Pieter Bruegel: engraving, *The Harrowing of Hell*. Christ gestures; the door of Hell collapses on its guards; and the redeemed souls pour out. Bibliothèque Albert I, Brussels.

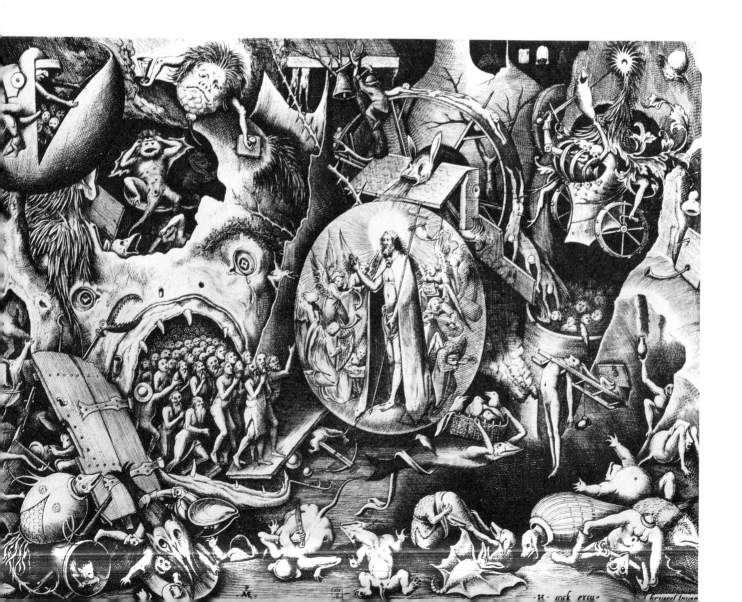

indicated by an illumination from one of the 'moralised' texts of Ovid, published in 1484 (p. 208). Here is the entrance to Hades, Christianised as Hell; it is guarded by Cerberus, and just within the iron-bound portal a guardian devil with bat-wings and claw feet can be discerned against the flames. If it seems inconsistent that Hermes should survive both as Christ *and* as Satan, one should remember that many classical gods developed this sort of split personality when they were taken over by Christianity. At the very moment when surviving Italian fertility cults of Venus and Demeter were being digested by the cult of the Virgin Mary as *Mater Dei*, St Martin, the bishop of Tours (316–400) had visions of the devil as Venus – and as Jupiter, Minerva and Hermes as well.

By the sixteenth century it seemed perfectly natural to artists that they should fuse the once distinct images of Leviathan and of Hermes at the half-open door to Hell into a fresh and exceedingly horrible synthesis: Leviathan seen as fleshy architecture. In Pieter Bruegel's engraving, *The Harrowing of Hell* (opposite), Leviathan is still recognisable; he has kept part of his

Pieter Bruegel: *Dulle Griet*, 1563. Antwerp Museum. The mouth of Hell is seen as part organic matter, part ruinous masonry and brickwork.

The Mouth of Hell changes from beast to building. **opposite above** Herri met der Bles, *Hell*: Rijksbureau voor Kunsthistorische Documentatie, The Hague. **opposite below** Joachim Patinir: *Charon crossing the Styx*. The round tower, through which the black river flows, is guarded by Cerberus; though it is recognisably a Hell-Mouth, it is also the ancestor of fairground entrances to the Tunnel of Love. **above** Niccolo di Pietro Gerini: *Temptation of St Anthony*, Castellani Chapel, Sta Croce, Florence. Leviathan has become an architectural ruin, whose windows and arch distantly allude to eyes and mouth.

traditional fish-shape and his sunken eyeballs goggle opaquely at one like those of a stale cod on a fishmonger's slab; through the gaping fish-mouth pour jubilant flocks of redeemed souls, raising their arms towards the mandorla in which Christ has floated down to them. But the edge of Leviathan's jaw has been equipped with sockets to take the hinges of two iron-bound timber doors. These, wrenched away, lie on top of various discomfited fiends.

Bruegel carried this disturbing transformation further in the Hell-Mouth which yawns on the left-hand side of *Dulle Griet* (p. 195). The thin, ragged sheet of bark-like substance which partially enclosed the Hell-Mouth in *The Harrowing of Hell* has turned into the curve of a ruined masonry wall. The head is half masonry and half flesh; flesh becoming brick, stiffening, turning into battlements, with saplings rooted in its decayed joints like the plants that grow on a castle keep. One still living eye, round and unblinking, glares out beneath a wooden awning fixed beneath what looks like an eyebrow but proves, on closer inspection, to be a string of empty flasks hanging on the wall. In an Inferno by an unnamed member of the School of Bosch, now in the Metropolitan Museum in New York, the

The Mouth of Hell as Mannerist decoration for buildings and gardens, **left** Doorway to Palazzo Zuccari, Rome. **opposite** The *bocca d'Inferno* at Bomarzo, built by Pierfrancesco Orsini in the mid-16th century. The inscription round the upper lip reads: 'All thought flies', and the steps lead up to a dining-room inside the mouth.

Hell-Mouth has become even more architectural; it lies half-sunk in the mire of Hell, the mouth yawning in a smooth parabolic arch – one thinks of a hippopotamus basking in a river – and the back of its head has been converted into a ramshackle lean-to, with window and door and a tree, parodying the Tree of Life in Eden, thrusting its blasted limbs up through the roof. A Hell-Mouth ascribed to Herri met der Bles (p. 196) is even more an architectural ruin. Light gleams through its mouth, reflected from the landscape in the background; the left side of its forehead is a brick buttress, and the eyes are empty windows, from one of which a figure leans, holding a lantern. The river of Hell, presumably the Styx, flows through its open mouth. And when we come to Joachim Patinir's *Charon crossing the Styx*, in the Prado (p. 196), we can see the last transformation of Leviathan; he has ended up as a kiosk in the infernal park, an unpleasant and claustrophobic little building but not a very alarming one. The mouth is now an arch, nothing more – though it is ornamented with a string

Ylape.   S. paul.   Walachias.

ous qui entendons a par
ler du iour du derrenier
iugement ce qui lui
plaira et afferner icelui
encontre les mauuais z
mescreans (deuós mettre
premieremét aussi cöme
ou fondement de ledifice les tesmoingnages
duins ausquelz ceulp qui ne veulent croire
sefforcent de venir au contraire par petites raisós
humaines faulses z fallacieuses a fin quilz de
batent le tesmoingnage lequel est prins des sai
ctes escriptures ou signifier autre chose ou met
qui soit dit estre de par dieu. Car ie ne cuide voit
quil soit aucun hôme mortel qui ne saccorde et
consente a iceulp tesmoingnages quát il aura
entendu cöment ilz sont dictz z recitez, et quil
croira quilz soient dictz et prononcez p les saintes
ames du dieu souuerain et vray Soit quil con
fesse aussi celle chose de bouche, soit quil ait hö
te ou paour par aucun vice de le confesser ou soit
encores que par obstinacön tirssemblable a for

senerie) Il sefforce de deffendre tres hoteusement
ce quil scet et croit estre vray. Ce doncques
que sainte eglise croit et tient en vraye cöfession
et profession de vray cestassy que Ihucrist est a
venir pour iugier les vifz et les mortz, nó disons
ce estre le derrenier iour du iugement duin, cest
a dire le derrenier temps. Car Il nest mie certain
par quantz iours Icelu iugement duren, mais
tout hôme qui lit selon le coustume des escriptures
saintes combien q negligemment on scet que iour
est souuent mis pour temps, Et iour ce quát
nous disons le iour du iugement de dieu nous
adioustons le iugement derrenier (Car Il iuge
desmaintenät et iugera des le cömencement de
lumain lignage en mettant hors de paradis ter
restre, et en separant du fruit de vie ses pmiers
hommes qui firent le grant pechie. Mais q
plus est Il iugea quant Il nesppargna mie aux
anges qui pecherent, et desquelz se pnce diceulp
anges subuertist hors les hômes de soy mesmce
sans le iugement hautst et Iuste dicelui. Lame
des hommes et des diables nest mie z malheurse

of toads to establish its infernal uses; the eyes of Leviathan have shrunk to one *oeil-de-boeuf* window; Cerberus, the three-headed dog of Hades, crouches in a lean-to shed tacked on to the wall; and the Styx, across which Charon is steering his coracle, flows into the mouth and out the other side.

Patinir's gazebo is the ancestor of the fairground Tunnel of Love, into whose mouth one rides in a little boat, floating down an artificial stream. It is also connected with the decorative Mouths of Hell which were used as fireplaces in Palazzo Thiene, as windows and doors on the façade of Palazzo Zuccari in Rome (p. 198), and as outdoor pavilions in such gardens as Bomarzo (p. 199). These follies were meant to terrify no one. Local legends have attached themselves to the *bocca d'inferno* at Bomarzo; according to one, the mask will announce the time of one's death if one approaches it at midnight on a certain March evening. But we may surmise that no such disturbing fancies were intended by the duke who had it built. It is the measure of the decay of the symbol that the mouth through which souls were once propelled at the point of a pitchfork into the stinking fumes and everlasting torments of Hell had now become the stone portal leading into a cool rock-hewn chamber, with benches and a table on which the duke, Pierfrancesco Orsini, drank his Orvieto wine on a hot afternoon, comfortably watching shadows move across the urns and carvings in his enchanted garden. Some images lose their power with use. Hell-Gate was one of them.

The Nine Circles of Hell

Let us assume, in any case, that the soul has got to Hell. He emerges blinking from the darkness of Leviathan's mouth, picks himself out of the pond of hot pitch into which he fell from the Bridge of Judgment. What landscape does he see?

A difficult question: there is no single landscape of Hell. Its topography varies from a simple chasm full of fire to the immensely detailed and complex map of the Pit which Dante developed in the *Inferno*. Dante's scheme of Hell may be briefly summarised, since a number of *Inferni* painted by fourteenth- and fifteenth-century artists derive from it.

Hell extends to the centre of the earth. It is like the conical hollow of a boil in flesh. The pit is arranged in nine circles, exactly balancing the spheres of the heavens, and arranged in a similar order: that is, the lesser sins find their punishment on the top, exterior rings of Hell, and turpitude increases the lower one goes, just as in Heaven the sublimest essences are reserved for the Empyrean and coarse matter for earth. The mediaeval universe was, in fact, infernocentric. Upper Hell is formed of five circles. The first circle is Limbo, containing the souls of unbaptised people and virtuous pagans. The second circle is reserved for the lustful; the third for gluttons. In the

The damned are consigned to Hell and the waiting devils in a French illustrated MS of *De Civitate Dei* from the Bibliothèque Ste Geneviève, Paris.

fourth, misers and spendthrifts are punished, while the fifth circle is full of souls damned for the sin of anger, grappling and shrieking at one another in the marshes of the Styx. Within this circle are the walls of the City of Dis, which contains the whole of Lower Hell. In Lower Hell, sins of the will against God are punished (the sins of lust, gluttony, avarice and rage are treated by Dante as weaknesses, not as deliberate rebellions).

Circle six, then, lies just inside the adamantine walls of Dis and contains the burning tombs of heretics. From it, a cliff drops to another river, the Phlegethon, which flows outside Circle seven, in which the 'violent against nature and self' are punished: suicides and, running forever on a ring of burning sand, homosexuals. From the edge of this circle, an even deeper cliff plunges down to Circle eight, which is divided into ten concentric *bolge* or trenches: a funnel of stone, *pietra di color ferrigno*, containing the fraudulent: souls damned for perverting language, law, social custom and love. Finally Dante arrives at Circle nine, the frozen lake of Cocytus, the bottom of Hell, in which the souls of

The tortures of the damned. **above** Luca Signorelli (c. 1441–1523): fresco in Orvieto Cathedral. Punishment by garrotte, blows and rending of flesh. **opposite** Mathias Grünewald, *The Damnation of Lovers*, Strasbourg, Cathedral Museum. Possibly the most loathsome image produced by a 15th-century artist, Grünewald's vision of the punishment of lust involves emaciation, running sores, penetration of the rotting flesh by serpents, and a clammy toad attached to the woman's genitals.

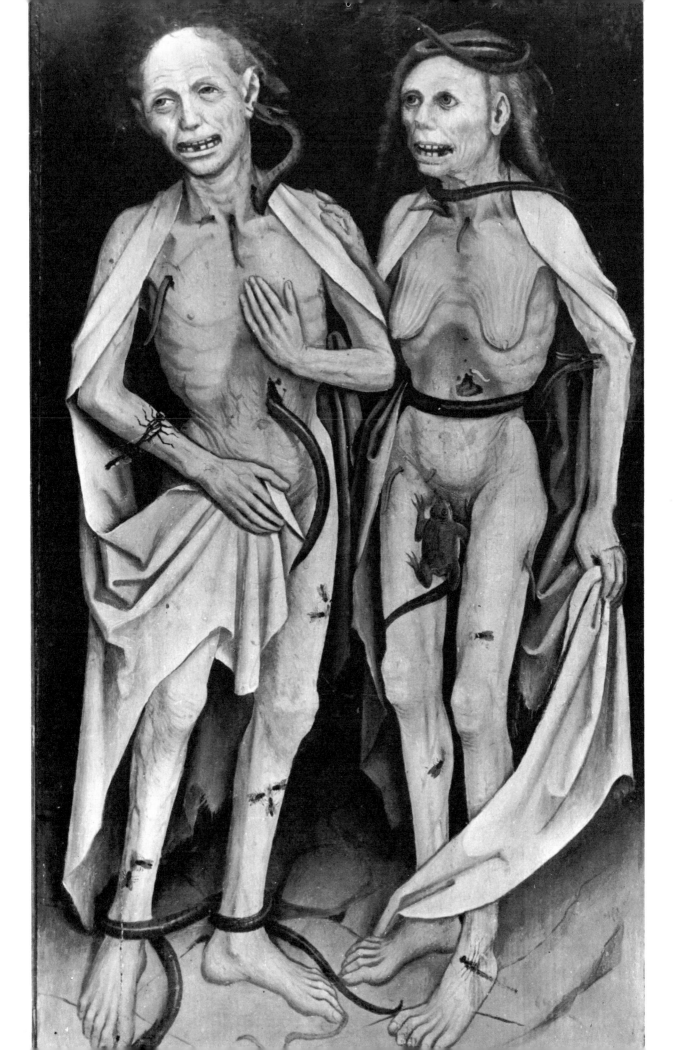

traitors stand up to their necks in ice, presided over by Satan himself.

Much of Dante's material for the geography of Hell was taken from earlier authors – from the Visions, from Islamic and eastern sources, and especially from Virgil. The culminations and sub-divisions of his Inferno made up a structure so grandiose in its complexity that no single painting could contain them, though several artist, including Botticelli and Blake, made series of illustrations for the *Divine Comedy*. However, one feature of Dante's Hell was to be of great importance for the depiction of Hell in general. This was his separation of the pit into circles or cells, each of which contained a group of sinners undergoing torment for a different sin. There is no suggestion anywhere in the Bible that Hell is portioned out in this way, and popular eschatologists from the sixteenth century onwards tended to view Hell as a compressed *pâté* of souls, all being equally roasted, as in the frightful sermon which a Jesuit preaches to Stephen Dedalus in *Portrait of the Artist* :

Hell is a strait and dark and foul-smelling prison, an abode of demons and lost souls, filled with fire and smoke. The straitness of this prison-house is expressly designed by God to punish those who refused to be bound by His laws. In earthly prisons the poor captive has at least some liberty of movement . . . Not so in Hell. There, by reason of the great numbers of the damned, the prisoners are heaped together in their awful prison, the walls of which are said to be four thousand miles thick : and the damned are so utterly bound and helpless that, as a blessed saint, Saint Anselm, writes in his book on similitudes, they are not even able to remove from the eye a worm that gnaws it.

All very indiscriminate: the authors of early Christian visions were more subtle in making the punishment fit the crime. The earliest of them, the *Apocalypse of Peter* (late first century), tells of blasphemers hung up by their tongues, murderers eaten by snakes while their victims – who, one hopes, are immune to Hell-fire – look on, slanderers and perjurers biting off their own lips and tongues, and

women, hung by their hair over that mire that bubbled up ; and these were they that had adorned themselves for adultery : and the men that had coupled with them in the defilement of adultery were hanging by their feet, and had their heads in the mire : and all were saying, 'We believed not that we should have come into this place'.

Some of the tortures assigned to Hell by visionary writers were – however relative a term this may be – quite straight-forward: suspension, strappado, flaying, crushing, rolling spiked rocks up and down a red-hot iron hill, immersion to the genitals in molten lead (a favourite for adulterers, on whom the Christian Fathers were quite maniacally strict) or burning sulphur or ordi-nary hot mud, breaking on wheels, strangulation, impalement, disembowelling, invasion of the orifices by toad, worm, newt or

Demons and their victims. Flying devils toss souls about in mid-air. Detail from *The Damned*, fresco by Luca Signorelli, Orvieto.

opposite Sinners locked in the mouth of Hell by an angel. Psalter of St Swithun's Priory, c. 1150, British Museum. **overleaf** Fra Angelico, *The Last Judgment*. Museo di S. Marco, Florence.

Ey commence se diziesme liure de ouide
dont la premiere fable est de Orpheus
a de Erudice

¶Inde per immensum :c.
Essus auez oy comment pphis de
uint ung beau iouuencel. Et co-

ment il espousa yeute samye. Le dieu hymen fut assis auec plusieurs autres dieux
a deesses. Et quant hymen se partit:par-
lait sen Vola grat erre en Lyconie/ou sc
mos estoit de par orphe' q deuoit espou-
ser erudice.a ses nopces Vint sas bon eur

Fiends stir the pots in Hell's kitchen with pitchforks. German woodcut, 15th century.

opposite An illuminated page from a 14th-century Ovid '*Moralisé*'. Here Orpheus and Eurydice are standing at the door of Hell with a demon in the pose of Hermes Psychopompos, the conductor of the souls of the dead.

blackbird; and of course plain roasting, the staple method of infernal cuisine, and to Joyce's Jesuit profoundly effective:

. . . each lost soul will be a hell into itself, the boundless fire raging in its very vitals. O, how terrible is the lot of these wretched beings! The blood seethes and boils in the veins, the brains are boiling in the skull, the heart in the breast glowing and bursting, the bowels a red-hot mass of burning pulp, the tender eyes flaming like molten balls.

Other tortures achieved a high pitch of ingenuity. The *Vision of Thespesius* – a curious document which, though composed after the birth of Christ, was written by a pagan and thus refers to a non-Christian Hell – was recorded by Plutarch and read by later topographers of the *Inferno* and has many parallels with the Christian visions. Among other things, Thespesius sees three lakes, one of molten gold, another of lead, the third of iron. In them, the avaricious are punished:

For the flame of the golden furnace having rendered these souls of a fiery and transparent colour, they plunged them into that of lead, where, after they were congealed and hardened into a substance like hail, they

209

Duree que les deux cites
dont liue est de dieu et
lautre du dyable sont par
uenues a leurs fins dues
par nir sauueur jhucrist.
nous auons a disputer
diligement en ce liure
tant come nous pourrons
par layde de dieu de quele condicion soit le tourmet que
nir au dyable ꞇ a tous ceulx qui lui appartiennent.
Et ay mieulx ame a tenir ceste ordre ace que apres
Je truitte de la beneurte des saintz pour ce que le dit
tourment ꞇ beneurte pardurable sont auquiect les
corps ꞇ semble estre non croiable chose que les corps

puissent pourir en tourment que iceulx demourer sans
aucune douleur en beneurte pardurable. et par ce est
le auray demonstre que icelle paine ne soit mie a non
croire. er maindra monlt a demonstrer que on doye
plus legierement croire ꞃ limmortalite des corps soit
auenir auv saintz aucune tristesse. Ne ceste ordre de
proceder ne sa point contre les diuines escriptures
esquelez aucunesfois la beneurte des bons est mise
deuant. Si comme est ce ou jl est contenu ꞃ ceulx ꞃ
bien feront jront en la resurrecion de vie. ꞇ ceulx qui
mal feront en la resurrecion du jugement. mais y
est aucunesfois ordre contraintt ou contraire si com
me ou jl est ꞃ. Le filz de femme enuoiera ses an
ges ace quils cueillent ꞇ amassent tous les esclandes

Pieter Bruegel: *Dulle Griet*, Antwerp Museum. Detail of figure on roof, back turned to audience, excreting coins into street.

were again thrown into the lake of iron, where they became black and deformed, and being broken and crumbled by the roughness of the iron, changed their form ; and being thus transformed, they were thrown again into the lake of gold, in all these transmutations enduring the most dreadful and horrid torments. Those who suffered most were those for whose transgressions their children or posterity suffered. These were constantly rebuked and reviled by the souls of their offspring . . .

A great many of the tortures ascribed to Hell have no symbolic value at all, and as one authority remarked, 'When we come to the accounts of the twelfth and thirteenth centuries, when visions were at the height of their glory, we find the utmost nonchalance observed in the pairing off of punishments and crimes.' Instead, there is the feeling that Hell was a convenient repository into which artists and writers could pour all their sado-masochistic fantasies; a safety-valve for the Id of European culture. There is very little in today's pornography of sadism which, for sheer ingenuity and nastiness, even begins to approach the eschatological frenzies of the Church. Nevertheless, some images of torture do have a distinct symbolic content. One of these is a punishment often visited upon usurers, misers and the avaricious: they are forced to eat excrement, either their own or (as in Taddeo di Bartolo's *Hell* in San Gimignano, p. 33) a devil's. Now there is an essential and primitive connection between faeces and money. A baby's fascination with his own excrement is, as child psychologists never tire of pointing out, possessive: the child wants to keep the first substance he is conscious of producing. Presumably this kind of childhood experience lay behind Bacon's celebrated apothegm, 'Money be like muck, no good unless it be spread'. The Netherlands and Italy abounded in similarly pithy proverbs, all to the effect that money and dirt are the same; these found pictorial form in the work of Bruegel and Bosch. But when placed, as at San Gimignano, in the specific context of Hell, the use of excrement as torture becomes a brilliant parody of the use of gold as symbol of divine light in Heaven, and one of the more striking examples of the system of inverted correspondances which existed in Christian imagery between Heaven and Hell. (Alchemy regarded gold and excrement as things intimately connected, 'since the *nigredo* and the ultimate attainment of the *aurum philosophicum* form the beginning and the end of the process of transmutation'[6].)

The main counterpart to the light of Heaven is, however, the gloom of Hell – the 'exterior darkness, where there shall be weeping and gnashing of teeth'. The literature of Hell, from Virgil through the visions to Dante and Milton, repeats the theme of black fire, visible darkness, *lux atra*. Had artists taken this in too literal a way, there would of course have been nothing in Hell to paint. In mediaeval Dante illustrations, darkness and fumes are sacrificed for the sake of clarity, and this was also the custom throughout the Renaissance; in the Hells of

opposite Miniature from a 15th-century MS of St Augustine's *De Civitate Dei* : Hell. Bibliothèque Ste Geneviève, Paris. Note the souls, at lower right, boiling in a hot lake and lacerated by dragons; and the punishment of lovers, bound together face to face on a spit over coals fanned by demons.

Giotto, Taddeo di Bartolo, Traini, Nardo di Cione and – as far as one can judge from the surviving fragments – Orcagna, Hell's obscurity is schematically indicated by dark background spaces, iron-grey and earth-brown rocks, rings of dead unreflecting water and sudden bursts of fiery red; but the whole scene is bathed in an even light which gives equal weight to each of the crevices and cauldrons wherein souls are tormented. The first painter to make light a protagonist in Hell was Hieronymus Bosch. The vista of Hell in *The Garden of Earthly Delights* is the supreme work of animist landscape in western art (p. 63); everything in it, and especially the sky, is charged with malevolent fury. Green rags of light flap and shudder between the rolling smoke-clouds, and the black buildings on the skyline spit jets of sparks like Bessemer converters; behind them, a chain of mountains stretches away in a lunar desolation whose only parallel is the cold green peaks Leonardo painted in the background of the *Madonna of the Rocks*. But not even Traini's fearsome Judgments and Hells resemble Bosch's encyclopaedic vision of a perverted cosmos. No scheme of Hell based on Dante, with his exactly-placed rings and pits, could accommodate the sprawling profusion of Bosch's imagination. It demanded a new syntax, a discontinuous symbolic language. Curiously enough, this language seems to have come, in part, from classical antiquity: the myths, marvels and freaks of the east.

Tortures for each sin, from Taddeo di Bartolo's fresco of *Hell* at San Gimignano. **opposite** Lust: an adultress is lashed by a horned demon, while a sodomite is impaled on a stake from anus to mouth; one end of the stake is held in the mouth of another homosexual, while a devil turns the other end over the fire. **left** Gluttony: devils force the souls – including a corpulent tonsured monk – to consume inedible meats.

VPARBIA   TETSI   LVLV

AVARO

VSVRIO

LVXVRITIA

chapter 5

The Shapes of Satan

Prodigies from Distant Lands

Off known maps, in distant countries below the rim of the horizon, there is an anti-world where Nature spews forth monsters, marvels and hybrids in a state of delirious topsy-turveydom. Belief in the monstrous Antipodes was practically universal among Europeans of the Middle Ages, cultivated and illiterate alike. But it was not limited to that period. The fascination of oriental grotesques reached back to the fourth century BC, and forward to at least the sixteenth century. It produced a set of images whose ramifications, immense as they were, provide a context for the monsters with which artists like Bosch and Bruegel saw fit to populate their visions of Hell.

Othello wooed Desdemona by telling her about his wars and adventures, and he mentioned the prodigies he had seen in distant lands as proof of his wide travels –

The Cannibals that each other eat,
The Anthropophagi, and men whose heads
Do grow beneath their shoulders.

Desdemona believed every word. Why not? The marvels of the east were an inexhaustible source of entertainment for Europe and by the fourteenth century had been thoroughly moralised, with each freak made to signify some passion, virtue or allegory of the human soul. They were part of the accustomed language of symbolic forms. How did this happen?

The vision of a *monde à rebours* was transmitted to Christian art by the Greeks, who located it in the then incredibly distant regions of India and Ethiopia. Now as we have seen, classical culture had many religious monsters of its own, some demoniac and others harmlessly grotesque – satyr, sphinx, lamia, gorgon, harpy. But, as Wittkower observed:[7]

The Greeks rationalised [their instinctive] fears in another, non-religious form, by the invention of monstrous races and animals which they believed to live . . . in India.

The most famous classical account of these monsters was given in AD 77, by a man who never went there: Pliny the Elder. For him, the Asian freak-pen was proof of Nature's sportiveness:

See how nature is disposed for the nones to devise full wittily in this and such like pastimes to play with mankinde, thereby not only to make herself merry, but to set us a wondring at such strange miracles. And

Avarice: Taddeo di Bartolo, detail from *Hell* at San Gimignano. A miser, for his tightness, is strangled with a rope; the usurer lies in the flames whilst a demon excretes gold coins into his mouth.

215

I assure you, thus dayly and hourely in a manner playeth she her part, that to recount every one of her sports by themselves, no man is able with all his wit and memory . . .[8]

Some parts of Pliny's account are, just conceivably, verifiable today. Others we recognise at once. His 'Philosophers, whom they call Gymnosophists, who from the Sun rising to the setting thereof are able to endure all the day long, looking full against the Sunne . . . and from morning till night can abide to stand sometimes upon one leg, and sometimes upon the other in the sand, as scalding hot as it is', are quite obviously Indian *yogi*. His 'men with heads like dogs, clad all over with the skins of wild beasts, who in lieu of speech use to bark' could have been dog-faced baboons. But what are we to make of

a kind of people called the Monocoli, that have but one leg apeece, but they are most nimble, and hop wondrous swiftly. The same men are called Sciopodes, for that in the hottest season of the Summer, they ly along their back, and defend themselves with their feet against the Suns heat . . .

or the Choromandae,

. . . a savage and wild people; distinct voice and speech have they none, but instead thereof, they keep a horrible gnashing and hideous noise; rough they are and hairy all over their bodies, eyes they have red like the owlet's, and toothed they be like dogs . . .

or others 'without heads standing upon their necks, who carry eies in their shoulders'? What of the race who lived near the source of the Ganges and were, it seems, the first hippies? Pliny called them

the Astomes, for that they have no mouths; all hairy over the entire body, yet clothed with soft cotton and down that come from the leaves of trees; they live only by the aire, and smelling to sweet odours, which they draw in at their nosthrils: No meat nor drinke they take, only pleasant savours from divers and sundry roots, flowers and wild fruits growing in the woods they entertaine: and those they use to carry about with them when they take any farre journey, because they would not misse their smelling.

Pliny took all this material from much earlier reports by two Greek writers, Ctesias and Megasthenes. Ctesias of Cnidos was a doctor at the Persian court of Artaxerxes in the late fifth century BC. Megasthenes was sent to Patna, as ambassador of Seleucus I to the court of King Chandragupta, in 303 BC.

It was Ctesias who first reported the parasol-footed Sciopodes, the dog-headed men, the satyrs which haunted the central Indian plateau, the pigmies, the originals of Othello's headless wonders (a race of monsters who carried their faces on their chests and their eyes in their shoulders, duly copied by Pliny and read by Shakespeare), and a weird tribe of men and women with only eight fingers and eight toes, white hair which turned to black in old age instead of vice versa, and floppy elephantine ears. There was also the *martikhora*, a dangerous brute mentioned by

Lorenzo Maitani: *The Damned in Hell*, Orvieto Cathedral, façade. The lost souls are wreathed in serpents and brutally torn by demons.

216

Orcagna: fragment of *Hell* fresco;
Museo Sta Croce, Florence.

Detail of lintel, showing a pigmy
mounting a horse.

Romanesque tympanum, La
Madeleine, Vézelay. The theme is
the universality of Christ's teaching;
and fabulous creatures, believed to
live in India, are included among the
races to which his word will reach.

Aristotle and transferred, like the classical satyr, to India: head of man, body of lion, and venomous tail of scorpion: habitat, rocks and deserts: diet, raw travellers.

Megasthenes, in his account of Indian marvels, swelled the population of this troublesome zoo with bat-winged snakes, savage men whose feet grew backwards on their ankles, the flower-sniffing Astomes in their cottonwool pelts, the Hyperboreans – whose life-span was a thousand years – and a race of cyclopses with dogs' ears and one eye in the middle of their foreheads. Ants dug up gold, and unicorns – which must, originally, have been rhinoceroses – guarded it. Never before had a landscape been so drenched in fantasy.

Pliny has been rebuked for his uncritical acceptance of this enchanting farrago of old wives' tales, local Indian legends, transferred Greek myths and mistaken natural observation. But one must remember that he issued a warning before he wrote it: 'I will not pawne my credit for many things that herein I shall deliver, nor bind them to believe all I write as touching strange

opposite Detail from Vézelay showing the huge-eared denizens of India, and **right** detail of the Cynocephali.

and foreign nations.' And Pliny's credulity is nothing compared to that of the many commentators who succeeded him and copied his account of the marvels into their books until by the ninth century it had turned into a self-ramifying myth. The legend of Antipodean monstrosity was strong enough to survive every trade contact that Europeans had with India for more than a thousand years. It became a fixed *schema*. Just as the first Australian colonial artists saw the scrubby flat foreshores and odd plants of Sydney Harbour in the 1790s through the eyes of Claude, so visitors to India and those who heard their accounts could not imagine the place except in terms of Pliny, Megasthenes and Ctesias.

India was the Id of Europe. Its monsters existed *absolutely*, in the sense that no mediaeval thinker supposed that they were biological variants on existing species. God had created them directly, just as he created the mumbling hunchback in the village square. They were the products of a specific, though patently inscrutable, divine intention. St Augustine thought that by

'. . . a kind of people called the Monocoli, that have but one leg apeece, but they are most nimble, and hop wondrous swiftly . . . They ly along theur back, and defend themselves with their feet against the Suns heat.' – Pliny. Carving on main entrance of Sens Cathedral, France, 13th century.

opposite Monsters as decorative grotesques: Luca Signorelli, *grotteschi* in Orvieto Cathedral.

making whole races of freaks God had intended to show his faithful that individual deformities were not the result of a failure of skill on his part; that everything in the world, from hydrocephalism to club feet, conformed to some aspect of the divine plan.

Christian belief in this integrity of marvels lies behind one of the greatest works of Romanesque sculpture: the tympanum of the main doorway of the Abbey Church at Vézelay (p. 219). It is encrusted with monsters, whose presence has led several writers – including André Breton and Arnold Hauser – to see it as a work of wildly irrational fantasy. Émile Mâle was the first modern scholar to identify it as a map of the world[9], and although the significance of a number of the images has not yet been worked out, there is enough evidence in the carvings to suggest that this is the correct interpretation. The theme of the tympanum is the Church's power of universal teaching, conferred on the apostles by Christ – 'Go, therefore, and teach all nations, baptising them the in name of the Father, and of the Son, and of the Holy Ghost'. And the artist made the point about *all* nations as vivid as possible by showing that the Church could save even the monsters of India. The family of three naked creatures, mother, father and child, with their vast ears (p. 220) is nothing other than the Indian tribe mentioned in Ctesias. The diminutive man scrambling up a ladder to get astride his horse is one of the '*Pygmaei Spythamei*' – 'called they are so, for that they are but a cubit or three shaftments high, that is to say, three times nine inches' – whom Pliny took from Ctesias. Here, too, are the fierce dog-headed men of India, the Cynocephali (p. 221). On the Cathedral of Sens, other familiar marvels were carved, with the same purpose of symbolising the universality of Catholic teaching – one of the Sciopodes, for instance, sheltering himself from the sun with his single big foot (left).

It does not necessarily follow that all the mediaeval artists who produced versions of these classically fixed Indian types had read Pliny or Megasthenes – though probably the clerics who worked out the symbolic programmes for the cathedrals had done so. Illuminated codexes from the ninth century onwards are rich in Antipodean monsters, all of which follow the Plinian scheme; by the eleventh and twelfth centuries this existing visual tradition had been assimilated by Church art. There is no fundamental difference between the monsters depicted in a miniature to a ninth-century edition of Solinus (a commentator on Pliny), and those at Vézelay and Sens. That the types survived unmodified for several more centuries is shown by an illustration in a fourteenth-century *Livre des Merveilles*, where a naked warrior, armed with a shield, nervously challenges a

222

Escendat qs do
mine deus ni
sps tuus scs sup hoc
altare qui q populi
tui dona scificet q su
mentium corda pu

dedicat non tii sup
uacui est sequentem
birdictionem fien.
S7 et pleniq;. Cum
tena siit ad ecclia se
pta nec omes ecce

Sciopod and a headless man in a rocky landscape. In the same book appear the Astomes, who do not crop up in Church art – minute, vulnerable figures, sniffing at their flowers and fruits with the air of strangers who have blundered back into Eden by the rear gate.

Monster as *divertissement* : miniature from the Pontifical of Bourges, French, 14th century. Bibliothèque Ste Geneviève, Paris.

The Freak as Symbol

It is most unlikely that anyone in the fourteenth century could have been frightened by these timid ancestors of the Noble Savage. Few of the freaks and marvels from India found their way directly into the populace of Hell. Some of them were 'moralised' and became images of specific types of sin; with this symbolism tacked onto them they could be used as part of the infernal landscape, and we will consider this process shortly.

By far the more important aspect of the demonisation of freaks, however, was their assimilation into the general nimbus of associations which surrounded the idea of a monster.

For monsters are mixtures: a jumble of parts, fragments, alien anatomies brought together. Their significance was usually negative, as far as antiquity and the Renaissance were concerned. They could be as it were defused, by incorporating them into a decorative scheme: the grotesques of Raphael or Signorelli, sprouting with curlicues, vegetables growing into torsos, satyrs, grotesque heads and animal hybrids, are cases in point (p. 223). But the hybrids of the *grotteschi* were not used symbolically. Neither, as a rule, were the sphinxes, griffins, sirens, twin-tailed lamias, satyrs, harpies, salamanders and mermen which infest the lintels, consoles and decorative panels produced at this time.

But when a monster was perceived as a symbol, it took on a different character. You could interpret it seriously, as something menacing, thrown up by fate or the Pit: a portent. Every time a hermaphrodite calf was born in Nuremberg, or a pin-headed baby in Fiesole, it could be taken to indicate some dreadful or prodigious event that was about to occur: the end of the world, the arrival of Antichrist or the Messiah, the fall of the Holy Roman Empire, or the loss of a horse race. Traditionally, the conjunction of opposites which monsters represented was brought about by an unfortunate combination of zodiacal patterns; the same astrological causes swayed the form of animals and the patterns of the body politic, and so the ancients (and their heirs, the humanists) took monsters very seriously indeed. The literature of the fifteenth and sixteenth centuries abounds in manuals on portents and how to interpret them. When a Siamese pig with two bodies, eight legs and one head was born in the German village of Landser in 1490, the Emperor Maximilian is said to have attached some political importance to its arrival at a crucial point in one of his diplomatic transactions. Albrecht Dürer recorded the pig, with fascinated and meticulous disgust, in an engraving (left). For, as one of the portent-manuals said, God created freaks

Monster as portent: Albrecht Dürer, *The Monstrous Pig of Landser,* engraving. Author's collection.

with a particular significance, since the beginning of the world, in the form of peculiar creatures, monsters, phenomena in the sky, on the earth and in the sea, as an admonition and a horror for mankind.

Mediaeval objectivity about monsters did not perish altogether; the Schedel's *Nuremberg Chronicle*, published in 1493, illustrates (p. 226) twenty-one of the fabulous creatures of India, ranging from our old friends the Sciopodes and satyrs to some races not mentioned in Pliny, including one of a species 'who have such a large lower lip that they cover all their face with this lip when they sleep'.

Schedel made no effort to provoke horror with these freaks; his attitude was one of detached biological curiosity, flavoured with myth and showmanship. But by the turn of the century this was rare; and it would be true to say of the Renaissance that its attitude to freaks and portents was grossly superstitious compared to that of the relatively enlightened Middle Ages. The freak was feared because it was a manifestation of evil, a drop thrown up by the cauldron of irrationality that bubbled underneath civilisation.

Bosch, Bruegel and their imitators inherited this attitude to monsters. But it might not have affected their paintings as it did, had it not been tempered by a view of freaks which intervened between St Augustine's tolerance of them and the Renaissance's fear. This view arose from the late mediaeval passion for 'moralising' the world and its contents. As we have seen earlier, the mediaevals tended to experience the world as a symbol in itself and each of its elements as an image of some type of virtue, sin or belief. Naturally, they extended this allegorising habit to the marvels of India. The Cynocephali, or dog-headed men, became symbols of quarrelsomeness. The pigmies, being tiny, personified humility. So could the headless men with faces in their chests, because the head was taken to be the seat of pride. Now if one is confronted by a set of monsters which demand to be given some allegorical moral meaning, and which at the same time belong to a class of freakish beings popularly regarded as menacing, enigmatic, portentous and even demoniac, one will naturally tend to transform them into images of sin. This, it seems, is exactly what the great northern eschatological painters of the late fifteenth and sixteenth centuries did. In Bosch and Bruegel the demonisation of the freak is accomplished and Hell is endowed with its own animal kingdom, a loathsome parallel to the innocent beasts which graze on the lawns of Paradise.

Now it must be admitted that the significance of the freak-zoo which Bosch and Bruegel elaborated was lost on some of their contemporaries, especially in Italy. Vasari seems to have mistaken the freaks for witty ornamental grotesques. Writing of Jerome Cock, the sixteenth-century engraver, he mentions 'a painter who got him to engrave the seven mortal sins with various demons, a fantastic and laughable thing ... with many other fancies which it would be tiresome to recount'. The painter was Pieter Bruegel, and when today we look at one of the prints Vasari spoke of (opposite), it would seem perverse to find it 'laughable'; though one can very well sympathise with Vasari for finding its details tiresome to list. A Spanish priest, Fray Joseph da Siguença, was more accurate about such imagery when he wrote, on Bosch, in 1605:

... And I should like to point out that these pictures are by no means farces, but books of great wisdom and art, and if foolish actions are shown in them, they are our follies, not his, and, let us admit it, they are a painted satire on the sins and fickleness of men.

Siguença continues with a remark which Surrealist inter-

above Monsters as personified sins: Jerome Cock, after Pieter Bruegel: *The Sin of Avarice*, engraving.

opposite 'Detached biological curiosity, flavoured with myth and showmanship.' 21 marvels of India, from Schedel's *Nuremberg Chronicle*, 1493. Compare the third figure from the top of the left column with the demon on p. 228. The motif of the face in the chest (or belly, or buttocks) was readily transferred from Eastern freaks to the Devil.

preters of Bosch, determined to read his paintings as unrestrained effusions of the subconscious, might seize on as text and verse:

In my opinion, the difference between the paintings of this man and those of others is that the others try as often as possible to paint man as he looks from the outside, while this man has the courage to paint him as he is inwardly . . .

But it is clear that Sigüença, when he says inward man, is thinking of the state of his soul, not of his Id: he means that Bosch painted sin, personified, at work on the soul of men. 'But when did man' (except, by implication, in Bosch's paintings) 'show such a fullness of sins?' Today, Bosch and Bruegel are praised as great psychological painters on the evidence of their visions of Hell and its monsters. Yet it may not detract from their real stature as artists to suggest that neither of them, in their eschatological works, was much concerned with what we understand to be the problem of psychology: the motions of the individual mind as shown by the study of behaviour. The gallery of monsters and freaks was a means of locating vice *outside* the psyche: of showing that sin had an objective existence, not to be discussed in terms of individual weakness. Men are

227

Jan Mandyn: *Aeneas and the Cumaean Sibyl in the Underworld*, The Hague. An example of the wholesale stealing of motifs from Bosch's altarpieces by his followers: the skull with a pola in its eyesocket, from which hangs a key, is taken from the Hell panel of *The Garden of Earthly Delights* (see pp. 62–3).

Studio of Hans Memling: *Hell*, detail of a polyptych. Musée des Beaux-Arts, Strasbourg. Satan, with goat's horns and hairy satyr's legs, capering in the mouth of Leviathan.

reduced to soft forked worms, floundering in slime or spitted on the strings of a harp; but sin, in its thousand demoniac forms, is what dominates Hell. Sin is more real than the sinner. And the insane grotesqueness of the monsters suggests with ineluctable power the deformations which sin itself works on the human soul. Sin does not cause damnation; sin is damnation; and the wan souls in Hell are surrounded by these obscene proofs of their existence, capering a saraband in the foreground.

The individual meaning of each freak in the Hells of Bosch and Bruegel is (and will remain for some time) open to endless speculation. Are they simply *fantasie*, dreams of painters, without allegorical meaning? Most scholars reject this view, pointing to the fact that many such demoniac motifs were illustrations of popular Flemish and Dutch proverbs, that others derive from traditional symbols for sins – a monstrous hare, for example, which recurs in Bosch's paintings, is a well-known mediaeval symbol of lust, and occurs as such in the bestiaries – and that others are readily decipherable in terms of their own allegorical clues. But nonetheless, a discord rules over Bosch scholars which is barely less than the *nacht und nebel* of Hell itself. For Tolnay, an image of a key, through whose grip a naked body is hanging, 'betrays the desire for marriage, which is forbidden to the clergy' (p. 63); for Fraenger it signifies the punishment of wicked priests who lock up knowledge from their congregations.

Vom vrsprung vnd herkunfft des Antichriſt.

ORTVS ET ORIGO PAPAE

Hie wird geborn der Widerchriſt
Megera ſein Seugamme iſt:
Alecto ſein Kindermeidlin
Tiſiphone die gengelt jn.
M. Luth. D.

154.

below Anti-Lutheran woodcut: the Devil plays on Luther's head as on a bagpipe, c. 1535.

Popular anti-Papist woodcuts and caricatures. **above left** The Pope as Antichrist, 'inspired' by the breath of devils; at right, more demons reduce monks in a crushing-vat. **above** A she-devil, amid gusty farts, gives birth to a litter of Popes and clergy, while witches tend and suckle other popelets.

Pope Alexander vi, woodcut with
trick fold: **above** first position,
right second position – the Devil
unmasked.

231

One scholar thinks that the great face on the white eggshell which rears above the swamps of Bosch's Hell is 'a lecherous idiot's head' (p. 63); another concludes that it is Bosch's self-portrait. Bosch's bagpipe (p. 63) is identified in Tolnay's text as an 'emblem of the male sex', and in his notes as a womb-symbol. Though it can hardly be both, it may be neither; the cornemuse, or bagpipe, with its sack and drones, was – literally – a windbag; a popular German woodcut, made for propaganda against Protestantism *c.* 1535, shows a devil playing Luther's head as a bagpipe (p. 230), to produce his vain and wicked rhetoric. The satanic overtones of bagpipes are attested to by the instrument's German name, *bock*, or he-goat[10]. Conceivably then, Bosch meant his bagpipe as a symbol of perverted discourse. But one cannot be sure; and there is hardly one symbol or event in Bosch's demonomachies which does not present the modern viewer with equally distressing uncertainties. The miracle is that despite the immense gap of background and belief across which we now look at the Hells of Bosch, Bruegel and their Schools, the monsters do communicate their basic meaning with such vitality; grappling, howling, rending one another, they are 'all Hell let loose', the grotesques to which nothern Europe transferred its primitive fears of Chaos and anti-world which, in classical times, it had loaded on to the marvels of the east.

The Evolution of the Devil

But the devil remained the Lord of Hell, the quintessence of aggression. Compared to the freaks, which were either personified sins or minor demons, his form was relatively stable. But how did it evolve and what were its sources?

In a famous passage, Isaiah prophesied the ruin of Babylon, at the cataclysmic moment when 'the earth will be shaken out of its place, at the wrath of the Lord of hosts on the day of his fierce anger':

And Babylon, the glory of kingdoms,
  the splendour and pride of the Chaldeans,
will be like Sodom and Gomorrah
  when God overthrew them.
It will never be inhabited
  or dwelt in for all generations;
no Arab will pitch his tent there,
  no shepherds will make their flocks lie down there,
But wild beasts will lie down there,
  and its houses will be full of howling creatures;
  there ostriches will dwell,
  and there satyrs will dance.
Hyenas will cry in its towers,
  and jackals in the pleasant palaces . . .
                    [Isaiah XIII, *19–22]*

232

below Bronze figure of Pan.
opposite Riccio: Satyr and Satyress.

233

This is one of the few biblical references to a creature long associated with the Christian devil and largely responsible for his shape: the classical satyr. He appears again in the prophecy:

For the Lord has a day of vengeance,
a year of recompense for the cause of Zion.
And the streams of Edom shall be turned to pitch,
and her soil into brimstone;
her land shall become burning pitch.
Night and day it shall not be quenched;
its smoke shall go up for ever.
From generation to generation it shall lie waste,
none shall pass through it for ever and ever.
But the hawk and the porcupine shall possess it,
the owl and the raven shall dwell in it,
He shall stretch the line of confusion over it,
and the plummet of chaos over its nobles.
They shall name it No Kingdom There,
and all its princes shall be nothing.
Thorns shall grow over its strongholds,
nettles and thistles in its fortresses.
It shall be the haunt of jackals,
an abode for ostriches.
And wild beasts shall meet with hyenas,
the satyr shall cry to his fellow;
yea, there shall the night hag alight,
and find for herself a resting place.   *[Isaiah* xxxiv, *8–14]*

Who would not find in these verses a description of Hell, the prototype of Dante's *città dolente?* Whether or not Isaiah meant the ruins of Babylon and Edom to be taken as metaphors of Hell, successive interpreters of the Bible, including many artists, had no hesitation about using these texts as the raw material of their Infernos. Just as beautiful Lucifer fell from Heaven and, disfigured by rebellion, became the Lord of Hell, so the fabulous cities of Chaldea become the inverted realms of chaos through their sin of pride: infernal cities balancing the celestial city. That is why so many elements of Isaiah's account are familiar from descriptions of Hell itself – the burning pitch-streams and sulphur soil of Edom, the everlasting fire and smoke, the thorns and strangling weeds, the loneliness, the 'howling creatures' and the bestiary (composed of animals unclean in God's sight. See *Leviticus* xi, *passim :* these include animals that 'swarm upon the earth' – lizards, rodents, chameleons, geckos – and numerous birds, including hawks, vultures and all raptors, ostriches, owls, wading birds, 'every raven according to its kind', the bat, and, rather obscurely, the hoopoe), jackal, hawk, porcupine, hyena, owl and raven, the melancholy-voiced ostrich, the spirit of the night-hag, Lilith, revisiting the bones of the city which formerly sustained her cult; and the satyr. All these

opposite Luca Signorelli: *The Damned*, Orvieto Cathedral.

ከመ፡ኒ፡ተምቃሕኩ፡ወመ   ሥአሙ፡ለእሰ፡በθ ጋም፡   ናክ፡ር ኁ፡በክ፡ወኢ፡ያብ
ጸአ፡ሙ፡ ነቢየ፡ወ እ፡ነበ   ኋጉን፡እንዝ፡ይ ብሎ፡   ላ ዕ ና፡ አ ቅ አ ው ፡ ጸ ሙ ዳ

Pan playing the double flute. Attic red-figure vase-painting.

creatures, except for the ostrich, found their way into the fauna of Hell in Christian art, though often changed and rendered grotesque to the point of unrecognisability. For the satyr, however, was reserved the most important role of all. He was transformed into the devil himself. (How different the moral history of Europe might have been if Satan had come to be represented as an ostrich!)

Satyrs are among the more familiar creatures in the landscape of classical mythology but comparatively little is known about them. The satyr is a hybrid (p. 232), half man, half goat. In this he resembles other mythological creatures like sileni and centaurs. His goatish nature shows itself not only in his looks – horns, cloven hoofs, frisky stub of a tail, goat's legs with thick shaggy hair on the flanks – but also in his personality and behaviour. To Hesiod, satyrs were 'good-for-nothing and mischievous'. They are forest-dwellers, sharing their sylvan haunts with nymphs, dryads, hamadryads and centaurs. Satyrs are shy, inarticulate creatures, and their wild timidity, as of deer, was exquisitely captured by Riccio (p. 233). Unlike the sileni, who were always depicted in antiquity as either drunken greybeards or wise old horse-men whose potato faces bore a marked resemblance to Socrates', satyrs are always young, randy and practically illiterate. Apollo wrought a particularly horrible vengeance on one of them, Marsyas, who learnt to play the flute, challenged the god to a musical contest and lost. Marsyas was strung up and skinned alive. This draconic punishment had an interesting point, as myth. It represented the absolute mercilessness of Apollo, the incarnation of reason, sunlight and clarity, towards any foray into his own domain by the irrational and the visceral. It is not necessary to imagine a modern equivalent (Mozart, perhaps, flaying Mick Jagger?) to perceive the force of this myth or its relevance to a later Christian culture which wanted to personify those forces of darkness, chaos and formlessness which were summed up in the demons of Hell.

Nevertheless, satyrs were not demons; their tendency to get drunk, trample down grape-trellises, consort with Maenads, steal fruit and sneak up on the unsuspecting mistresses of Augustan poets may have been inconvenient but it was not satanic: the demonisation come later, and the reasons are curious. They have to do with the most important association of satyrs: their relation to Pan, the Horned God, and Dionysus.

Pan's habitat, and the original centre of his cult, was the rural district of Arcadia in Greece. He was a fertility god, the son of Hermes and an unknown mother. Pan's special task, initially, was to protect and increase the fecundity of cattle. (It has been pointed out that Arcadia was not a good district for raising cows, so that most of its flocks were goats; Pan's goatishness is partly traceable to this, and partly to the existing traditions of horned

Bronze head of Pan. British Museum.

gods in the Near East whose characteristics he inherited.) It was appropriate, if Pan was to make the animals multiply, that he should be a phallic god. This he became. The main association of Pan, in antiquity as today, was a prodigious appetite for sex.

Like the satyrs, Pan was a woodland creature, who preferred to gambol and trill his syrinx in caves, secluded valleys and dense forests. He also shared their shape, or more properly speaking, they his: the goat-feet, hairy flanks and horns, as well as the ever-erect and sharply pointed penis, are customary equipment for Pan in all his manifestations (p. 237). So is the faun-face, with its pointy ears, large snuffly nostrils, wide mouth and slanting eyes (left). One of Pan's skills was instilling 'panic' into people whom he disliked – precisely as the English word suggests, a wild unreasoning fear, a group hysteria, which caused those who felt it to revert to the most primitive animal instincts and run for their lives, leaving (in an apposite cliché) the devil to take the hindmost.

Pan's irrationality and phallicism connect him to the major ecstatic cult in ancient times: that of Dionysus, a god of vegetation and fertility. His worship began in Thrace and Phrygia and was to spread over Greece. To women, Dionysus had a special attraction: bands of them, the Maenads, were reputed to roam the countryside in an exaltation of hysteria, dancing uncontrollably and waving wreaths of leaves. It was the Maenads who in a counterpoint to Apollo's gory punishment of Marsyas put the supreme musician Orpheus to death:

Looking from the crest of a hill, these maddened creatures, with animal skins slung across their breasts, saw Orpheus. One of them . . . flung her spear at the poet Apollo loved, at the lips which had produced such melodies. Her weapon, tipped with leaves, left its mark, but did not wound him. Another picked up a stone, and hurled it at Orpheus; but even as it flew through the air it was charmed by the blending harmonies of voice and lyre, and fell at his feet, as if to ask pardon for so daring an assault. None the less, the women's rash attack increased in violence, till all restraint was lost, and maniac fury had them under its sway. All their weapons would have been rendered harmless by the charm of Orpheus' songs, but clamorous shouting, Phrygian flutes with curving horns, tambourines, the beating of breasts, and Bacchic howlings, drowned the music of the lyre . . .

It was like the scene in an amphitheatre when, for a morning's entertainment in the arena, a doomed stag is hunted down by dogs . . . To provide real weapons for their mad intent, it happened that there were oxen ploughing in the fields, and not far off sturdy farmers were digging the hard ground, toiling and sweating to secure their harvest. When the farmers saw the horde of women, they fled, leaving their implements behind, so that hoes and heavy rakes and long mattocks lay scattered about the deserted fields. Savagely the women seized hold of these, tore apart the oxen which threatened them with their horns, and rushed once more to the destruction of the poet. He stretched out his hand towards

238

Illumination from a Coptic manuscript of demons leading sinners to purgatory. Lady Meux Collection, British Museum.

his assailants, but now, for the first time, his words had no effect, and he failed to move them in any way by his voice. Dead to all reverence, they tore him apart, and, through those lips to which rocks had listened, which wild beasts had understood, his last breath slipped away and vanished in the wind. [Ovid, *Metamorphoses* XI]

The Dionysiac cult had a curious affinity with Christianity: the Thracians held that their god could enter the body of an animal – ox, sheep, goat – or, on occasions, a human being; the rite was then to dismember the creature alive and, as a sacrament, to eat the god, thus absorbing his power. *Hoc est enim corpus meum.* Dionysus was a horned god; his familiars were the bull, the stag, the goat; and it was as a symbol of the preternatural strength got by magical association with the animal kingdom that the Maenads wore their animal skins. The god had also a

239

strong connection with the Underworld, thanks to his aspect as a giver of fertility, which by extension meant that he could also give men life after death. Some of his cults appear to have worshipped Dionysus as Lord of the Dead.

Now as Margaret Murray has shown,[11] the worship of totemic gods akin to Dionysus was not confined to the Mediterranean basin. Fertility cults, involving a horned god, phallic rituals and ecstatic dances, had spread all over Europe in palaeolithic times and survived the birth of Christianity. Dionysus was one of these gods. It is likely that Strabo, writing in the first century AD, had one of them in mind when he wrote that 'in an island close to Britain, Demeter and Persephone' (the goddesses most closely connected, in Greek mythology, with fertility and death, and hence with Dionysus himself) 'are venerated with rites similar to the orgies of Samothrace'. Three hundred years later, a Greek geographer reported that 'in islands near Jersey and Guernsey, the rites of Bacchus' (Dionysus as god of wine) 'were performed by the women, crowned with leaves; they danced

Sassetta: *Temptation of St Anthony*, Siena, Pinacoteca.

240

Miniature from illuminated codex of
Life of St Anthony, c. 1435.
Laurentian Library, Florence.

and made an even greater noise than the Thracians'. And in the seventh century we find the famous prohibition in the *Book of Penitences*, by Theodore, Archbishop of Canterbury: an entire chapter of these ecclesiastical laws is spent describing and anathemising the practices of the ancient fertility worshipers:

> . . . *not only celebrating feasts in the abominable places of the heathen, and offering food there, but also consuming it. Serving this hidden idolatry, having relinquished Christ. If anyone, at the kalends of January, goes about as a stag or a bull – that is, making himself into a wild animal and dressing in the skin of a herd animal, and putting on the heads of beasts; those who in such wise transform themselves into the appearance of a wild animal, penance for three years because this is devilish.*

This, compared to the flayings alive and burnings at the stake with which clerics of the 'enlightened' Renaissance punished devil-worshippers, is a remarkably mild sentence.[12] Nevertheless, the *Book of Penitences* is only one of many documents showing the survival of Pan and the problems it raised for the Church.

241

Christianity was a palimpsest. It took over fragments and myths from numerous other religions – Mithraism, Judaism, the cult of the Great Mother, and so forth. If it struck an obdurately-rooted local cult in the course of its expansion throughout Europe, Christianity would often absorb it like an amoeba, digest it, and thus legitimise the pagan myth. The hagiology of the Catholic Church contains many saints for whose existence there is not a shred of historical evidence, because they were pagan cult-figures adapted for the use of new converts who could not break easily from their old religious practices. Gods of wind, of local springs, of leaves and harvests, gods who presided over market-places in Bithynia and burial-grounds on the Maremma, Venus cults in Turkey and Apollo cults in Illyria – all, after the missionaries arrived, bequeathed the name of a saint to the Church and a few ounces of sacred chicken-bones or dog-ribs to the reliquaries of the local basilica.

The Church could absorb these scattered cults because they were not powerful enough to menace it. Not so with Pan, Dionysus and their northern relatives. Especially in northern Europe the old fertility religions were the most serious alternative to the worship of Christ. Christianity therefore could not incorporate them as benevolent features of its mythological landscape. They had to be given a totally negative aspect. Once the Christians had transformed the old cults into objects of fear and loathing, they would have rid themselves of a large part of the opposition. And so the Church did to Pan what Stalin did to Trotsky – and for precisely the same reasons. It turned him into the epitome of absolute evil, the Lord of Misrule: the devil. The attributes of Pan were given, in art, to the Christian Satan.

And yet to put it in this way, without qualification, makes an immensely complicated process unreally simple. There was no single, fixed form for the devil; instead, there was a variety of iconographical types. Confronted with the task of inventing a shape for the Lord of Chaos, artists were apt to fill it with every nauseating detail they could think of; and these details varied, through psychological necessity, from one artist to another. By the end of the thirteenth century the commonest type of devil is the one that can still be seen, much defaced by pious finger-nails and pocket knives, in Sassetta's little panel of the Temptation of St Anthony (p. 240): a man-like creature with a hairy body, horns and claws, but equipped with black wings and quadrilobe clawed feet. He appears again – this as an almost literal transcription of a satyr – in an illuminated codex of the *Life of St Anthony*, datable *c.* 1435 (p. 241); the demon has the classical goat's horns, cloven feet (which seem to be evolving into claws) and a curved stubby tail, and the sensual grin of Pan has widened into a gummy and repulsive leer. But all sorts of other undesirable creatures contributed at one time or another to the image of the devil. Fish, bat, snake, scorpion, dog, cat,

Detail from *The Triumph of Death*, by Francesco Traini. Camposanto, Pisa. Note composite form of devils, who are dragging souls from the mouths of the dying: eagle's head, membraneous bat wings, hairy flanks, human torso, snake tail, four-clawed feet.

griffin, hydra, toad and harpy rendered up bits of their anatomy, which were fused in a monstrous and wavering Identikit portrait whose constitution depended as much on the painter's imagination as on any programme of representation that he had inherited. However, some types do remain traceable, and it may be interesting to look at them.

The earliest known figure of the devil in Christian art is a third-century fresco in the Catacomb of Saints Peter and Marcellus in Rome. But here the devil appears in his original form as the serpent coiled around the Tree of Knowledge in Eden. In early Christian paintings the devil never seems to take on a terrifying aspect even when he is represented as a man or an angel. Probably the first picture of Satan in human form is a rather feebly-drawn figure in the sixth-century Egyptian frescoes at Bawit. One might expect to find this sort of head in any provincial representation of Apollo at the time; if anything,

'A monstrous and wavering Identikit portrait' – the composite forms of the Devil. **upper right** *The Temptation of St Anthony*, by Martin Schongauer. The saint carried aloft by demons. **right** *The Temptation of Christ*, by the Master L. CZ. Engraving. **opposite** *The Temptation of St Anthony*, by Lucas Cranach. Engraving.

Rex abiſſi

The fifth angel of the Apocalypse blows his trumpet. 'In appearance the locusts were like horses arrayed for battle; on their heads were what looked like crowns of gold; their faces were like human faces; their hair like women's hair, and their teeth like lions' teeth; they had scales like iron breatplates . . . They have tails like scorpions, and stings, and the power of hurting men for five months lies in their tails. They have as king over them the angel of the bottomless pit; his name is Abaddon . . .' – *Relevations* IX, 7–10. Miniature from *Liber Floridus*, c. 1448, French: Musée Condé, Chantilly.
below Andrea Parentino: *The Temptation of St Anthony*, Galleria Doria, Rome.

this demon is angelic, idealised and attractive. There is no trace of the hideous deformity one finds in later pictures of the devil, and certainly the Bawit fresco has nothing to do with Pan. For here is Satan in his role of Antichrist.

The symbolism of Antichrist is enormous, but his nature and activities can be briefly described. In the Last Days, before the reappearance of Christ 'in his clouds of power and glory' which will herald the Last Judgment, a super-human tyrant will appear on earth and set his reign up against the reign of God. (This fantasy emerged from earlier Persian and Babylonian myths – the destruction of the arch-demon Ahriman at the End of Days in an appalling cosmic battle with his adversary, the omniscient and perfect Lord of Creation; or even, outside this Zoroastrian myth, the dualistic Babylonian idea that the outcome of the universe would be decided by a final battle, the most terrible of all, in which the forces of good and evil would confront each other.) He is the 'false Messiah', Antichrist. Working hand-in-glove with Satan (with whom, by the tenth century, he was

often identified) he will produce all kinds of fake miracles and prophecies. His beauty and apparent kindness will be irresistible, except to a few chosen faithful. But Antichrist's conjuring-tricks and Apollonian camping will at last be undone:

> *. . . the lawless one will be revealed, and the Lord Jesus will slay him with the breath of his mouth and destroy him by his appearing and his coming. The coming of the lawless one by the activity of Satan will be with all power and with pretended signs and wonders, and with all wicked deception for those who are to perish, because they refused to love the truth and so be saved. Therefore God sends upon them a strong delusion, to make them believe what is false, so that all may be condemned who did not believe the truth but had pleasure in unrighteousness.*
>
> *[2 Thessalonians* II, *8–12]*

Most pictures of the devil up to the end of the tenth century depict him as the noble Lucifer, crowned or flying, altogether kingly. He is the Antichrist seen by St Ephraim in the fourth century, 'like a God, flying on the air, surrounded by demons who appear as angels of light'. He is the Miltonic creature who appears in the *Quadriregio*, by Federigo Frezzi, bishop of Foligno (d. 1416):

> *I thought to see a monster, foul, uncouth;*
> *I thought to see a realm all waste and sad,*
> *And him I saw, triumphant, glorious.*
> *Stately his manner was, and fair, and so benign*
> *His aspect, and with majesty so filled*
> *That of all reverence he seemed most worthy.*
> *And three fair crowns he wore upon his head:*
> *Joyous his countenance, and blithe his brow,*
> *And in his hand the sceptre of great power.*
> *And though his height might well exceed three miles*
> *His features and his form such balance showed,*
> *Such harmony, I wondered much thereat . . .*

Such effusions as this from the early *quattrocento*, coupled with earlier visions of Antichrist, might seem to indicate that it was beautiful Lucifer who dominated devil-imagery through those centuries. But of course this was not so. The appearance of Satan changed abrupty somewhere around AD 1000. He became a repulsive imp in art, and his switch of form was faithfully recorded in the visions of countless hallucinated monks and virgins. Raoul Glaber, a monk of the monastery of St Leger, reported in the early eleventh century that

> *I saw, at the end of my cot, a little monster in human shape. He had – as far as I could see – a pockmarked neck, a thin face, very black eyes and a wrinkled, low forehead. His nose was flat; his mouth, enormous, with swollen lips. He had a short, sharp chin, a goat's beard, erect and pointed ears, tangled hair standing up on end, the teeth of a dog, and a pointed head. He was pigeonbreasted and humpbacked, his clothes were filthy, and he hopped about, he skipped insanely around.*

above Ghiselbertus: *The Last Judgment*. Typanum of central door, St Lazare, Autun. **left** Demon on Romanesque capital at Vézelay.

Demons from capitals at Vézelay.

This could serve as a faithful description of the demons carved on the capitals and tympanums of French Romanesque cathedrals, at Vézelay, Autun or Souillac (p. 249). Romanesque devils ran to type. They had enormous heads supported on spindly, ape-like bodies. Their eyes bulged with rage and had bags under them. Instead of horns they had masses of hair rising in fiery whorls and clumps, as if the malice and heat compressed in their wiry frames were sending emanations out through their scalps. Their orifices – mouth, nostrils, ears, anus – were extravagantly large. This in itself was a symbol of malevolence and aggression; the big mouth like the fairy-tale wolf's, 'all the better to eat you with'; the nostrils for scenting the victim; the anus for adding a gift of diabolic farts to the already insupportable stench of Hell (a habit noted by Dante in *Inferno* XXI, 139; each member of the preposterous cohort of demons in the Fifth Bolgia blows a raspberry at his leader who, in response, 'made a bugle of his bum' *[ed elli avea del cul fatto trombetta]*); a whole body designed, like a waste disposal unit, to chew up its victim and eject him again. An obsession with holes and lips is usual in demonic art and especially prominent in Goya (opposite); and, Rabelaisian though it may have become, Jacques Callot managed to retain a great deal of its nastiness in his *Temptation of St Anthony* (p. 255). Devils corrupt their environment any way they can and their wind bloweth where it listeth.

Why Antichrist changed to imp so quickly and universally is uncertain but it may be no coincidence that he did so after the Council of Cluny in 956. The Council was an early version of the Council of Trent, designed to tighten Church discipline and lay down methods of binding the faithful more rigorously to their beliefs. Is it possible that, thanks to Cluniac influence on ecclesiastical thought, a need for an image of fear which would polarise the love of virtue was felt more acutely, and satisfied by the devil in his superbly horrible new guise?

In any case, once the devil was given an ugly form, his fusion with the Horned God was an easy matter. The nimbus of flaming Romanesque hair vanished from his head and was replaced by horns. His wide mouth and distended nostrils amalgamated with the sensual features of Pan. The 'Wild Hunts' on which he rode at the head of a mob of worshippers, furiously galloping over the Brocken on boarback (p. 258), were survivals of the legend of the Maenads in their carnivorous ecstasies. His relation to the classical satyr is made quite clear by a miniature in a fifteenth-century Antonine codex in the Laurenziana, which shows a devil offering St Anthony a palm in the course of one of that saint's many temptations; the creature is in no way distinguishable from a satyr and is described in the text as *capris formam habens*, 'having the shape of a goat'. An interesting sidelight on this is afforded by one of the woodcuts in the *Nuremberg Chronicle*, made in the late fifteenth century; the

'An obsession with holes and lips.' Goya: *Soplones*, from *Los Caprichos*, 1799.

satyr, which is Pliny's Indian-dwelling variety, is one of a tribe that 'have horns on their foreheads, and goat-like feet, like the creatures St Anthony Abbot saw'.

Moreover, the devil as satyr was enriched from another source – the Wild Man of mediaeval mythology.[13]

Unlike the satyr, the Wild Man actually was a man, not a goat with human torso. But he had been debased almost to the level of the beasts by living in woods. This is an important point, for if the Wild Man were a fallen human and not a risen satyr (still less a risen ape, an idea which would not have occurred to mediaeval chroniclers), his state paralleled the fall from grace of Adam – out of the garden, into the wilderness – and, more significantly, the rebel angels' fall from Heaven.

But the Wild Man was not a social rebel who had known more comfortable things and turned his back on them. He belonged to a distinct species which had always lived in woods and forests. As such, he had much in common with other shy inmates of the boskage – fauns, satyrs, sileni. He was *homo silvestris* (from which comes the modern surname Sylvester). This caused some earlier writers to confuse him with the faun; for instance, an eighteenth-century authority on classical prototypes in art, Bernard de Montfaucon, treated *sylvestres*, *satyres* and *faunes* as virtually interchangeable.

He exists, of course, only in art and myth. The type was fully described by Bernheimer:

It is a hairy man curiously compounded of human and animal traits, without, however, sinking to the level of an ape. In exhibits upon its naked human anatomy a growth of fur, leaving only its face, feet, and hands, at times its knees and elbows, or the breasts of the female of the species. Frequently the creature is shown wielding a heavy club or mace, or the trunk of a tree; and, since its body is usually naked except for a shaggy covering, it may hide its nudity under a strand of twisted foliage worn around the loins . . . The creature itself may appear without its fur, its club, or its loin ornament. Any one of its characteristics may be said to designate the species.[14]

Of the durability of this hirsute creature there is no doubt. He existed before biblical times, and mad King Nebuchadnezzar turned into one:

He was driven from among men, and his body was wet with the dew of heaven till his hair grew as long as eagles' feathers, and his nails were like birds' claws. [Daniel iv, 33]

The legend of the Hairy Anchorite derives from him, since it was assumed that you grew a thick mat of hair if you lived in the open. Such was the fate of St John Chrysostom.[15] The saint met, in his civiller days, a woman in the forest. He made love to her; and then, overcome with remorse, 'atoned' for his sin by picking her up and throwing her off a cliff. (Watch out for priests on picnics.) St John then took up permanent residence

Jacques Callot: *The Temptation of St Anthony*. British Museum.

in the woods, living on berries and water, and soon developed a profuse and home-grown hair shirt. Some years later, crawling about on his hands and knees, he met the girl again. Miraculously saved from injury when she fell, she had borne St John a son. This incident was frequently depicted by artists, notably by Albrecht Dürer. And in our own day, the Wild Man flourishes in mythological but popular figures like the Wild Man of Borneo and the Abominable Snowman, not to mention the mummers, who in remote districts of Bavaria and the Carpathians still deck themselves in leaves and hair and clubs to act out rituals of wood-spirit invocation whose history is almost as old as the Horned God himself, and which have been going on, undeterred by the most violent efforts of Christianity, since before the time of Pieter Bruegel (p. 260).

The personality of the Wild Man is, to a degree, strong, dim-witted and aggressive. He cannot speak; not even the most primitive monosyllables (me Tarzan, you Jane) escape his lips; he converses with his mate in grunts, and being solitary by nature does not seek the company of such other Wild Men as may lurk in the forest. His brain is so degenerate that he is in-

255

Michael Pacher: *St Wolfgang with the Devil*, 1483. The face on the Devil's buttocks has two origins: first, in the witch's practice of the anal 'devil's kiss'; second, in the legendary monsters of India. Note the stag's horns and hooves.

Devils enraged at the death of a virtuous man. Woodcut, from '*L'art de bien vivre et bien mourir*', 15th century. Paris, Bibliothèque Ste Geneviève.

capable of rational action; he is, in fact, an ogre. We are apt, fortunately, to be much more tolerant of madmen than our mediaeval ancestors were. The madman, until quite recently but especially in the Middle Ages, was an object either of fear or of derision: the slavering maniac rattling his chains, the giggle-witted court fool. It was a common practice in mediaeval Europe to expel the mentally afflicted – once their paranoia or schizophrenia had destroyed their powers to fit into village society – into the fields, where they ran wild, huddled in caves, and eventually (one supposes) died a miserable death. There can be little doubt that the image of the Fool contributed something to that of the Wild Man; and should one compare any representative picture of a Wild Man (p. 265) with Jacquemart de Hesdin's miniature of a Fool in a landscape with trees (p. 266), their relationship will be clear. The golf-club shaped stick which the Fool holds (appropriately, since he is lost in the rough), and the stone he is biting in mistake for bread, are standard mediaeval

attributes of lunacy; the club resembles the Wild Man's club, and though the Fool is not hairy the tatter and swirl of his rags suggest an excessive energy.

What the Wild Man lacks in brain he makes up for in brawn. His strength is superhuman. He can uproot trees, tear animals apart with his bare hands, and leap across mountains. A Wild Man in Spenser's *Faerie Queen*, Sir Satyrane, learns in childhood to attack

> *the Lyon and the rugged Beare,*
> *And from the she Beare's teats her whelps to teare.*

Hence the symbolic importance of the Wild Man's pelt. Abundant hair implies domination by baser forces, a slip down to the beasts. (On a Romanesque capital at Estibaliz in Spain, Adam is shown beardless before the Fall and hirsute after it.)[16] And until it was taken over by the hippies as a sign of mild loving-kindness, hair also connoted strength and aggression. (Except of course in women, where it is [or was] one of the chief symbols of feminity. Long hair was taken to accentuate the basic properties of *either* sex in the Middle Ages and the Renaissance.) Shakespeare's soldier is full of strange oaths and bearded like the pard; and, as everyone knows, Samson lost his strength to Delilah's shears. Aggressiveness and lust are the main passions beneath the Wild Man's woolly pate. Northern mythology and folk-tales are full of Wild Men who erupt, snorting, from the woods, devastate farms, murder

The Wild Hunt: a devil riding on a boar. Southern Tyrol, 11th–12th centuries.

258

their occupants, destroy whole villages and occasionally carry off maidens to some uncomfortable cave where, bruised and impregnated, they ensure the future supply of Wild Babies. (They may, if they enjoy this life, which some apparently did, become Wild Women themselves – very bad for the figure; Wild Women, according to folklore, had long sagging breasts which, when on the move, they slung over their shoulders. However, the rape of a damsel by a Wild Man was a popular motif on mediaeval love-caskets.) Another widespread legend of the Wild Man, that he led whole mobs of his followers on a demonic rampage, mounted on boars, stags, mountain goats and suchlike animals, through the forests and over the mountains, is a significant reappearance of the Wild Hunt of devil-worshippers and the Pan-drunk revels of the Maenads.

And so the Wild Man became an exceptionally compact and powerful symbol. He was misrule personified. He arose, as Bernheimer puts it, from

> ... *the need to give reckless expression and symbolically valid form to the impulses of reckless physical self-assertion which are hidden in all of us, but are normally kept under control.*

In other words: the Wild Man was *all* libido. And as such, he corresponded perfectly with that arch-symbol of the darkest and least controllable layers of man's mind, the devil. Some of the most appalling images of the devil ever made are the result of his fusion with the Wild Man, to produce a vision of Satan, *prince de notre monde, prince de l'enfer*. In 1545, Melchior Lorch made an engraving of the pope as Antichrist (p. 269), dedicated to Martin Luther. Did more venom ever drip from a political cartoon? The pope has the attributes of the Wild Man – hair all over his body, unkempt beard, and a club which has turned at the handle into a triple cross. His left hand grips the key of St Peter, the papal tiara is on his head, and from his mouth there bursts a black stream of toads, scorpions and other horrid organisms, vomited out across the world to do the Church's diabolic work of lies and false witness to Christ. His bat wings flap and his barbed tail sweeps between his legs to encircle a diabolic cardinal, who simultaneously vomits a bishop into the air and drops a turd on to an inscription which reads: 'Take yourselves off, God and men; the Devil and I are masters.'

But the greatest, and on art the most influential, adaptation of the Wild Man in demonic imagery was produced some two hundred and fifty years before Lorch's engraving. It is Dante's description of Satan locked in his lake of ice at the bottom of Hell, and one need, I think, make no apology for quoting it in full:

Lo 'mperador del doloroso regno
 del mezzo il petto uscia fuor della ghiaccia;
 e più con un gigante io mi convegno,

che giganti non fan con le sue braccia :
vedi oggimai quant'esser dee quel tutto
ch'a così fatta parte si confaccia.

S'el fu sì bello com'elli è or brutto,
e contra 'l suo fattore alzò le ciglia,
ben dee la lui procedere ogni lutto.

Oh quanto parve a me gran maraviglia
quand'io vidi tre faccie alla sua testa !
L'una dinanzi, e quella era vermiglia ;

l'altr'eran due, che s'aggugnièno a questa
sovresso 'l mezzo di ciascuna spalla,
e sè giugnèno al luogo della cresta :

e la destra parea tra bianca e gialla ;
la sinistra a vedere era tal, quali
vegnon di là onde 'l Nilo s'avvalla.

opposite Goya: *Saturn eating his Son*,
Prado, Madrid. An example of the
demoniac power which the Christian
imagination tended to associate with
hirsute and therefore other-world-
creatures. It is but a short remove to
the Wild Man and the Devil himself.

260

previous page The Master of the
Triumph of Death fresco in the
Camposanto, Pisa. opposite
Michelangelo: *The Last Judgment*,
Sistine Chapel, Rome.

Jean Bourdichon: Wild Man, Wild
Woman and baby outside their cave.
Miniature, 15th century; École des
Beaux-Arts, Paris (Compare with
p. 266).

Jacquemart de Hesdin: *The Fool*.
Bibliothèque Nationale, Paris.

Sotto ciascuna uscevan due grand'ali,
  quanto si convenià a tanto uccello :
  vele di mar non vid' io mai cotali.

Non avean penne, ma di pipistrello
  era lor modo ; e quelle svolazzava,
  sì che tre venti si movean da ello :

quindi Cocito tutto s'aggelava.
  Con sei occhi piangea, e per tre menti
  gocciava 'l pianto e sanguinosa bava.

Da ogni bocca dirompea co'denti
  un peccatore, a guisa di maciulla,
  sì che tre ne facea cosi dolenti.

A quel dinanzi il mordere era nulla
  verso 'l graffiar, che tal volta la schiena
  rimanea della pelle tutta brulla.

'Quell'anima là su c' ha maggior pena',
  disse 'l maestro, 'è Giuda Scariotto,
  che 'l capo ha dentro e fuor le gambe mena.

266

Hairiness as symbol of aggression: detail of demons, from *The Triumph of Death*, by Francesco Traini: Pisa, Camposanto.

Delle altri due c' hanno il capo di sotto,
  quel che pende dal nero ceffo è Bruto
  – vedi come si storce e non fa motto ;

e l'altro è Cassio che par sì membruto.
  Ma la notte risurge, e oramai
  è da partir, chè tutto avem veduto.'

Com'a lui piacque, il collo li avvinghiai ;
  ed el prese di tempo e luogo poste ;
  e quando l'ali fuoro aperte assai,

appigliò sè alle vellute coste :
  di vello in vello giù discese poscia
  tra 'l folto pelo e le gelate croste.

Inferno XXIV, 28–75: 'The Emperor of the woeful kingdom stood forth at mid-breast from the ice, and I compare better with a giant than giants with his arms ; see now what that whole must be in proportion to such a part. If he was as fair as he is now foul and lifted up his brows against his Maker, well may all sorrow come from him. Ah, how great a marvel it seemed to me when I saw three faces on his head ; one in front, and that was red, the two others joined to it just over the middle of each shoulder*

267

above and far right Two studies for Satan, from Sandro Botticelli's illustrations to Dante. Note the three heads, each with horns and a mouth chewing a sinner, and the heavy coat of Wild Man's hair.

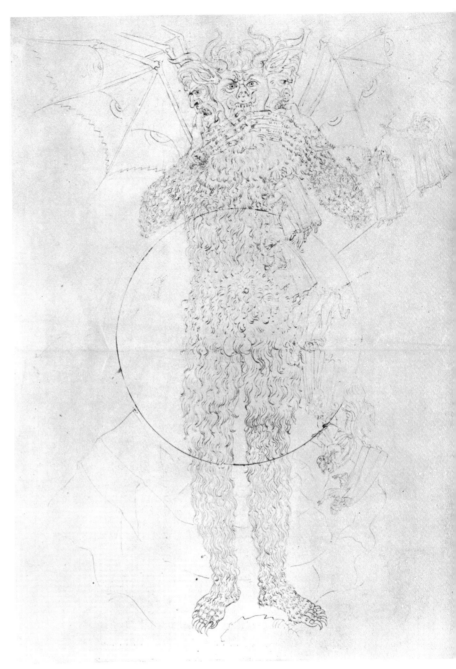

Melchior Lorch: *The Pope as Antichrist*. Engraving, 1545. The Pope is given the attributes of a Wild Man – thick matted body-hair, beard, and a tree-trunk club.

269

and all joined at the crown. The right seemed a colour between white and yellow; the left had such an aspect as the people from where the Nile descends. [That is, black.] Under each came forth two great wings of size fitting for such a bird, I never saw sails at sea like these; they had no feathers but were like a bat's, and he was flapping them so that three winds went forth from him, by which all Cocytus was kept frozen. With six eyes he was weeping and over three chins dripped tears and bloody foam. In each mouth he crushed a sinner with his teeth, as with a harrow, and thus he kept all three of them in pain; to the man in front the biting was nothing to the clawing, for sometimes the back was left stripped of skin.

'That soul up there which has the greatest punishment,' said the Master, 'is Judas Iscariot, who has his head inside and kicks his legs without. Of the other two who have their heads below, the one that hangs from the black muzzle is Brutus – see how he writhes and utters not a word – and the other Cassius, who looks so stalwart. But night is rising again and now it is time to go, for we have seen all.'

At his bidding I clasped him round the neck; and he watched his chance of time and place and, when the wings were spread open, caught hold of the shaggy ribs,[17] then descended from tuft to tuft between the matted hair and the frozen crusts. [trans: John D. Sinclair]

Satan's body, then, is covered with hair. It cannot be the thigh hair of the satyr, since it extends all over his skin, and Virgil and Dante are able to climb down on its matted, icy handholds. The probability is that Dante was acquainted with Wild Man legends and had adapted the smelly, goatish fleece of strength and incoherent energy to his culminating vision of the Lord of Misrule. It is certain however that artists who represented Satan enthroned or frozen at the centre of Hell frequently endowed him with a Wild Man's pelt. Thus, in a miniature by the Brussels Initials Master, under a Gothic structure at the bottom of a landscape in whose sky flying demons chase sinners and truss up a king with rope, and on whose earth horned, shaggy fiends are bringing carts and wheelbarrows full of the wicked (including a bad monk) to a fiery hole, Satan sits enthroned; he is covered in green hair from head to foot, and stuffs a sinner into his mouth (opposite). This need not be taken as a specific reference to Dante's Satan, though it belongs to the fourteenth century; but the Brussels Initials Master, whose identity is not known, was an Italian artist,[18] and his image of Hell is close in spirit and detail to the *Inferni* produced by Italian artists of the fourteenth century. We have seen these tortures in Traini, Nardo di Cione, Taddeo di Bartolo: the sodomite *en brochette*, cranked over the fire by a devil; the molten metal poured from a ladle on to the genitals; the courtesans in their tub, not of asses' milk, but of hot oil; the man dragged upside-down by a noose; the disembowelling and scratching, the penetration of the body by snakes. (This image is one which Freudians are apt to take as purely phallic. It may not be – birds, as one naturalist[19]

The Brussels Initials Master: *Satan Enthroned in Hell*. Book of Hours, use of Paris, British Museum, London.

omme ne m furo
ir tuo arguas me
neqs m ua tua cor
rupias me.

Mathias Grünewald: *The Temptation of St Anthony*, Colmar Museum, 1513–15.

pointed out, have no penis and yet exhibit the same horrified fascination with reptiles as we do. The snakes which burst forth from the wretched, putrescent flesh of the couple in Grünewald's *Damnation of Lovers* (p. 203) may signify a general corruption: at that time, worms and serpents were popularly thought to appear by spontaneous generation in rotting bodies and then poke their way out.)

The Satan who rises up in the eschatological frescoes of the Italian *trecento* has, for unmitigated horror, no equals in art except the demons of Bosch, and the ghastly metamorphic brutes which – in a landscape of broken beams, dead trees

272

Anonymous, c. 1270–1300: *The Inferno*. Mosaic on cupola of Baptistery of S. Giovanni, Florence.

dripping with moss and mountain crags like slimy icicles –
assail Mathias Grünewald's St Anthony (opposite). But he is a
different kind of demon and the difference reflects itself in the way
he is depicted. We have seen how for Bosch, evil and sin were
totally diffused throughout the world; and how he found an
image for this universe, pullulating with motes of evil, in the
spectacle of crowds of jabbering and freakish demons, with no
single dominant figure around whom they revolve. (The
white egg-man in *The Garden of Earthly Delights* Hell panel may
be taken as an exception to this. But its control over the picture is
formal, compositional. As an image, it is not of a different order
of intensity to others in the foreground. Moreover, it does not
represent Satan; as Fraenger has shown, it is a parodic inversion

273

Detail of Satan from Giotto's *Last Judgment*, Padua. Early 14th century.

of the Tree of Life.) The principle of evil is manifested in nature as a whole, perverting each of its forms impartially. The same is true of the monsters in Grünewald's *Temptation of St Anthony*. They do not suggest a hierarchy of evil. Italian Hells do imply precisely such a hierarchy. They make a clear distinction of rank between Satan and his minions, and this is shown by Satan's central position, huge size and different attributes. This corresponds exactly to the central position which Christ takes at the Last Judgment or in the 'All Saints' Pictures' (pp. 148–51), flanked by angels (for which read, in Hell, demons) and by saints (in Hell, the damned). Even the formal way in which the various pits, cauldrons (it is not impossible that these cauldrons may have been recognised – if not intended – as Hell's version of Paradisal fountains) and barbecues of Italian Hells are portioned off, stacked neatly one above the other, puts one in mind of the organised rows of heavenly choirs in the *Allerheiligenbilder*. Just as the disposition of the Italian masters' Celestial Paradises and Golden Cities was designed, among other things, to show the organised flow of grace and light from its source, God, down through all layers of existence, so the scheme of Hell provided Italians with the sight of evil, concentrated in its Satanic fount, radiating outwards through the hierarchy of Hell.

One of the obvious questions about Hell's iconography is whether Dante took his vision of Satan from earlier painters, or painters got it from Dante. The former is probably true – though this is not to say that artists who read the *Inferno* were not influenced by the description of Satan. As we shall see, they followed it minutely. What evidence have we for supposing that Dante took his Satan from art? It is on the ceiling of the Baptistery in Florence: the mosaic of the Last Judgment. In some ways this Satan is not like Dante's – he has no wings, and the two heads which issue on long reptilian necks from his ears belong to dragons, quite unlike the ugly human face in front. But each mouth chews a sinner – though they are not identifiable as Brutus, Cassius and Judas. It is unlikely that so odd an image was invented, full-blown, by the artist who designed the mosaic. We may guess that it was based upon the classical image of three-headed Cerberus, the hound at the gate of Hades, and assume that Dante too had seen representations of Cerberus, who is one of the main figures in his *Inferno*. He may have seen early thirteenth-century images of Satan with three faces. But he probably saw the Baptistery *Last Judgment* too. The mosaics were completed between 1270 and 1300. Dante did not leave Florence until 1302, when, on the 27th of January, he was sent into exile after a Guelf party purge, for alleged conspiracy. (There is a tradition [but no real evidence] that Dante had written the first seven cantos of the *Inferno* by then.) It is therefore possible that the description of Satan in the Thirty-Fourth Canto was inspired by this unforgettable mosaic

William Blake: Cerberus.
Watercolour illustration to Dante's
Divine Comedy, 1824–7.

with its triple-headed Fiend. It is interesting to note that Giotto, who completed the fresco cycle in the Arena Chapel somewhere around 1306, painted a Satan of precisely the same kind, with dragons issuing from his ears – though the Baptistery version is positively athletic compared to the bloated monster which emits its necrotic glow through the murk of Giotto's Hell (opposite). Traini's Hell in the Camposanto (p. 189) was however as influential on fourteenth-century painters as Giotto's or the master of the Baptistery mosaics. Its impact on Nardo di Cione's *Hell* in Santa Maria Novella, *c*. 1351–7 (p. 158) was considerable. Both these frescoes are of course directly modelled on the *Divine Comedy*; Nardo's was more faithful to it. So close did *trecento* artists stick to Dante that Taddeo di Bartolo actually labelled the sinners whose legs protrude, like strands of spaghetti sucked by a gluttonous *carabiniere*, from Satan's lips: *Bruto* (Brutus), *Giuda* (Judas), *Cassio* (Cassius).

Myth and Reality

The three-faced Satan completes our panorama of the anti-world. For here is the highest blasphemy against and inversion of the heavenly order. Satan's three faces are a parody of the Trinity.

275

A hydria showing Herakles
confronting Eurystheus with
Cerberus, the watchdog of Hades.
Louvre, Paris.

There is an ancient association between triune gods and the underworld, which may have affected the form of three-headed Satan. Two images of Hecate, Queen of Darkness: **right** from Cartari's *Imagini dei Dei*, 'signifying the three aspects of the moon, and lunar power over the elements'; **opposite** a 16th-century bronze.

The Hells of Traini, Orcagna, Nardo di Cione and Taddeo di Bartolo are, no less than those of Bosch and Bruegel, the sublimely eloquent results of the meeting of reality with a myth. With the Tuscans, the myth, or religious belief if you prefer, was the eschatological doctrine of the Church, imprinting its absolute certainty of the existence of Hell on the minds of their whole audience. The reality was the social climate of the middle decades of the fourteenth century. Between May and September of 1348, the epidemic of bubonic plague known as the Black Death struck Florence, Siena and other Tuscan cities. In that summer half the population of Florence, forty-five thousand people, died. In Siena, sixty-five per cent perished, leaving no more than fifteen thousand terrified citizens alive (these figures are conservative). In Florence, a plague epidemic of 1340 had already killed by the reckoning of its chronicler, Villani, fifteen thousand people; and now,

. . . the priest who confessed the sick and those who nursed them so generally caught the infection that the victims were abandoned and deprived of confession, sacrament, medicine, and nursing . . . and many lands and cities were made desolate. And this plague lasted till –.

Villani left the date blank, hoping to record it when the Black Death had gone. It was never filled in. Villani too died in the epidemic of 1348. Then two more epidemics, milder but still disastrous, followed in 1363 and 1375.

The social and economic consequences of the Black Death were incalculable. Crops and industries failed; Florentine banks collapsed; society (what remained of it) was ripped apart. The gulf between the Haves and the Have-Nots became, if anything, greater, for a wave of spending, frivolity and hedonism was triggered off among the rich by the fear of imminent death. (And a very understandable reaction too; you can't take it with you.) But to the vast majority of Tuscans, the significance of the Black Death was obvious. It was the rage of God: a God offended by the sins of fourteenth-century society, determined to avenge his insulted majesty by loosing on Italy the shocking reality of another of Traini's frescoes in Pisa: the Triumph of Death (p. 262–3). Millard Meiss has pointed out a subtle change this produced in the art of the late *trecento*:[20] Christ, enthroned on his mandorla in Heaven, no longer gazes straight ahead or, with a gesture of benediction, to the blessed on his right; he has turned on the wicked, dismissing them into eternal punishment with a terrible gesture of rejection. The motto of the Tuscan artists in these fearful decades might well have been Savonarola's: *Gladius domini super terram*. To paint Hell, you must know you walk on a thin crust.

Bruegel and Bosch knew they did. They had witnessed (or Bruegel certainly had; the facts of Bosch's life are so scanty that, like Jesus Christ between the ages of twelve and thirty, we can only make guesses at what he was doing on the basis of what, later, he declared) starvation, usury, the vandalism of *landesknecht* and prince; the corpse in the ditch, the public hanging and the burning roof cannot have been strange sights to them. Indeed, it is hard to think of any period in history (except our own) in which one could have looked about and seen more savage cruelties, more grotesque social inequities and a denser landscape of hysteria than in northern Europe between 1480 and 1550, with its warrior dukes and rebellious, ill-led mobs of peasants, its poverty, pogroms and religious wars, its screeching flagellants and deranged messiahs proclaiming the imminent arrival of Armageddon. It is not perhaps too facile a connection between history and art to say that Bosch and Bruegel, unlike nearly every other great painter in the west, painted what they saw. Here, the myth and the reality intersected again, but not as it did in Tuscany. For Bruegel and Bosch were not confronted with a grandiose act of God, like the Black Death. What

John Martin: illustration to *Paradise
Lost*, 1827. The adamantine vaults
of Hell.

they saw was the acts of men, which were enough to collapse
any faith in humanism and disrupt any order that you could not
make for yourself on a canvas.

With these painters the art of Hell reached a peak of intensity
and moral persuasiveness which, with one grand exception, it
was never to regain again. That exception is of course Michelangelo's *Last Judgment* (p. 264). But his is a Hell of a different
kind. No three-headed Satan presides over his hive of tiny
sinners; the sulphur-pits and tongs, the spits and forks, have
vanished. (It may be remarked in passing that Brutus, torn by
Satan's fangs in the traitors' pit of Hell, would have been a most
unlikely subject for Michelangelo, who sculpted Brutus as a
figure of the highest republican virtue, and remarked [or was
quoted as doing so, in the *Dialogues* of Gianotti], that 'he who
kills a tyrant does not commit homicide, killing a man, but
rather a beast. Brutus and Cassius did not sin, then, when they
killed Caesar.') Instead, Hell is a mass of writhing nudes, whom
Charon is flailing out of his coracle on to a dun-coloured, dark
shore, where they stumble in despair as if, by some lobotomy,

279

their minds were no longer able to sustain the vast energy of their muscles. In its discontinuity, its centrelessness, its jabbing and frustrated sublimity of movement, Michelangelo's *Last Judgment* is, as has so often been observed, one of the great monuments of pessimism in western art. The historical circumstances surrounding the time it was painted are too well known to require mention here, except that Michelangelo seems to have found, in the sack of Rome and the slow collapse of Humanist confidence, the tragic reality to match the horrid myth of Hell. *Io sto rinchiuso*, he once scribbled, and the lines come back unbidden when one looks at the Sistine Hell:

> *I am mewed up like the pith in its rind, poor and alone, like a spirit enclosed in a phial ; and my dark tomb affords little flight.*

This is the first modern Hell. It is tragically subjective. We can deduce nothing reliable about the personalities of Giotto or Bosch by scrutinising their Hells, except in the field of their aesthetic responses. After all the Bosches have been seen, all we can discuss – and then most tentatively – is his obsessions. Not why he had such obsessions or what he thought about when not painting or even what his religious beliefs were. But Michelangelo has left particles of his psyche behind on the Sistine wall, like a paste dragged by the brush.

Without Michelangelo's drawing, we cannot imagine Blake's Dante illustrations (p. 275). But I would prefer to leave the complexities of Blake's eschatological vision to another book. And we need not linger over the metamorphoses of Hell since Michelangelo. The only thing of any significance which happened to its iconography was that Lucifer, as beautiful devil, revived; an event of more significance in literature than in painting, again with the exception of Blake. Generally, the best that viewers of Hell could expect were series like John Martin's illustrations to Milton, done in 1827 (p. 279), with their gloomy adamantine vistas which, though undeniably charged with poetry, are somewhat reduced by the tiny, narcissistic nudes who, as Lucifer, pose unconvincingly within them like the standard-little-figure-of-a-traveller one always sees pointing at the Parthenon in eighteenth-century travel sketches. And with illustrators like Gustave Doré we are down to the penultimate rung of banality – an insipid and overworked melodrama with the stage-wires barely concealed. By the end of the nineteenth century, all Satan could do was whisk rabbits from hats and dance the mazurka at fancy-dress balls. Yet he was still capable of frightening children when some Victorian father unrolled the horrible future of spinal meningitis, death and damnation which awaited his masturbating son; and so he was not quite dead; only in art.

At the end of such a book as this, it is, I suspect, thought obligatory to write a disquisition on Satan and Hell in the twentieth century. There would seem enough ground to pick over. Sartre's *Huis Clos*: 'Hell is others'. *Saison en Enfer*. The Surrealists on Lautréamont. Artaud, *Fragments of a Journal in Hell*: 'I am human by my hands and my feet, my guts, my meat heart, my stomach whose knots fasten me to the rot of life.' The paralysing *angst* of the English community at Connollie-sur-Mer. Bad acid trips.

But Hell is not so easily reduced. Try, and it vanishes into a figure of speech. Our culture uses Hell as a metaphor based on another metaphor; it refers to painful states of consciousness, to despair or to alienation. But to pretend that these depressions and traumas have any real relation to the Hell envisaged by Christian artists between – let us say – the third and sixteenth centuries, is nonsensical. And it is that Hell with which I have been concerned here. To extend it to the twentieth century would be like producing *Don Giovanni* without the Statue, the Spirits and the trapdoor.

There is however one area of art in which Satan survives, though in a reversed and namby-pamby form. This is the comic strip. In Batman, Superman, Captain Marvel, Captain America and the rest of their muscle-bound, cloaked, masked and quick-changing tribe, we catch the last flicker of Satanic omnipotence and Luciferian, if prognathous, beauty. Batman, leaping his way through the Underworld in that scalloped black cloak, with his belt full of paralysing gases and bullet-proof shields (right), is said to have been inspired by a photograph of Luca Signorelli's *Damned Souls* (p. 204) which his late creator saw in a Los Angeles magazine. When Superman stops a charging locomotive with his chest or conjures up a tornado with his little finger he does so in memory of Antichrist the wonder-worker. Unlike Satan and Antichrist, the super-heroes end up in the last frame getting a warm handshake from J. Edgar Hoover for their defence of Democracy; but this is not the first time in art that a classical survival has found its meaning reversed in a new context, and Satan, if he is still listening, should be grateful for any crumbs of attention that still fall from the feast of reason, enlightenment and progress whose guests have dispensed, for the time being, with the need for eschatology. Perhaps in a century or so, when the sluggish mutated survivors have formed their primitive communities by the Thames and the Potomac, a myth of Hell will be reborn out of that passionate human instinct, to believe in something infinitely worse than what one has already.

Antichrist into super-hero: Batman.

Part 1

1   Rev. R. O'Kennedy.
2   Resolutions of the Ecumenical Council of Florence, in the Papal Bull *Cantate Domino*, 1441.
    See Encyclical of Innocent IV, 6 March 1254, Thirteenth Ecumenical
3   Council: *Circa Ritus Graecorum*.
4   *The Decline of Hell*.

Part 2

1   *Anabasis I*, II, 7. For two excellent and detailed studies of the Paradise myth, see A. Giamatti, *The Earthly Paradise and the Renaissance Epic*, and Howard Patch, *The Other World According to Descriptions in Mediaeval Literature*.
2   A. Giamatti, pp. 52–3.
3   It should be noted that some recent authorities discount the connection between hashish and eastern Paradises invariably made by eighteenth- and nineteenth-century authors. See Bernhard Lewis, 'The Assassins', *Encounter*, November 1967, p. 39.
4   R. A. Jairazbhoy, in *Oriental Influences on Western Art*, p. 246.
5   In *The Millennium of Hieronymus Bosch*, Faber & Faber, 1952. Fraenger's basic contention, that Bosch was a member of the Adamite sect, or Brethren of the Free Spirit, and that 'The Garden of Earthly Delights' was painted for the leader of that sect, is without documentary evidence of any kind and has been discredited by later historians; there is no point in belabouring it here. However, his study is immensely useful on many specific points of Bosch's imagery.
6   Charles de Tolnay, *Hieronymus Bosch* (trans. Michael Bullock and Henry Mins), Methuen, London, 1966, p. 204.
7   Edward Lucie-Smith, 'Hieronymus Bosch', *Art and Artists*, January 1967, p. 47.
8   Pomponius Mela, *De situ Orbis* 1, 9.
9   Bede, *Hexaem.* i.
10 Quoted in Patch, p. 144. On the source of the Nile, see Alan Moorehead, *The Blue Nile*, Hamish Hamilton, p. 1.
11 Most recently in A. Cislot, deriving from Jung.
12 Erwin Panofsky, 'Poussin and the Elegaic Tradition', published in *Meaning and the Visual Arts*, Doubleday, 1955.
13 *Ibid*.
14 Michael Levey, *Rococo to Revolution*, Thames & Hudson, 1966, p. 70.
15 For a popular and brilliantly argued account of the Australopithecine origins of *homo sapiens*, see Robert Ardrey, *African Genesis*, Collins, 1961.
16 Aristotle, *De Coelo*, IV., 3.
17 Stephen Toulmin, 'The Mediaeval World-Allegory' in *The Discovery of Time*, Hutchinson, 1965.
18 Suger and his writings are the subject of a famous essay by Erwin Panofsky, first published by Princeton University Press in 1946 and reprinted as 'Abbot Suger of St Denis', in *Meaning and the Visual Arts* Doubleday, 1955.

[19] All quotations from Abbot Suger's writings are taken from volume I of *A Documentary History of Art*, by Elizabeth Gilmore Holt, Doubleday, 1957.

[20] Cirlot.

[21] For a full treatment of the mandorla in Christian art, see Otto Brendel, 'Origin and Meaning of the Mandorla', *Gazette des Beaux-Arts*, ser. 6, vol. xxv, no. 923 (Jan. 1944).

[22] For an exhaustive treatment of the halo through all phases of Oriental and Western art, see Marthe Collmet-Guerin, *Histoire du Nimbe*, Nouvelles Editions Latines, 1961.

[23] Collmet-Guerin.

[24] Based on *Revelations* xv, 6: 'And out of the temple came the seven angels with the seven plagues, robed in pure bright linen, with their breasts girded with golden girdles'.

[25] See Gustav Davidson, *A Dictionary of Angels*, Collier-Macmillan, 1968.

[26] *Allerheiligenbilder* have been discussed by Panofsky, on Van Eyck, in *Early Netherlandish Painting*.

Part 3

[1] In *The Romantic Agony*.

[2] *De Coelo* 2.

[3] *Pahlavi Texts*, *Dâdistân-i Dinik* xxi, 5–8; quoted in Patch, *The Other World*, p. 9.

[4] From the Persian *Viraf-Nameh*, quoted by Alger in *History of a Future Life*, p. 136 ff.

[5] The reference to the Bridge of Judgment in the apocryphal *Vision of St Paul*, which dates from the fourth century, is now considered to be a ninth-century interpolation based on St Gregory's *Dialogues*.

[6] Cirlot, p. 94.

[7] See R. Wittkower, 'The Marvels of the East', *Warburg* V, 1942, pp. 159 to 179. This is the definitive study of the subject.

[8] Pliny, *Natural History*, 7,2 trans. Philemon Holland.

[9] Émile Mâle, *Religious Art in France: XII Century*, See also Wittkower.

[10] See Emanuel Winternitz, *Musical Instruments and Their Symbolism in Western Art*, Faber, 1967, pp. 75–8 and fig. 10.

[11] Margaret Murray, *The Witch-Cult in Western Europe*, O.U.P., 1921.

[12] See Hugh Trevor-Roper, 'The European Witch-Craze of the Sixteenth and Seventeenth Centuries', in *Religion, The Reformation and Social Change*, Macmillan, 1967.

[13] On Wild Men, the definitive essay is Richard Bernheimer, *Wild Men in the Middle Ages*, Harvard, 1952.

[14] Bernheimer, pp. 1–2.

[15] See E. Wind, 'The saint as monster', *Journal of the Warburg Institute*, I (1938), p. 183.

[16] This carving, which I have not seen, is mentioned by Cirlot, p. 129.

[17] Sinclair's translation has 'flanks'. Dante's word is *coste*, which means ribs.

[18] See Millard Meiss, *French Painting in the Time of Jean de Berry: the Late XIV Century and the Patronage of the Duke*, Phaidon, 1967, where the works and the problem of the identity of this miniaturist are exhaustively studied.

[19] Robert Ardrey, *African Genesis*.

[20] Millard Meiss, *Painting in Florence and Siena after the Black Death*, Princeton, 1951 (issued as a Harper paperback in 1964).

List of Illustrations

of S. Giovanni, Florence (Alinari-Mansell).

192 (top) Giovanni Bellini (?): *Christ's Descent into Limbo*, City Art Gallery, Bristol.

192 (bottom) Orpheus and Euridice at the entrance to Hades. 14th-century MS illumination from a moralised Ovid's *Metamorphoses* in the Bibliothèque Nationale, Paris (Roger Viollet).

193 The kingdom of Hades, French MS illumination to Ovid, Bibliothèque Nationale, Paris

194 Jerome Cock after Pieter Bruegel: *The Harrowing of Hell*, engraving in the Bibliothèque Albert I, Brussels.

195 Pieter Bruegel: *Dulle Griet*, Antwerp Museum (Giraudon).

196 (top) Herri met der Bles: *Hell*, Rijksbureau voor Kunsthistorische Documentatie, The Hague.

196 (bottom) Joachim Patinir: *Charon crossing the Styx*, Prado, Madrid.

197 Niccolo di Pietro Gerini: *Temptation of St Anthony*, Castellani Chapel, Sta Croce, Florence (Alinari).

198 Doorway to Palazzo Zuccari, Rome (Alinari-Mansell).

199 Mouth of Hell at Bomarzo (Edwin Smith).

200 Judgment from a French illustrated MS of St Augustine's *De Civitate Dei*, Bibliothèque Ste Geneviève, Paris (Roger Viollet).

202 Luca Signorelli: The Tortures of the Damned from the fresco in Orvieto Cathedral (Scala).

203 Mathias Grünewald: *The Damnation of Lovers*, Strasbourg Cathedral Museum (Giraudon).

204 Luca Signorelli: The Damned, from Orvieto Cathedral (Scala).

209 Fiends stirring the pots in Hell's kitchen. 15th-century German woodcut (British Museum – Freeman).

210 Hell, from a 15th-century French MS of St Augustine's *De Civitate Dei* in the Bibliothèque Ste Geneviève, Paris (Giraudon).

211 Pieter Bruegel: *Dulle Griet*, detail of figure on roof, Antwerp Museum (Giraudon).

212 Gluttony, from Taddeo di Bartolo's fresco of *Hell* at San Gimignano (Anderson-Giraudon).

213 Lust, from the *Hell* fresco at San Gimignano (Anderson-Giraudon).

214 Avarice, from the *Hell* Fresco at San Gimignano (Alinari-Giraudon).

219 (top) Detail of the lintel from the main doorway at Vézelay (Roger Viollet).

219 (bottom) Typanum over the main doorway at Vézelay (Roger Viollet).

220 The huge-eared denizens of India from the tympanum at Vézelay (Giraudon).

221 The Cynocephali from the tympanum at Vézelay (Giraudon).

222 The Monocoli from the main entrance of Sens Cathedral (James Austin).

223 Luca Signorelli: *grotteschi* in Orvieto Cathedral (Raffaello, Orvieto).

224 Miniature from the Pontifical of Bourges, 14th century, Bibliothèque Ste Geneviève, Paris (Roger Viollet).

225 Albrecht Dürer: *The Monstrous Pig of Landser*, engraving in the Author's Collection (Freeman).

226 21 Marvels of India from Schedel's *Nuremberg Chronicle*, 1493 (Foto Marburg).

227 Jerome Cock, after Pieter Bruegel: *The Sin of Avarice*, engraving, Bibliothèque Albert I, Brussels.

228 Studio of Hans Memling: *Hell*, detail from a polyptych, Musée des Beaux-Arts, Strasbourg (Giraudon).

229 Jan Mandyn: *Aeneas and The Cumaean Sibyl in the Underworld*, Rijksbureau voor Kunsthistorische Documentatie, The Hague.

230 (top left) The Pope as Antichrist (British Museum – Freeman).

230 (top right) A she-devil gives birth to a litter of Popes and clergy (British Museum – Freeman).

230 (bottom) The Devil plays on Luther's head as on a bag-pipe, c. 1535 (British Museum – Freeman).

231 (left) Pope Alexander VI, woodcut with trick fold (British Museum – Freeman).

232 (right) Pope Alexander VI unmasked as the Devil (British Museum – Freeman).

232 Bronze figure of Pan (British Museum).

233 Riccio: Satyr and Satyress (Crown copyright – Victoria and Albert Museum, London).

237 Attic red-figure vase-painting, Pan playing the double flute (British Museum – Freeman).

238 Bronze head of pan (British Museum).

239 Illumination from a Coptic MS of demons leading sinners to purgatory (British Museum – Freeman).

240 Sassetta: *Temptation of St Anthony*, Siena Pinacoteca (Alinari-Mansell).

241 Miniature from an illuminated codex of the Life of St Anthony, c. 1435 in the Laurentian Library, Florence.

243 Francesco Traini: *The Triumph of Death* (detail), Camposanto, Pisa (Anderson-Giraudon).

244 Lucas Cranach: *The Temptation of St Anthony*, engraving (British Museum – Freeman).

245 Martin Schongauer: *The Temptation of St Anthony* (British Museum – Freeman).

245 (bottom) Master L. CZ: *The Temptation of Christ*, engraving (British Museum – Freeman).

246 Illustration to the Apocalypse from *Liber Floridus*, c. 1448, Musée Condé, Chantilly (Giraudon).

247 Andrea Parentino: *The Temptation of St Anthony*, Galleria Doria, Rome (Anderson-Giraudon).

249 (top) Ghiselbertus: *The Last Judgment*, tympanum of the central door of St Lazare, Autun (Giraudon).

249 (bottom) A Demon on a capital at Vézelay (Giraudon).

250-1 Demons from capitals at Vézelay (Giraudon).

253 Goya: *Soplones* from *Los Caprichos* (British Museum – Freeman).

255 Jacques Callot: *The Temptation of St Anthony* (British Museum – Freeman).

256 Michael Pacher: *St Wolfgang with the Devil* (Bayerische Staatsgemäldesammlungen).

257 Devils enraged at the death of a virtuous man, from *L'art de bien vivre et bien mourir*, Bibliothèque Ste Geneviève, Paris (Roger Viollet).

258 The Wild Hunt, a devil riding on a boar. Southern Tyrol, 11th–12th centuries (Otto Swoboda, Vienna).

260 Pieter Bruegel: Wild Man Masquerade (Bibliothèque Albert I, Brussels).

265 Jean Bourdichon: Wild Man, Wild Woman and baby outside their cave. 15th-century miniature, Ecole des Beaux-Arts, Paris (Giraudon).

266 Jacquemart de Hesdin: *The Fool*, Psalter in Latin and French of Jean de Berry, Bibliothèque Nationale, Paris.

267 Francesco Traini: *The Triumph of Death* (detail), Camposanto, Pisa (Alinari-Giraudon).

268 Sandro Botticelli: Study for Satan, illustration to Dante (British Museum – Freeman).

269 (left) Melchior Lorch: The Pope as Antichrist, Engraving 1545 (British Museum – Freeman).

269 (right) Sandro Botticelli: Study for Satan, illustration to Dante (British Museum – Freeman).

271 The Brussels Initial Master: *Satan Enthroned in Hell* (British Museum – Freeman).

272 Mathias Grünewald: *The Temptation of St Anthony*, Colmar Museum (Giraudon).

273 Anonymus c. 1270–1300: *The Inferno*, mosaic on cupola of Florence Baptistery (Alinari).

274 Detail of Satan from Giotto's *Last Judgment*, Padua (Alinari).

275 William Blake: Cerberus, watercolour illustration to Dante's *Divine Comedy* (Tate Gallery).

276 (left) Hydria showing Herakles confronting Eurystheus with Cerberus, the watchdog of Hades (Hirmes).

THE ILLUSTRATIONS ON PAGES 180 AND 205 SHOULD BE TRANSPOSED.